The Great Logo Adventure

Discovering Logo on and off the computer

By Jim Muller

Doone Publications

7950 Hwy 72W, #G106
Madison AL 35758 USA
Tel: 1-800-311-3753
Fax: 205-837-0580
e-mail: asmith@doone.com
web: http://www.doone.com

Welcome to *The Great Logo Adventure*!

Maybe you were introduced to the Logo language in school. Maybe you had, or still have one of the older Logo packages.

Well, times have changed.

Today, Logo offers a very rich programming environment that includes multimedia tools, robotics and network access. Full-featured Logo packages now offer hundreds of commands for exploring all sorts of applications, from the simplest turtle graphics to artificial intelligence, even Windows programming.

Best of all, some of the best Logo packages are free! MSW Logo, which was used to develop this book, provides a full set of multimedia tools plus an excellent introduction to Windows programming. You'll find it on the enclosed CD.

What is *The Great Logo Adventure*?

The Great Logo Adventure is the latest in a series of cartoon-illustrated family activity books that introduce young people of all ages to the fun and excitement of exploring Logo on and off the computer. Logy, our turtle mascot, and her irrepressible rabbit friend Morf, have added a number of new activities to this book. In addition to free Logo software for most desktop computers, the CD included with this book offers a wide range posters, pictures, and projects for all ages.

While The Great Logo Adventure has been written using MSW Logo, you can use this book with just about any version of the language. We talk about some of the differences between Logo packages in these pages.

What is Logo

Logo is an interactive programming language for adventurers of all ages. It has borrowed the techniques of symbolic computation - the manipulating of words and ideas - from LISP, the programming language in which Logo was originally written. These techniques are combined with other powerful ideas such as the use of procedures, recursion, and the manipulation of programs as data to provide a unique interactive programming environment.

Why Logo

Logo has been designed with "no threshold and no ceiling." You begin by controlling the actions of a cybernetic turtle in a graphic environment that provides immediate feedback. These immediate actions let you "see" how you are thinking. When your sequence of thoughts does not make the turtle do what you want, the descriptive nature of Logo lets you easily trace your thoughts to "debug" your thinking.

As you grow, so does Logo, from the immediate graphic environment into a structured, procedural programming environment for exploring mathematics, language, science, the computer, number systems, and so much more. While the threshold for Logo is exceptionally low — as young as two years old — the ceiling is limited only by your imagination.

Planting Some Seeds

Like the gardener, we plant some seeds on these pages. You are the one to feed these ideas, to nurture them, and to make them grow.

As with any seed, you have to be patient!

You may be tempted to rush over the details. Just remember that the younger the explorers, the more dependent they are on imitation and repetition. Time may seem to be your enemy — but it's the turtle's friend!

So join your young people at the computer and explore this book together. Cultivate their imaginations. Give them the time to explore. Just don't be surprised if you are the one who ends up being cultivated.

There's an old Bambera proverb from the drought-ridden country of Mali in West Africa:

"Mogho Kelen Te Sira Be!"

Loosely translated, this says that "one person cannot make a trail." To accomplish a common task, the multiple talents of a group working together can be more productive than the finite talents of the individual — which tells you why the focus of this book is on groups and group activities.

OK, ready to start?

Good! It's time to enjoy your very own *Great Logo Adventure*!

About the Author

Jim Muller has had a lifelong interest in translating high technology into understandable, practical, and enjoyable applications – especially for young people. He began working with Logo in 1979 while public relations manager for Texas Instruments Incorporated.

After introducing TI Logo, the first commercial Logo package, in April of 1981, Muller went on to organize the first Logo users group. What started as eight junior high students exploring TI Logo around a ping-pong table in the Muller garage grew into the Young Peoples' Logo Association, Inc. (YPLA). Organized by and for all the young peoples of the world, the association quickly grew to 6000 members in 42 countries. In 1985, the YPLA joined CompuServe as The Logo Forum. Now they have a Logo web page at http://www.cyberramp.net/~jmul.

In addition to a monthly newspaper, the YPLA published these books, some in multiple editions:

- 1,2,3 My Computer and Me
- The Turtle's Sourcebook
- The Turtle's Discovery Book
- The Misadventures of Mrtle
- The Logo Library
- Learning Logo On and Off the Computer

and this interactive software:

- Logo Island Adventures
- Voyages of The Turtle Shell
- Escape From Logo Castle
- DoodleBug Logo

The author has since published *The LadyBug's Discovery Book* for LadyBug Logo, *The Turtle's Discovery Book* for PC Logo and Logo Plus, and *The Logo Sourcebook* for MSW Logo.

Acknowledgments

There are far too many! There's my son Larry and his friends. Without their curiosity and enthusiasm, the Young Peoples' Logo Association never would have happened.

There are many, many young people from around the world who shared their own Great Logo Adventures with us. Some of those adventures are in this book.

Thanks to Brian Harvey for UCB Logo and most certainly to George Mills for putting it into the Windows environment as MSW Logo.

There's the late Charles Micha, the cartoonist who made The Great Logo Adventure come to life.

Special thanks to the many educators who helped develop and validate the YPLA approach to Logo, and from whom we learned so much. Dorothy Fitch, Judi Harris, Joan Randolph, and Kathleen Martin are but a few. More recently, there's been Jenny Betts of Brisbane, Australia, and Toby Epstein of the LaDue School District in St. Louis, Missouri. Through our cybernetic conversations, I've again discovered how much fun learning can be, on and off the computer.

And, of course, there's Audrey Muller, who has survived the invasion of Turtle androids into her home and still managed to maintain a sense of stability all these years.

Contents

The Tortoise and the Hare.... A Logo Fable

Once upon a time, there was a tortoise who moved along very slowly. The tortoise liked this slow, easy life. It was fun watching the birds, the trees, and the flowers. There was lots of time to learn from each new thing he saw as he wandered about.

Once upon that same time, there was a hare who liked to hop and leap about.

Now, the hare was always teasing the tortoise about his slow, steady pace. But the tortoise never replied. He just kept minding his own business, enjoying each new sight and sound.

One day, the hare teased the tortoise one time too many.

"Hare," said the tortoise, "I challenge you to a race. Whoever can get to the other side of the forest first is the winner. And if I win, no more teasing!"

The hare laughed so hard he fell down. He held his sides as he rolled around on the ground. Of course, the hare agreed. Race day came and the big race began.

The tortoise started off at a slow, steady pace – step, step, step – never faster, never slower.

The hare leaped and hopped all over the place. He even did cartwheels around the tortoise and then sped off to have some fun before he got to the other side of the forest.

He even stopped to take a nap. He knew he had plenty of time before the tortoise would ever catch up.

I bet you know what happened. Maybe someone read you the story about the tortoise and the hare.

The tortoise won the race and the hare felt very foolish. He never teased the hare again.

1

I bet you think that's where the story ends. Well, not quite!

Once upon a much later time, just a few years ago in fact, there was a turtle who lived near a forest. This turtle was a distant cousin of the great-great-great grandchild of that famous tortoise. The turtle had a friend who was a rabbit, a distant cousin of the great-great-great grandchild of the not-so-famous hare.

One day, the turtle and the rabbit were each given a computer and Logo. They were both very happy and could not wait to see what they could each do with their new presents.

The turtle opened the Logo book and began to read, one page at a time.

The rabbit opened his Logo book and just skipped over the first chapter.

It looked too easy. He wanted to find the "good stuff." He hopped and leaped all over the place. When he glanced over at the turtle, she was still reading the first chapter.

"Hey, that's the easy stuff," the rabbit said. "Look at this!"

The turtle liked what the rabbit did, but she was having lots of fun doing her own thing. She knew she'd soon be able to do the things the rabbit copied from his book.

Time passed, and the rabbit was still bouncing from one thing to another. By now, the turtle had finished Chapter 2.

More time passed. The hare took another look at what the turtle was doing. He was just about to tease the turtle for going through the book so slowly when he stopped.

"Hey! How'd you do that? That isn't in the book," the rabbit said.

The turtle explained slowly, step by step, what she had done to make the pretty picture on the screen. But the rabbit was still puzzled.

"I know, rabbit," explained the turtle, "this isn't in the book. I made it up from what I read about in the first chapters."

"But how'd you know what to do?" asked the rabbit?"

"Gee, I thought you knew all about Logo and computers, rabbit," laughed the turtle as she turned the page.

"Logo is the most fun when you start with what you know and discover new things as you move along.

"Logo isn't just something to do at the computer. It's really about exploring new ideas – about discovering new ways to do things."

"If I want to learn things, I'll go to school," said the rabbit. "That's what school is for!"

"The computer and Logo are for learning things, too," answered the turtle.

"They're tools just like paper and pencils are tools."

"Tell me something, rabbit. When you're in school and you make a mistake on your spelling test, do you blame the spelling book? Do you blame the pencil and the paper?" asked the turtle.

"That's silly. The book doesn't take the test. And the paper and pencil can't do anything without me. If I make a mistake, that's my fault. And if I get all the words right, I'm the one who gets the Gold Star!"

"If the teacher asks you to write a story, do you copy that story from a book?

Or do you use the words you learned how to spell to write a story of your very own?"

"I write my own stories, of course!" answered the rabbit.

"Well, rabbit, why should the computer and Logo be any different. Logo is the language you use, just like English. The keyboard is your pencil and the screen is your paper. Now why don't you see what you can do with them – all by yourself."

The poor rabbit was embarrassed enough for one day. He was angry, too; angry at himself for being so silly.

"Computers aren't that tough," thought the rabbit. "All I have to do is teach it what I want it to do."

So the rabbit sat down with his book again and began to read. Soon he was doing his own thing, not the things the book told him to do. Sure, he made mistakes. But he found that's found that's where the fun begins.

When he finally got his procedures to do the fancy things he wanted them to do, he did a couple of cartwheels over to the turtle.

"Come see! Come see!" he said very excited and he ran back to his computer.

"Yes, that's the idea," said the turtle.

"I'm beginning to see what you mean," Morf said excitedly. "But how did you know all this so fast?"

"Rabbit," answered the turtle, "I have to be honest with you. See that small shape there in the center of the screen?"

"Sure, that's the turtle."

"Yes, and that's also my cousin, Ernestine. She's the one who makes everything happen.

"Let's just say it runs in the family."

Using This Book

Are you new to Logo?

Then this book is for you. We really don't care which Logo package you use.

Start with what you know. Add bits and pieces together until you can do whatever you want to do with each new command you come across. If that sounds like a lot, don't worry. Logy and Morf will guide you on your Great Logo Adventure.

As you will see, our friends each took their own path to discover Logo. Logy, being the slow, more methodical type, spent her time at the computer with her book, one page, one chapter at a time. Morf likes to jump around a lot, especially to do Logo activities off the computer. He skipped over some of the geometry exercises early on, but came back to them when he needed them.

While both Logy and Morf enjoyed their Logo books, they didn't stop with just those activities. Along the way, they made up there own pictures, videos, games, and music. And when they finally got to the end, you should see what they could do. In fact, they're going to write the next book. Wait and see.

Getting Started

"Hey, Logy, whatcha doing?"

"What's it look like I'm doing. I'm cleaning the windows so we can get started on our new adventure."

"Can't you leave the housekeeping until later. We've got Logo work to do!"

"I don't like dirty windows!" replied Logy. "I don't care if they are on the house or on the computer. If we're going to discover new things to do with Logo, we're going to have clean windows.

"Did you know that Ernestine brought along her whole family, over 1,000 turtles. And you can now play music through your new sound card. You can even use Logo to make up your own Windows stuff for your friends to use. Just wait until you see the trouble you can get into!"

"Yeah, yeah, yeah" Morf said, bounding around excitedly. "What do we have to do? When can we get started. I've got lots of ideas I want to try out!"

Which Logo Are You Using?

First things first!

This chapter is for those using MSW Logo, the Logo for Windows package on the CD that comes with this book. It tells you all about the MSW Logo windows and menus. You don't need to know all about these to get started. Just remember that the information is here when you need it.

Installing MSW Logo

The first thing you need to do is install Logo on your computer. Make sure that you select the correct MSW Logo kit from the CD that came with this book.

msw32b52.exe This is the 32bit kit for Windows 95 and Windows NT.

msw32s52.exe This is for those running Win32s in Windows 3.1x. Win32s is not included.

msw16b52.exe The 16bit kit for those running Windows 3.1x or Windows 95 in 16-bit mode.

msw16s52.exe This is for those running Windows 3.1 on IBM XT and other 286 computers.

mswsrc52.exe The source kit.

mswtut52.exe An on-line video tutorial for beginners 3.5 MB compressed.

1. Turn on your computer and get Windows started.

2. Double-click the File Manager in Windows 3.1 or Windows Explorer in Windows 95. Double-click means to quickly press the left mouse button two times. But you already knew that, didn't you?

3. Double-click on the MSW Logo kit to be installed. Then follow the instructions on the screen.

MSW Logo Directories

When MSW Logo is installed, three directories are set up:

- **Mswlogo:** This is the main directory or folder. This is the where you will save your own procedures. You can also make a separate procedures directory if you want.

- **Examples:** This directory includes a number of subdirectories with different types of MSW Logo sample procedures. Be sure to   read the README.TXT file. This provides a description of all the example procedures.

   MSW Logo procedures are regular ASCII text files that you can read using a text editor or word processing software. If you change them at all, it's best to save them using another name.

- **Logolib:** This is a file of special Logo primitives – that's the Logo word for commands – used by MSW Logo.

What's on the CD?

The CD that comes with this book includes the listed versions of MSW Logo plus UCB Logo for those using DOS or a Macintosh computer. In addition to free Logo software, you will find all the procedures from this book plus many other projects: MSW Log procedures and files to read using Acrobat Reader. That's included in the Util directory.

For a more complete listing of what's on the CD, check out the Appendix at the back of this book.

Installing UCB Logo

UCB Logo is also provided on your CD.

It is best suited to those more advanced users who are familiar with DOS and DOS file structures. It is more like "classic Logo" in that it does not include multiple turtles, music, or multimedia features. Two UCB Logo packages are included on the CD:

ucblogo_seax.hqx Compressed files for the Macintosh.

blogo.exe   Compressed files for the PC.

Blogo.exe includes three Logo programs:

- **ucblogo.exe**   runs in MS-DOS on 286-and-up PCs. It uses extended memory if you have it, so you can run large Logo programs.

- **bl.exe**   runs on any MS-DOS PC, but is limited to 640K.

- **ucbwlogo.exe**   runs on Windows 95 and Windows NT only.

Copy the UCB Logo file for your computer into an empty directory on your hard drive and then inflate it. To install UCB Logo, type Install. Read the Readme and UCBLogo.txt files for more information on how to setup and run UCB Logo.

Opening Logo

When you install MSW Logo, Windows puts it in its own program group or folder. Left-click on the program group or folder and there's the MSW Logo icon in its own little window.

Double-click on the Logo icon in that little window to open MSW Logo. The MSW Logo Screen appears.

Parts of the Screen

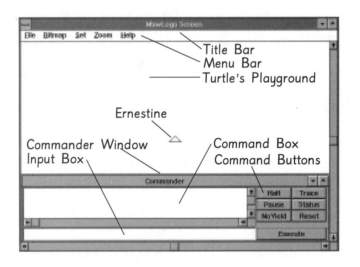

There's Ernestine sitting at right in the middle of her playground. Ernestine looks like a pointed arrow but she's really a turtle who does just about anything you ask her to do. If she doesn't understand, she'll tell you.

First, let's take a look at the rest of the MSW Logo screen.

It's like many Windows screens. The Title Bar is at the top. This tells you what window you're looking at.

The Menu Bar is right below the Title Bar. It holds the names of menus we'll describe a bit later.

Down below the playground is the Commander window. This is where the action is.

The big space in the Commander window is the Command Box. This box keeps a list of what's going on. If something goes wrong, you'll see a message here.

Below the Command window is the Input Box. This is where you type your instructions to the turtle.

Over on the right side, there are a bunch of buttons that can make things a little easier.

Commander Buttons

Morf loves buttons and things. So here's a list of the Commander buttons. We'll talk more about each of them later as we go along.

Halt
This stops the Logo action right away. It does the same thing that the HALT command does.

Trace
This turns the Trace command on. Left-click on it to turn the Untrace command on.

Pause
Logo stops the action temporarily and waits for the Continue command.

Status
The Status button brings up a Status window that tells you what's going on.

Yield
This tells Logo not to allow other programs to run while Logo is running.

Reset
This button is like the Clearscreen command. It resets or clears the screen.

Execute
This is like pressing the Enter key. It tells the turtle to run or execute your procedure.

Commander Window

The Commander window is separate from the MSW Logo window. That means you can move it around, make it smaller or larger, or you can change it into a little icon. We work with this window a lot. So if you want to practice moving it around or changing its size, go ahead.

1. Left-click in the Title Bar where you see the word, Commander.

   The title bar of the Commander window changes color.

2. With the cursor in the Title Bar, press and hold the left mouse key down. Then drag the Commander window around the screen.

   The Commander window moves with the mouse.

3. Move the Commander window back where it is supposed to be and release the mouse button.

   You're back where you started.

MSW Logo Menus

There are five menus in the Menu Bar. You know what a Menu is, don't you? You left-click on the word and up pops a list of choices. MSW Logo menus give you lists of commands you can execute. We describe the commands throughout this book. We also tell you to look back here to read about the menu commands.

— This is the File menu

File

This menu shows you a list of things you can do with your procedures. There are also commands that do the same thing. You'll read about these as they come up later on.

When we want you to pay special attention to something, we use this Special Note box. Right now, we have a special note about this book that we want you to read before we get started.

When reading about menus and what you can do with them, you may see things like File/Edit or Edit/Copy. This is just a short way of saying open the File menu and left-click on Edit, or open the Edit menu and left-click on Copy.

Sometimes you may see instructions like File/Edit/All. You got it. That means open the File menu, select Edit, and then left-click on All in the box that appears.

Load...

Left-click on Load to display the Open dialog box in which you can select the procedure to load, just like you do with any other windows program.

Save

This saves any procedures that you may have loaded along with any new procedures you wrote and any procedures you changed. If you are saving new procedures, the Save As dialog box is displayed. Give the procedure a name in the File Name: box. Left-click on OK to save it.

Save As...

The Save As dialog box is displayed. This gives you the chance to save any procedures that you have in memory under a new name. Type a name for your procedure in the File Name: box. Left-click on OK to save it.

Edit

The Edit Procedure dialog box is displayed showing any procedures currently in memory. Either type the name of the procedure you want to edit in the box above the list of procedures or left-click on the procedure name. The name you select is then displayed in the box. Left-click on OK to display the procedure in an Editor window. Left-click on All to display all the procedures in your workspace. You already know what Cancel means, right? If not, try it out and see.

Erase

Erase acts a lot like Edit except that the Erase Procedure dialog box is displayed showing any procedures currently in your workspace. Either type the name of the procedure you want to erase in the box above the list of procedures or left-click on the procedure name. The name you select is then displayed in the box. Left-click on OK to erase the procedure. Left-click on All to erase all the procedures.

Exit

Left-click on Exit to leave MSW Logo.

Bitmap

Bitmap is a computer term that describes the pictures you create. This menu includes commands for loading, saving, and printing the pictures that you create. There are a wide variety of Bitmap commands that you'll learn about as you move through this book. Here's what the menu commands do.

New

Left-click on New to erase the picture that is displayed on the screen. The turtle remains where it stopped.

Load

Left-click on Load on the Bitmap menu. The Open dialog box is displayed with a list of bitmaps you can load. These are graphic files with the *.bmp extension.

Save

Left-click on Save to save the current screen as a picture file. The entire screen is saved making this a very big file. To reduce the size of the file, reduce the Active Area as described below.

Save As...

The Save As dialog box is displayed. This gives you the chance to save a picture under a new name. Type a name for your picture in the File Name: box. Left-click on OK to save it.

Print

Left-click on Print to send the current screen to your printer. This works like the regular Windows command. A dialog box is displayed that lets you change your printer setup if you want.

Print Setup

This is just like the regular Windows Print Setup option. You can change printers, paper size, and all sorts of other things here.

Set

Using the Set menu, you can change the type of letters and numbers that Logo uses by setting the "font" in this menu. You can also set colors. There's a lot more on fonts and colors in the Color, Music, and Pizzazz chapter.

Pensize

Left-click on Pensize to change the size of the turtle's pen. You can select on of the pictures of different line thicknesses or use the slide to get just the line thickness you want.

Font

You can change the font that is used with the Label command to display text on the graphics screen. This does nothing for how text is displayed in the Editor and Commander windows.

Left-click on Font to display a list of all the fonts you have installed. You know what a font is, don't you? It's a set of letters, numbers, and punctuation marks in one size and style. The Font dialog box gives you the choice of font sizes and styles from which to select.

PenColor
FloodColor
ScreenColor

These three options each display the same basic window from which you can select the color of the turtles pen, the color the turtle uses to "flood" or fill closed shapes, and the color for the screen background.

Zoom

You can Zoom in on your pictures to make them fill more of the screen. Or you can Zoom out so that you can see more of the screen's active area.

In
Go ahead. Left-click on the Zoom menu and then on In. What happens? Left-click on In again. And again. See what happens?

Normal
Now left click on Normal to get things back to the way they should be. Then try doing the same thing only zoom out.

Out
Zooming out is very handy if your screen does not display all of the pictures from the procedures on the CD. Just zoom out to see the whole thing.

Help

If you have questions about how to do something in MSW Logo, you can left-click on Help.

The Help Menu gives you some choices:

Index
Left-click on Index to see a list of the chapters in the MSW Logo On-line Help.

MCI
That stands for Media Control Interface. This is a group of special commands for controlling sound, video, and other multimedia devices. There are some good examples of these commands included in the Examples directory. We talk about them later in this book.

Using Help

This is a neat section. It will help you if you need help using Help. Does that make sense?

Tutorial

There is a video tutorial on the CD that comes with this book. Other than that, this book will have to do.

Demo

Select Demo to see a neat demonstration of some of the things that MSW Logo can do.

Examples

Examples displays the Readme file in the MSW Logo Examples directory. You can discover lots of other things you can do with MSW Logo.

Release Notes

This tells you all about the things that MSW Logo has to offer. It's the same as the MSWLOGO.TXT file in your MSW Logo directory.

About Logo

This tells you who developed MSW Logo. It also provides e-mail addresses where you can contact the developers.

Ready to Start

Ready to get started? Fine, it's time to...

Meet the Turtle

It's time to get down to business!

Look down in the Commander window. If you don't see a blinking line over on the left side, left-click (that means press the left button on your mouse) in the Input Box. That blinking line you see is "the cursor." It moves every time you type something in a window, dialog, or text box.

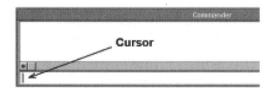

But you probably knew that already. So, let's get on with the fun!

Ernestine carries a pen that she uses to create all sorts of colorful drawings. Sometimes we call the lines that she draws turtle trails.

But remember, you are the one who has to tell her exactly what to do.

Turtle Directions

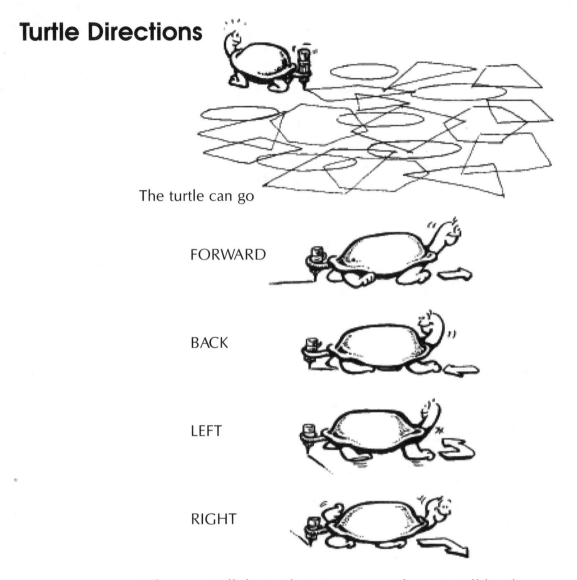

The turtle can go

FORWARD

BACK

LEFT

RIGHT

When you tell the turtle to move, you have to tell her how many turtle steps to take. Go ahead. Try it.

1. Type FORWARD.

   In this book, we sometimes use italics like this to make sure you know what's going on. Also, we type commands in UPPERCASE so you'll know what's a command and what's not. However, when typing MSW Logo commands on the computer, you can use either upper or lower case letters, or both.

2. Press the Space bar.

3. Then type a pretty big number, like 200 maybe.

4. For the turtle to hear you, you have to press Enter.

If you accidentally hit the wrong key and end up with something like FORWRD 200, the turtle sends you a message such as:

I don't know how to FORWRD

She's nice about it. So just type the command again, but without any more accidents.

Turning the Turtle

To turn the turtle, tell her to turn RIGHT or LEFT. Again, just as you have to tell her how many steps to move forward or back, you have to tell her how many turtle turns to make.

RIGHT _____

Go ahead! Type in a number – not an itty-bitty number. Make it a pretty big one.

What happened? The turtle turned to look in another direction, right?

OK, now turn her back to the direction she was heading before.

Type LEFT _____ and use the same number of turtle turns that you used before, when you turned right. Remember to press Enter.

Now the turtle is looking up toward the top of the screen again. How many turns does the turtle have to make to look at the side of the screen?

What do you think?

This is the cool part of Logo. You get to discover all sorts of new things all by yourself. You found that the turtle had to turn 90 turtle turns to look at the side of the screen.

Now, turn the turtle back to the top of the screen. What do you have to type to do that?

If you said LEFT 90, give yourself a double-dip ice cream cone!

Turning Around

Now, what do you have to do to get the turtle to face the bottom of the screen?

Well, you could tell the turtle to face the side and then face the next side, right?

RIGHT 90 RIGHT 90 (Yes, you can type more than one command on a line. Just remember to press Enter when you're done!)

RIGHT 90 RIGHT 90 should work, shouldn't it?

What would happen if you add the 90 and 90 together? Did you get 180? Morf did. Why not give that a try.

RIGHT 180 Then press Enter.

That did it, also! There's the turtle facing in the opposite direction.

Things to Remember

So, when you tell the turtle to go FORWARD or BACK, the turtle moves forward or back the number of turtle steps you tell her to go. When you tell the turtle RIGHT or LEFT, she turns the number of turtle turns you tell her to turn — but she doesn't move.

Get the idea? Try a few moves on your own.

Why not just mess up the screen with turtle trails? As you type in commands numbers, watch what the turtle does. Pretty soon, you'll be telling the turtle just where you want her to go.

Cleaning Up After Yourself

By now the screen is either a work of art or a big mess. So you'd better clean it off. To clear the MSW Logo screen, type:

CLEARSCREEN

Everything on the graphics screen is erased and the turtle goes HOME.

Some people use CLEARGRAPHICS. Others just use CG. Sometimes, the command CLEARSCREEN is like the CLEAN command described below. In MSW Logo, CLEAN clears the screen but the turtle stays where she is.

Awfully simple? Or simply awful?

Yep, that's the turtle's home, right there in the middle of the Graphics window. OK, so maybe HOME on the screen doesn't look exactly like our picture. But you get the idea.

When you tell the turtle to go HOME, she goes back to the middle of the screen and faces the top of the screen.

Remember this!   You'll use the HOME command a lot.

"That's fine, but what about erasing all the typing in the Commander window?"

Just type CLEARTEXT. The text disappears. In MicroWorlds, type CC to Clear the Command Center.

Some Logo packages have a very useful command that clears out everything and puts the turtle back like it is when you first start up Logo. It's the DRAW command.

- DRAW clears the screen.

- Sends Ernestine HOME.

- Shows Ernestine.

- Puts the pen down.

- Sets the pen color to black.

- Sets the background color to white.

- Sets the turtle's width to 1.

- Resets the turtle's font to the system font.

- Sets up the WRAP mode.

After you've learned how to do all that stuff and what it all means, you'll learn how to create the RESET command for MSW Logo. It does the same thing.

Rabbit Trail

1

Turtle Games Off the Computer

Now it's my turn to shine! Logy likes doing things at the computer. But I have to get away every once in a while and do things off the computer. So join me on my Rabbit Trails throughout the book. Here's one to get you started.

Have you ever played Simon Sez or Mother, May I? Why not try these games using Logo commands instead of the regular things you do. Logo commands add some new fun to the old game.

Simon sez FORWARD 5
Simon sez RIGHT 90
FORWARD 5

For another change, let's take a turtle walk that's a lot like these games. This one is fun to play with your class in school or with your family or friends at home.

One player is the turtle and one is the computer operator. The idea is to tell the turtle how to walk through a big letter or shape. The others in the room have to guess what the turtle is drawing.

The turtle starts in the middle of the room. The operator then tells the turtle how to move. The commands listed below will give you an idea.

FORWARD 10   turtle steps.
Make them little steps if you are in a small space.

RIGHT 150   turtle turns.

Remember how you turned right before? You tried RIGHT 90 to turn to the side. Then you tried RIGHT 180 and you turned around to face the opposite direction. 150 is closer to 180 than it is to 90. So you can make a good guess about how far to turn. It will do just fine.

FORWARD 11   turtle steps
LEFT 150   turtle turns.

You don't have to be reminded about this one, do you? I bet you know which direction you should be heading.

FORWARD 10   turtle steps

Now type these steps on the computer. Of course, you don't need to type the "turtle steps" or "turtle turns."

What letter does this shape look like? If you can't see the picture very well, how would you make this shape bigger on the screen?

If you make the turtle move five times as many turtle steps forward, do you have to make the turtle do five times as many turns?

The words you type – FORWARD, RIGHT, BACK, and LEFT – are Logo "primitives." Primitives are the action words, the instructions or commands that Logo already knows. You use primitives to write procedures. They're the things you will teach Logo to do in the Writing Procedures chapter.

Let's experiment. Morf just loves experimenting.

Try this. And don't forget to press Enter when you're done.

FORWARD 10 * 5
RIGHT 150
FORWARD 11 * 5
LEFT 150
FORWARD 10 * 5

The * sign tells the turtle to multiply 10 times 5 and move that many turtle steps. You'll learn more about Logo arithmetic later on. However, if you want to practice a little now, try working with these arithmetic signs.

FORWARD 10 + 5   Addition
FORWARD 10 - 5   Subtraction
FORWARD 10 / 5   Division
FORWARD 10 * 5   Multiplication

But first, back to your experiment – what happened?

The shape got bigger when you changed the steps. But it still looks like the letter N, doesn't it. So I guess that means that turtle steps and turtle turns really are different!

- Changing the number of turtle steps without changing the turtle turns changes the size of the shape. But it's still the same basic shape.

- Changing the number of turtle turns without changing the number of steps changes the shape itself without changing the size of the lines.

Go ahead, change the number of turtle turns. Change 150 to 120. What happens when you change it to 180? Why not try 310? As you play around with numbers, you'll begin to see how you can make the turtle do just what you want it to do.

Now, think about this?

What would happen if you changed the FD 10 * 5 to a 10 * 8? No, don't do it on the computer. Draw the change you think this might make. Then do it on the computer to see if you were right.

Don't worry about what you're drawing or what the turtle's trail looks like. This is the time to explore, to discover what the turtle can do with the four commands FORWARD, BACK, RIGHT, and LEFT.

Learning Turtle Shorthand

Now that you know what the basic turtle commands are and what they will do, let's make things easy. Let's try turtle shorthand:

FD	is the same as	FORWARD
BK	is the same as	BACK
RT	is the same as	RIGHT
LT	is the same as	LEFT
CS	is the same as	CLEARSCREEN
CG	is the same as	CLEARGRAPHICS

Get the idea? Go ahead and try a few.

The Turtle's Pen

So far we've been talking about the turtle drawing all the time. Ernestine always has her pen down to draw on the screen.

But what if you want the turtle to move without drawing a line? What do you do to make that happen?

You guessed it! You tell the turtle to pick up the pen.

PENUP or PU in shorthand

FD 100 RT 90

PENUP or PU   **PENDOWN or PD**

To tell the turtle to start drawing, tell her to put the pen down.

PENDOWN or PD in shorthand

FD 50

Awfully simple?   Or simply awful?

But don't think you're going to get off this easy!   There's more to it than that. In MSW Logo, the turtle can do three things with the pen when it is down: paint (when the turtle's drawing), erase, and reverse lines.

PENPAINT

The turtle draws lines.

PENERASE or PE

The turtle erases its steps

PENREVERSE or PX

If there's a line in the turtle's path, it is erased. If there is no line, the turtle draws one.

Why don't you put these commands to work? Make up some things to do and experiment.

Hiding the Turtle

If you want to get the turtle out of the way, type HIDETURTLE and press Enter. Ernestine disappears!

You can abbreviate HIDETURTLE by typing HT.

To see the turtle again, what do you think the command will be? Sure, it's SHOWTURTLE or ST in shorthand.

Erasing

Did you ever type something you didn't mean to type? Sure you did! Well, all you have to do to change it is to back up and type over what you want to change.

You can use the Backspace key to back up. It's the one with the arrow pointing to the left. Put the cursor after the letters you want to erase. Then press the Backspace key. It moves to the left erasing one letter each time you press the key.

You can also use the Delete key. The cursor stays in one place while it erases the letter to the right. Go ahead, give both keys a try. You'll see the difference.

The other way to erase is to drag the mouse over the text you want to change. Drag means to put the cursor in front of the section you want to change. Press and hold the left mouse button. Then drag the cursor (move the mouse) over the letters to change. The section you marked reverses color. Then release the left mouse button. To change what you've marked, just start typing. The marked section disappears.

OK, you know you can erase things that you type.

But what about things you draw?

Think about this.

You have just finished a great drawing when you see a line that's too long. You don't want to start all over again. All you want to do is erase that one line.

Let's try it and see what happens. Draw this shape.

FD 50   RT 120
FD 50   RT 120
FD 60

Rather than erase the entire drawing because the last line is too long, just change what the pen is doing. Since you want to erase that last line, you just move the turtle back over it.

Try this:

PENERASE or PE in shorthand
BACK or BK 60

What happened? Just as important, what do you do now?

If you said to tell the turtle to PENPAINT, or to put her pen back down, CONGRATULATIONS! That's the kind of answer that sends Logy into tailspins.

Give yourself a huge Gold Star!   And throw in a double-dip ice cream cone too!

OK, now type FD 50. Now what do you see? It looks better, doesn't it.

"But what if people don't have a PE command?"

"Morf, you're jumping ahead again. If people don't have a PENERASE command in their version of Logo, they can change the color of Ernestine's pen to the same color as the background. Then when they draw over the line, it will seem to disappear just like it does with PENERASE. Then they have to change the pen color back to what it was before and continue drawing.

"We'll learn more about colors in the Color, Music, and Pizzazz chapter."

Sometimes it's fun to just play around on the screen to see what you

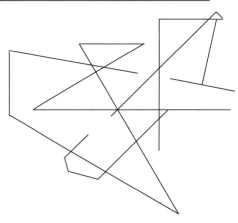

can do. At other times, it's fun to plan a drawing on paper first, and then put it on the screen.

Why not give that a try – first on paper, then on the screen?

If you run into a bit of trouble trying to figure out the Logo commands for your drawing, Morf has some ideas for you in his next Rabbit Trail.

Rabbit Trail

2

Making a Pencil Turtle

Sometimes it's hard to see how things work on the computer screen. To get things clear in your mind, you just have to go back to the good old pencil and paper.

But the pencil isn't the same as a turtle.

Here's an idea to help you make a turtle drawing on paper. Let's make a turtle for your pencil. You can use the one we did or you can make your own turtle. There's a page full of pencil turtles in \projects\chapt2 on the CD that came with this book.

Using your pencil, make a drawing of an egg on a piece of heavy paper or cardboard.

If you're at home, maybe you could ask your Mom or your Dad for help tracing a real egg.

But be careful, you don't want egg all over your drawing.

Hold the egg carefully and then trace around the egg to draw an oval shape. This looks like a turtle shell, doesn't it?

Now put a small circle, about the size of your pencil, in the middle of your turtle shell. At the top of the shell, draw the turtle's head. Then draw the turtle's right legs. Then draw the turtle's left legs.

To help keep directions straight, put R on the right front leg and L on the left front leg. Now you're ready to carefully cut out your turtle.

When that's done, slide the turtle up near the top of your pencil so you can hold it underneath the turtle. If it seems to slide around too much, use a piece of cellophane tape to hold it in place.

Ready to go? Make sure the turtle is looking at the top of the paper.
Then give the Pencil Turtle a command like:

FD 50

When you want the Pencil Turtle to turn, turn your pencil so the turtle
is facing where you want to draw your next line.

RT 90 FD 50
LT 90 FD 50

Get the idea?

Now try this.

RT 180

FD 100

LT 90

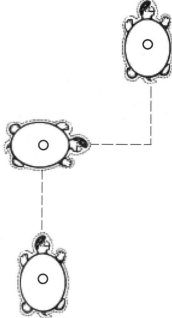

The turtle's going to turn to its left. But
which direction is that to you?

Your right? Or your left?

Since the turtle is moving down the paper,
the turtle turns to its left but your right. If
you've turned the Pencil Turtle like Ernestine
would turn, you can check this out by
looking at the front legs of the turtle. They
tell you which direction is which.

Remember, when you want to plan a drawing on paper, your Pencil
Turtle can help you think about the moves the turtle will have to make
on the screen.

To help you even more while you're making your drawing on paper,
make a list of the commands you give your pencil. This makes it easy
to remember when you type the commands on the computer.

Let's Review

You know how to tell the turtle to go FORWARD, BACK, LEFT, and
RIGHT. You can tell the turtle to draw with the PENUP or the
PENDOWN.

Remember where HOME is?

What happens when you tell the turtle PENREVERSE?

What about CLEARSCREEN? CLEARTEXT? CLEAN? PENPAINT?

OK! Time to do some more exploring off the computer!

Rabbit Trail

3

Exploring Turtle Town

Think about this for a moment. Where does your best friend live? From the front of your house, which direction do you turn to go to your friend's house, right or left? After you turn, how far do you go before you turn again?

Can you draw a map to his or her house?

Why not draw a turtle trail from the front of your house to the front of your friend's house? Pretend that each block is 100 turtle steps long and that each street is 10 turtle steps wide. After you have drawn the turtle trail, write down the Logo commands to make the trip.

Here's another challenge for you. Can you draw the map that would use the following commands?

    RT 90 FD 50
    RT 90 FD 100
    LT 90 FD 110
    RT 90 FD 100
    RT 90 FD 30

Pretend you are drawing a map to a friend's house. Once you get there, you can draw a picture of what your friends house looks like.

Here are a few blocks to give you a start. Use these or draw and color your own map.

27

Working with maps can be lots of fun, especially when they are done on the computer. There's a map of Turtle Town below that shows where Logy and Morf live.

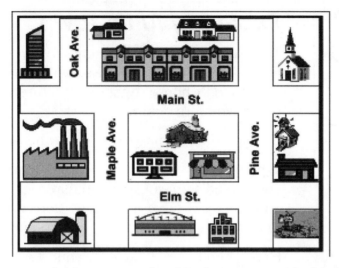

There is a copy of this map on the CD that came with this book. Why not load the drawing into Logo? It's called TOWN.PCX. Then we'll have some fun with it.

To load the Turtle Town map:

1. Select Bitmap/Load and load the TOWN.PCX file, or use the BITLOAD command.

2. To use the BITLOAD command, make sure that Logo is running and that the CD is in the CD drive. We'll call that drive "D." You should use the correct drive letter or path for your system.

3. Type BITLOAD "D:\\PCX\\TOWN.PCX and press Enter.

    The Turtle Town map is displayed.

"Why do you have to use two backslashes?"

The backslash is one of MSW Logo's special characters. It tells the computer to print the next character, but don't print the first backslash. To you, the command has two backslashes. However, Logo reads it like this:

BITLOAD "D:\PCX\TOWN.PCX

We'll talk lots more about backlashes, quotes, and other special characters later. Now let's have some fun moving around town.

Start by lifting the pen up. You remember how to do that, don't you?

1. Start from your home and find the farm.

2. Now find the factory.

3. Now it's time to go to school.

After you have had some fun moving around Turtle Town, why not get some friends together and see who can complete a trip in the least number of moves. For example:

1. Go to Morf's house. That's at the corner of Pine Avenue and Elm Street.

2. Take lunch to your Morf's father who works at the factory.

3. Go to see your cousin who lives in the apartments on Main Street.

4. Go get some candy at the candy store.

5. Go back home.

Rabbit Trail

4

Turtle Geography

Here's something else you can do with a group of friends or your class. Print the Turtle Town map. Then you can use your Pencil Turtle to move around Turtle Town.

Each of the Turtle Town buildings is on the CD that comes with this book as a separate file. They are all named TTBLDG*.BMP. The * is a number. Why not print them, cut them out, and make your own Turtle Town.

Or why not draw a map of your neighborhood and move your Pencil Turtle around on that.

Now let's get on with some Turtle Geography.

You've been moving around the Turtle Town map by going FORWARD, BACK, LEFT and RIGHT. Are these the directions you use to move around a map of the world, a map of your state, or your home town?

These other maps use the four directions, North, South East, and West. We'll talk more about these directions when we explore circles, clocks, and compasses. But for now, let's see what we can do with them using our map.

If you leave HOME and turn East on Main Street, what direction do you turn? Give yourself a big Gold Star if you said turn RIGHT.

Go East on Main Street to Pine Avenue and then turn South. Do you turn LEFT or RIGHT?

Go West on Elm Street to Maple Avenue.

Go North on Maple Avenue to Main Street.

What direction must you turn to find the skyscraper at the corner of Main and Oak Streets?

What else can you do with your Turtle Town map?

To get you started, add some puzzles to the map such as temporary construction barriers that you have to go around.

Turn the map into a maze.

Create a Turtle Town Game

Divide a group of friends into several teams. Each team must then design it's own turtle town game. When completed, teams play the games developed by each other and vote on which is the best game. This is also an activity that can be shared with other classes in the same or another school.

It's better if you draw your town on a large sheet of paper. You can make it a bigger and better game that way. If you need to find big sheets of paper, ask a local printer or newspaper if they have "proof sheets" or other scrap sheets or rolls you can have. Proof sheets will have printing on one side but you can use the other side for your game.

You can use your Pencil Turtle to play. Or why not try a Walnut Turtle?

Carefully crack open a walnut so that you don't break the shell. You can then glue the walnut shell to the pencil turtle shape and move it around to try out different actions.

If you don't have any walnuts, try cutting an egg carton apart. The sections that the eggs sit in make good turtle shells too.

Wrapping, Windows, Fences

No, you're not going to wrap fences around windows. This refers to three new commands you need to know about, especially when you're talking about Logo Geography.

Let's take a look at Wrapping first.

Let's say you're going on a trip. You're going to leave the continental United States and travel to Alaska. From there, you're going to make the short jump across the Bering Sea to Russia and then travel across Russia to Europe.

The only problem is that on this map, the jump from Alaska to Russia is no small jump. However, if you look at the globe, you'll see that it is only about 40 miles from Alaska to Russia.

So what happened here?

Simple, if you are mapping out your trip on the map, you have to "wrap" from the point where you leave the map on one side to where you pick it up again on the other side. If you want to see how this works on the computer, load the map that's on the CD that came with this book. Type

    BITLOAD "D:\\GRAPHICS\\MAP.BMP

Pick up the turtle's pen and drive the turtle up to Alaska and across to Russia. What happened?

The turtle wrapped around to the opposite side of the screen and appeared in Russia.

WRAP is the Logo command. It is usually ON when you load Logo. However, there may be times when you don't want the turtle to wrap around. Rather than wrap around the globe, maybe you want the turtle to fly off into space. If that's the case, use the command

    WINDOW

This command opens the window so the turtle can escape. The only way you can get the turtle back is to turn it around or just clear the screen.

It wasn't that many years ago that Russia and the United States were in a cold war. The two countries didn't like each other. But at least they weren't shooting at each other.

During that period of time, you couldn't travel from Alaska to Russia. It was like there was a Fence between the two countries.

Here's something to try. Bring the turtle HOME and then drive back up to Alaska on the map. Just before you cross over into Russia, type

FENCE

Now when try to cross into Russia, what happens?

It's like there's a fence that runs around the edge of the screen. You can't move beyond it. Logo gives you a message:

The turtle is out of bounds.

Check It Out

Now let's check this out to make sure you know just how these three commands work. Type

WRAP

Now type FD 2100.

The turtle draws a trail from bottom to top of the screen, stopping a ways up from HOME. The turtle WRAPped around the screen. Now type

FENCE

Now type FD 2100 again.

What happened this time? To find out, type BK 500. Now where's the turtle? It's right back HOME, isn't it? It only went to the edge of the screen and then printed the message:

The turtle is out of bounds.

One more test – type

WINDOW

Type FD 2100 one more time. Where'd the turtle go? To find out type

BK 1000   Nothing yet.

BK 1000   There it is, but it's not HOME. Try
BK 100   Where's the turtle now?

Type HOME just to be sure. Go ahead and play with these commands a bit. The next project is a good place to start.

How Big Is Your Screen

Here's a fun-type project for you. How big is your screen?

When MSW Logo was installed, it set the screen to 1000 turtle steps high and 1000 turtle steps wide. If you want to prove this, here's something to try. Type

    SHOW POS

and then press Enter.

[0 0] is printed, or shown, in the Commander window. That tells you that the turtle is HOME in the center of the screen at coordinates 0, 0. Don't worry about the SHOW and POS commands right now – or about coordinates. You won't use them for a while. Now type

    FD 1000 (Don't forget to press Enter.)

Wow! There's a line drawn up and down the screen. Now type

    SHOW POS (Press Enter here, too.)

Where are you? Does it say [0 0] again? Just so you know that Ernestine isn't teasing you, type

    FD 100 SHOW POS

Now what does it say in the Commander window? Morf got [0 100]. What did you get? This shows that you changed your coordinates to 0, 100. You went FD 100.

Now clear the screen – you remember how to do that don't you? Let's try the same thing in the other direction. Type

    RT 90 FD 1000 SHOW POS

Yes, you can type more than one command on one line. Just remember to press Enter when you want Ernestine to do her thing.

What happened? Are you back HOME again? If it says [0 0] in the Commander window, that's exactly where you are.

33

Fencing In Your Screen

"Logy, the screen on my notebook computer is much smaller than the screen on your computer. Ernestine may think that the screen is 500 steps from the center of the screen to the edge. But if I go forward more than 200 steps, the turtle disappears off my screen. How come?"

The size of your screen really has nothing to do with the size of the MSW Logo window. That window simply goes beyond the edge of your screen. If you want to change your screen so that it is the size of your screen, that's easy enough. But, first you have to measure your screen.

Morf found that the screen on his notebook computer was 660 steps wide by 400 steps high. Logy's screen is 970 steps wide by 660 steps high.

To change the Windows 3.1 screen:

1. Open the File menu and left-click on Exit to leave Logo.

   The MSW Logo screen closes.

2. Left-click once on the MSW Logo icon to highlight it.

   The icon changes color.

3. Open the Windows File menu and select Properties.

   The Properties dialog box is displayed.

4. Logy would change the Command line to read:

   logo.exe -h 660 -w 970

   Morf would type:

   logo.exe -h 400 -w 660

   Type the height (-h) and width (-w) of your screen.

5. Left-click on OK to change the settings for your computer.

To change the Windows 95/WIndows NT screen:

Those using Windows NT 3.5.1 or an earlier version need to follow the instructions for Windows 3.1. If you're using Windows NT 4.0, follow the instructions below.

1. Right-click (press the right mouse key) on the Start button in the lower right corner of your screen.

Left-click on Open *from the small menu that is displayed.*

2. Double-click (press the left mouse key two times very quickly) on the Programs icon or folder.

   A list of program folders is displayed.

3. Right-click on the MSW Logo folder.

   Another Open menu is displayed.

4. Left-click on Properties to open the MSW Logo Properties dialog.

   The MSW Logo Properties dialog is displayed.

5. Left-click on the Shortcut tab at the top of the dialog.

   The Shortcut page is displayed.

6. Add the height and width of your screen to the Target field following logo.exe using -h and -w as Logy and Morf did above. Left-click on OK to close the dialog.

   The MSW Logo Properties dialog is closed.

7. Close the other windows and then click on the MSW Logo icon.

   MSW Logo starts with your new screen dimensions active.

Turn on the Fence and check to make sure Ernestine goes out of bounds at the edge of the screen.

Designing Your Own Games

Now back to Turtle Town and other games. We talk a lot about games in our books. Games are fun, aren't they? Who ever said that learning can't be just as much fun?

Designing games can be lots of fun, too. Not only does it make you think through a whole series of Logo commands, it means you have to plan your game carefully so that players will understand what they have to do – and that it'll be fun!

What makes one game fun and another not so much fun? A good game is a challenge. It makes you feel good when you finish it, especially if you win.

A good game makes you think. If the game is too easy, it's not much fun, is it? After all, if you win all the time, that get's boring.

A good game is easy to understand. If you don't know what you're supposed to do, how can you win? So make sure that the rules to your game are clear.

What about playing a game?

Well, the same goes for players. They have to think very carefully to play and win! They have to plan their moves or they may find themselves getting lost or confused. It's good practice – and fun, too!

Here are some ideas some other players came up with when playing a Turtle Town game:

- One team added the feature that any player who drove off the road had to go to jail and miss three turns.

- Another team developed a game winning strategy when they turned the turtle into a helicopter so they could get across town directly, rather than move through the streets and making all those turns. (All they had to do was lift the pen up.)

Working with maps and developing games leads to all sorts of wonderful possibilities. Hopefully the ideas offered here will lead to many more of your own.

Connect the Dots

Have you ever played "Connect the Dots?" There are many different versions of this game. Let's make up a Logo version.

Draw some "dots" on the computer screen using an erasable marker. Then use the Logo commands you know to draw lines that connect the dots.

What did you draw? A crazy animal? Or just a crazy mess of lines?

OK, maybe your artwork isn't a masterpiece. But you can get some good practice with Logo commands this way.

A Dot Challenge

Clear the screen to erase the dots. Now draw some new dots in different places and number them. Can you move to Dot #1 in just one move? Can you guess the angle to turn to get to Dot #2? Can you guess how far it is?

This game is fun to play off the computer with a group. Use chalk marks or tape on the floor as the dots.

How about making it more interesting?

Put a small reward on each dot – maybe a prize or a piece of candy. Then you can see who can collect the most prizes or candy.

You know, this is sort of like a game of golf. In fact, when you get through this book, you can create your own Logo golf game.

Rabbit Trail

5

Logo Sports

Everybody likes baseball. Well, just about everybody.

Anyway, you'll find that playing baseball on the computer can be lots of fun.

Put four small stickers on the screen for bases. If you don't have stickers, use tape. Don't press too hard. You want the sticker or tape bases to stick but you also want to be able to unstick them.

Can you put the turtle on First Base in no more than three moves? (That's like three strikes.) Good, you're safe.

Now go to Second Base in three moves or less. Then go to Third. And now go back to Home plate.

Get some friends together and see who can run the bases in the fewest number of moves. To add some more fun to your game, move the stickers to different spots on the screen.

Logo Football

If you don't like baseball, why not try Logo Football? Logo and Morf live near Dallas, Texas, the home of the Dallas Cowboys. They're really big football fans.

Here's how to play Logo Football.

Draw a football field on the screen or on a sheet of clear plastic taped to the screen.

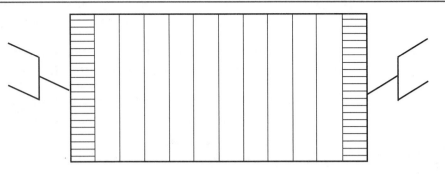

This picture of a football field is on the CD that came with this book. To load it into MSW Logo, make sure your CD is in drive D: and type:

BITLOAD "D:\\GRAPHICS\\FOOTBALL.BMP

How to Play Football

To play football, you need two teams. One team is the offense and one is the defense. The team that is on defense must place eleven small stickers on the screen to stop the offense from getting a touchdown. They can place the stickers anywhere on the screen. However, there must be enough room between the defense stickers to allow the turtle to go through without touching any of the defensive players.

The defense can also draw their defensive players on a piece of clear plastic taped over the screen, using an erasable marker. When the defense becomes the offense, all you have to do is wipe off the plastic and redraw the defense wherever you want it.

What about the offense?

The offense has to move the turtle from their goal line through the defense to the goal line on the other side of the screen without touching a defense sticker. The offense gets four downs, or four chances to make a touchdown. If they don't, they have to turn the ball over to the defense who then gets their chance to make a touchdown.

Logo football is a lot of fun, especially if you live in a big football town.

"But what about the extra point?"

"Well, why don't you make up your own rules about extra points after the touchdown."

Logo Soccer

There are all sorts of sports games you can think up for Logo practice.

Get your soccer fans to draw a soccer field on the Logo screen. Then save it as a picture. Now you can pick up teams to play soccer, or "football" as they call it in other countries.

You can use the same rules for Logo Soccer as you use for Logo Football. Or you can get as realistic as you want. That's up to you. If a player gets through the defense, he or she has to "shoot the turtle" through the goal.

You can make up the same type of game for ice hockey, too. We already have a basketball game that you'll discover later on.

Make Up Your Own Adventures

Now, why not make up some adventures of your own? To get you started, why not draw the letters of your name.

There are all sorts of things you can dream up, I'll bet.

Did you ever play "Blind Man's Bluff?"

Clear the screen. Then put a cover over it so you can't see what the turtle's doing. Then give the turtle some commands to draw a letter maybe. When you're finished, take the cover away and see how you did. Is the picture what you thought it would be?

There's a picture on the CD that came with your book called MAZE.BMP. It's shown below.

You can use this maze on the screen. Or why not make up your own maze.

Pick up the pen and move the turtle to where it says Start. Then put the pen down and see if you can move the turtle through the maze to the opening in the upper left corner.

If you want to make it tough for your friends, use colored erasable markers to draw pieces the turtle has to pick up before she leaves the maze. Erase each piece as the turtle lands on that spot.

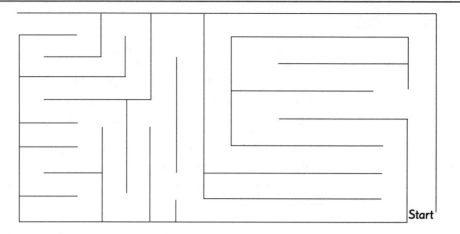

Start

Another challenge is to see who can get through the maze in the least number of moves.

All of these things are great practice using the turtle's direction and turning commands.

Go on, see what else you can do!

Printing and Saving Your Pictures

Everyone wants to see their work in print, right? That's very important, especially if you're working at school and you want your parents to see what you're doing.

All you need is a printer that is set up to print in your version of Windows. If you don't have a printer available at school, you can save your pictures and print them at home. Of course, you have to have a computer and a printer at home.

To print pictures:

The easiest way to print your pictures is to open the Bitmap menu and select Print.

Your picture is printed on your Windows printer.

To save pictures:

You have a choice: you can open the Bitmap menu and select Save or you can use the BITSAVE command. In either case, give your picture a name and type

BITSAVE "<picture name>.BMP

Your picture is saved in the MSW Logo directory.

To save your commands:

"How do I save the commands that drew the picture?"

You'll learn about writing and saving procedures in Chapter 3. In the meantime, since Logo doesn't let you save or print commands by themselves, you have to use Windows to do that for you. Here's one way to do it.

1. Expand the Commander window.

    Use the symbols on the right side of the Commander window title bar. Click on the up arrow (Windows 3.1) or the small square (Win95).

    The Commander window fills the screen.

2. Move the scroll bar at the right side of the window so that you can see that commands you want to see.

    The windows scrolls up or down to show your commands.

3. Drag the cursor over the commands you want to save.

    This means put the cursor in front of the first command you want to save. Press and hold the mouse key down as you drag the cursor over the commands you want to save.

    The commands are highlighted (they change color).

4. Release the mouse key after you have covered the commands you want to save.

    The commands stay highlighted.

5. Press Ctrl-C.

    The commands are copied.

6. Click on the down arrow (Windows 3.1) or the underscore [_] symbol (Win95) in the top right corner of the screen.

    MSW Logo becomes an icon at the bottom of the screen.

7. Open the Windows Notepad or your word processing software. When the software is loaded, press Ctrl-V or select Paste from the Edit menu.

    Your commands are copied to the screen.

8. Give the commands a file name and select Save from the File menu.

    Your commands are saved as a new file.

Learning to Say Good-bye

When you want to leave Logo, type BYE. Some Logo versions use GOODBYE

> *A message box is displayed asking if you really want to leave Logo.*

You can also select File/Exit to leave Logo. If you have not saved your workspace, the message box is displayed asking if you really want to leave Logo or not.

Writing Your Own Logo Journal

As you explore Logo, you're going to discover all sorts of things that you want to save or remember. It's a good idea to have your own journal or notebook where you can write down ideas and other things you want to remember.

That's important!

Just remember to take your time. Let the exercises in this book be the stepping stone to the many other things you can enjoy on your own

Great Logo Adventure!

Making Shapes

"What's that mean, Making Shapes?" asked Morf.

"It means that it's time to take all that you learned about moving Ernestine around the screen and put it to good use!" responded Logy. "We're going to start with simple shapes to make sure everyone knows what they are. Then we'll move on to some fancier stuff."

"Whadda you mean, fancier stuff?"

"There's a lot more to shapes than just lines. What makes one shape different from another? What's different? What's the same? What can you learn from that? What are the rules that make one shape different from another?

"The study of shapes is part of geometry, right? And that opens all sorts of possibilities!"

"Ok, Ok, Ok! How do we get started?"

Exploring Shapes

Let's play turtle. That's what I do best.

You can use your Pencil Turtle, you can use yourself, or you can use some of your friends. In fact, why not try all three?

Rabbit Trail

6

Body Geometry

Can you use your fingers to make a shape that looks like a square? It's not too easy, is it.

So try this one.

Get with a friend. Hold your arms out. Can you make a better square now?

Get a bunch of friends together and make a big circle. Now make a very small circle. In fact, why not have the group make all sorts of shapes?

What do you have to do to make a triangle? Can you make a triangle by yourself?

Or do you need some friends to help you out?

Playing turtle gives you an idea of just what it takes to make different shapes.

Exploring Squares

Let's start with an easy shape, like a square.

Do you know what makes a square different from, say, a triangle? Or a rectangle? Well, for one thing, all the sides of a square are the same size.

Tell the turtle to go HOME — not on the computer — you're still doing Body Geometry, remember? Pretend that HOME is in the middle of the room or the middle of your paper.

Now, what commands must you give the turtle to walk through a square?

1. FORWARD _____ TURTLE STEPS

Are you going to make a BIG square or a little square?

2. RIGHT _____ TURTLE TURNS

You can turn left if you want. But how many turns do you have to make for the corner of a square? 30? 67? 105? 298?

We've already done this. It was when we were talking about turtle turns. If you forget, why not turn back to Chapter 2 and find it again?

3. FORWARD _____ TURTLE STEPS

Fill in the blank with the same number of steps that you did in step 1.

4. RIGHT _____ TURTLE TURNS

How many turns should you make here? Should this be the same number of turns as you made in step 2?

5. FORWARD _____ TURTLE STEPS

You should already know how many steps to go this time.

6. RIGHT _____ TURTLE TURNS

How many turtle turns this time?

7. FORWARD _____TURTLE STEPS

8. RIGHT _____ TURTLE TURNS

What did you discover about a square?

Sure, the four sides have to be the same. But what about the corners? Do they have to be the same? Why?

That's simple!

If they're not the same, you'll end up going off in some strange direction and your shape will have too many sides.

Let's try this on the computer.

Get Logo up and running. Then type these commands.

FD _____   RT _____   FD _____

RT _____   FD _____   RT _____

FD _____   RT _____

Wow! All the sides and all the corners have to be the same. But that's a lot of typing when you do that four times. There has to be an easier way!

Repeating Commands

Look at all those commands. Do you see what you did? You repeated the commands FD _____ and RT _____ four times. So let's try a new command.

Here's what it looks like in Logo.

REPEAT 4 [FD 100 RT 90]

This tells the turtle to REPEAT the commands that are inside the brackets four times. Brackets look like square parentheses – [ ]. They hold lists of numbers, words, and things. You'll use brackets and lists a lot.

First, let's try some other squares. You fill in the steps. The number of turns has to be 90, right?

REPEAT 4 [FD _____ RT 90]

Make a great big square!

REPEAT 4 [FD _____ RT 90]

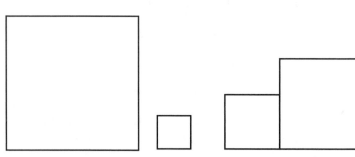

Make a little bitty square!

Morf tried the number 7 but decided that was a bit too itty-bitty. What are you going to use?

How about joining some squares together? Maybe you can think up a nice pattern using squares.

Terrific! Now for a tough one. Put a square inside a square?

That means you have to draw a big square, pick the pen up, move inside the big square, and draw a little square.

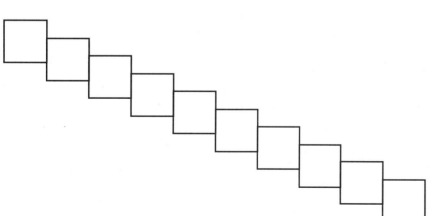

Whoops, one of the steps has been left out. Think about it. Which one is it?

Let's see. Draw a big square. Pick the pen up. Move inside the big square and draw a little square. You can't draw another square until you put the pen back down, right?

OK, no more tricks. Put the pen down and then draw a little square.

Don't forget! When you start exploring squares and things, it's good to write all your great ideas on paper or in your journal. Then you can use the same ideas again later.

More Adventures with Squares

There are lots of things you can do with squares.

Draw a little square first and then draw a big square around the outside. Draw a big square and then put a little square in the corner.

Draw a big square and then stack some other squares on top of it, like stacking up boxes.

What else can you do with squares? Take a look at the pictures below and on the next page. Can you make them on the computer?

How about some stairs?

What's the same about these pictures? What's different? What other things can you make?

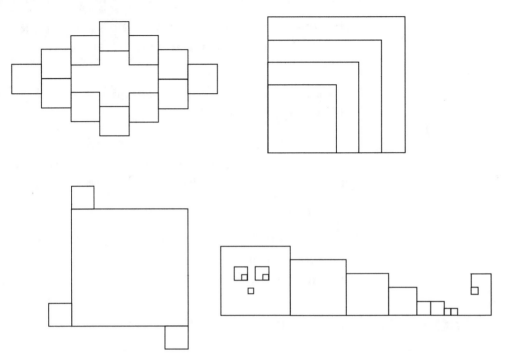

How about flags?

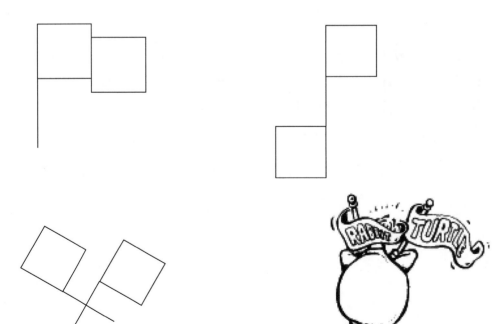

How about a windmill?

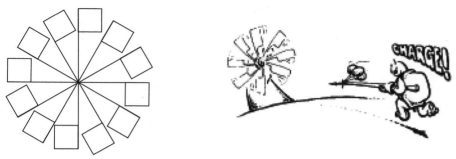

Don't forget to write down your ideas. You may just want to use some of these ideas later on.

Logo Puzzles

Here's a puzzle for you. Look at this picture.

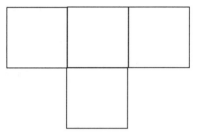

It looks like four squares hooked together, doesn't it.

Get some straws or some sticks and make this puzzle on a table top. Now, take away just one straw or stick so that there are only three squares left.

Can you do that?

You can also try solving the puzzle by drawing it on paper or on the computer.

Later, after you learn about writing procedures, we'll show you how to have the turtle solve the puzzle for you.

If you like puzzles, take a look at the puzzle projects on the CD that came with this book. You'll find lots in the Projects directory.

Exploring Triangles

Now, are you ready to tackle a triangle?

What makes a triangle different from a square?

For one thing, a triangle has three sides and three corners. A square has four of each — four equal sides and four equal corners or angles.

Adventures With Angles

There's a new word for you. Angles! Is that something like a corner?

Draw a line. Make a turtle turn of any size and draw another line.

Just like magic, there's an angle between the lines, right? But what about on the outside? Is that an angle, too?

Sure it is. It's just a big angle.

Wow! That's a lot of turtle turns!

Morf still likes to call them turtle turns. While Morf measures angles in turtle turns, most people measure angles in "degrees." More about degrees later.

Now, what about a triangle? Do all the sides and corners have to be the same or can they be different?

If you said the sides and the corners can be different, give yourself a big Gold Star!

But there's a funny thing about triangles. If all the sides are the same, can the angles be different?

Give yourself another Gold Star if you said, No!

But how do you know? If all the sides are the same, why do the angles have to be the same? Let's explore some triangles and see if we can figure this out.

Get Logo up and running. Let's start where we left off with the squares.

    FD 100
    RT 90
    FD 100

Adventures With Right Angles

OK! Now you have two sides and one angle on the screen. That angle has a special name. It's called a Right Angle.

"I know," Morf chimed in. "That's because the turtle goes to the right!"

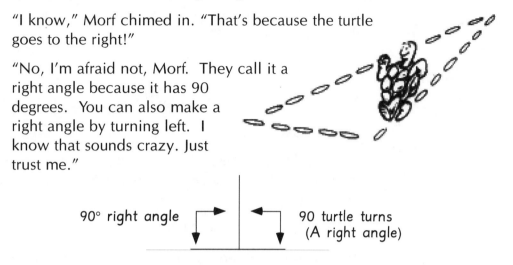

"No, I'm afraid not, Morf. They call it a right angle because it has 90 degrees. You can also make a right angle by turning left. I know that sounds crazy. Just trust me."

90° right angle   90 turtle turns
(A right angle)

When you talk about degrees, you use that little ° symbol. A triangle has three sides and three angles. So, let's make the corner you just made into a triangle.

The easy way is to just type HOME.

There's a triangle: three sides and three angles.

We know for a fact that two of the sides are equal. You typed FD 100 two times, right?

Look at the angle down near HOME. Compare that with the one in the upper right corner. Do they look to be the same? Are they the same as the corner you made when you went RT 90? Let's see.

With the turtle at HOME, type

    RT 90 FD 100

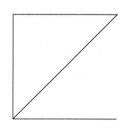

Hey! That looks like three sides of a square. What commands do you need to finish the square? RIGHT 90 sends you in the wrong direction. So why not try

    LT 90 FD 100

Now you should be at the upper right corner of a square that is also two triangles, correct? OK, now type HOME.

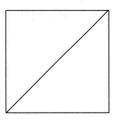

Look at the angles at HOME. Compare them with the angles in the upper right corner of the square. Do all four of the angles look the same?

You're right. They do look the same. Let's check this out.

Check It Out

Type CS to clear the screen and take the turtle HOME. Then type

REPEAT 4 [FD 100 RT 90] to draw a square.

Now turn RIGHT 45 and go FD 200. What happened? The turtle drew a line right through the upper right corner. Now type HOME and then type

REPEAT 2 [FD 100 RT 90]

This takes you to the upper right corner of the square with the turtle facing the bottom of the screen.

Turn RIGHT 45 and go FD 200 again, just as you did before. What happened?

The same thing, right? Only this time the turtle drew a line through the lower left corner.

Do you think we can make a rule from all this?

A Rule for Triangles

It looks like it. It seems that when a triangle has two equal sides, you're going to have two equal corners or angles.

In the example above, you turned RT 45 twice, correct?

Just to make sure, let's try another triangle. Clear the screen. Then try this

FD 100 RT _____ FD 100 HOME

Add any number you want. Do you see two equal sides and two equal angles on the screen? Try it a few more times, just to be sure. Use lots of different numbers for the turtle turns.

This idea seems to work, doesn't it. Do you notice anything else about your triangles?

First you went FD 100. Then you turned right and went FD 100 again. When you turn, you create the angles A and B as shown in the drawing above. Then, after going FD 100 the second time, you went home, creating the C and D angles.

Now let's try something else. Clear the screen and type

FD 100 RT 60 FD 100 HOME

Now you know that angle A is 60 degrees and angle B is 120 degrees, right? Why?

Now type

RT 60 / 2 FD 200

That's RT 60 divided by 2, then FD 200.

WOW! The angles C and D are half the size of angle A. Why? Type

FD 100 RT _____ FD 100 (Fill in a number.)

Now type RT 180 - _____ Fill in the number of turns you just made when you turned right. What happened? Is the turtle facing the bottom of the screen?

Hmmmmm! This is getting interesting. Now type

RT _____ / 2 FD 200

Fill in the number of turns you made above and divide it by two and then go FD 200. What happened?

DOUBLE WOW! You're discovering all sorts of things about triangles!

Take another look at the triangle drawing on the last page, the one with angles A, B, C, and D. What do you know now?

Angles A + B = 180
Angles C + D = Angle A
Angle C = Angle D

If all this is true, then

Angles B + C + D = 180

So, the sum of all the angles in a triangle equals 180. But before we look at more rules, try this one

FD 100 RT 120 FD 100 HOME

53

Do you see anything different about this triangle? Let's check this out. Type

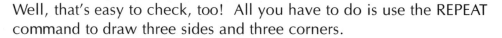

RT 60 FD 100

What happened? Where's the turtle? All three sides are equal now, aren't they? And if the sides are equal, what about the angles?

Well, that's easy to check, too! All you have to do is use the REPEAT command to draw three sides and three corners.

REPEAT 3 [FD 100 RT 120]

Wow! It works! And just to be completely certain, let's go back to the triangle with two equal sides. Clear the screen and type

FD 100 RT 90 FD 100 HOME

Now let's check that last line. Turn RIGHT 45 and go FORWARD 100. Did this take you back to the other corner?

More Rules for Triangles

No, not quite. However, it looks like you proved something about triangles.

1. If you have three equal sides, you'll have three equal angles.

2. If you have two equal sides, you'll have two equal angles.

3. If you have no equal sides, none of the angles will be equal.

4. The sum of the three angles in a triangle equals 180 degrees.

Looks like Logy got into a bit of trouble exploring triangles. How about you?

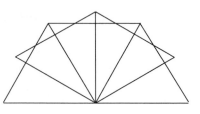

Can you make an hourglass?

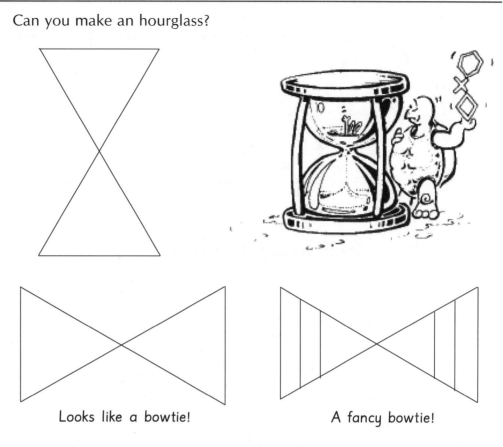

Looks like a bowtie!   A fancy bowtie!

Morf wanted to go find another caterpillar.

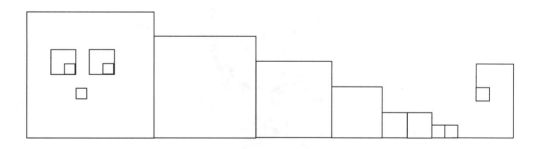

Can you draw a caterpillar with triangles for Morf?

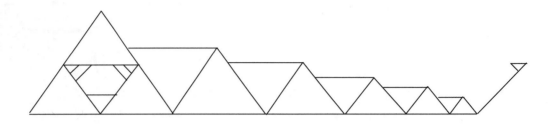

What do caterpillars turn into?

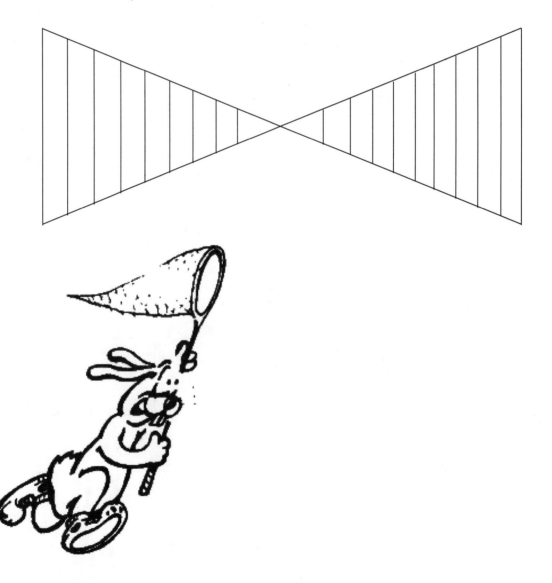

Better watch out for big butterflies!

Rabbit Trail

8

More Logo Puzzles

Here are some more Logo puzzles to do using a pencil and paper.

Draw each of these figures without retracing any line, and without lifting your pencil from the paper. Later on, you'll find Logo procedures that will solve the puzzles for you.

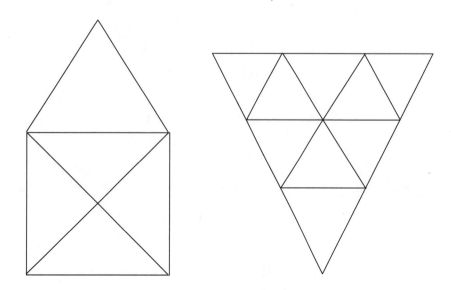

Adventures With Rectangles

Speaking of rules, what about squares and rectangles? We know a square has four equal sides. And, we know the four angles are all 90 degrees.

What makes a square different from a rectangle? Or is it different? They're both look like the side of a box. Some have square sides and some have rectangles for sides. I'm confused!

"Morf, seems like you got yourself into a box; I mean it looks like the box got into you!"

To start, let's draw rectangles. You know that this draws a square:

    REPEAT 4 [FD 100 RT 90]

How would you change that command to draw a rectangle?

Why not break it in half?

    REPEAT 2 [FD _____ RT 90 FD _____ RT 90]

Works for me! If you fill in the blanks with the same number, you get a square, right? Fill in different numbers and you get a rectangle.

What rules did you discover when trying to draw a rectangle?

Can you draw a rectangle where all four sides are different lengths? Not very easily, right? Wonder what that shape would be?

Can you draw a rectangle with only two equal sides? The other two would be unequal? No, that doesn't work either.

What about this blackboard? Is it a rectangle?

Can you draw a rectangle that has two sets of equal sides, where two sides are say, 100 steps long and two other sides are 200 steps long?

Yes! That's something you can do!

What does all this tell you about rectangles? If a square is a rectangle, then you're going to have four right angles. Right angles have to be 90 turtle turns, or 90 degrees.

Now, go ahead. Try stacking up some rectangular boxes.

Rules for Rectangles

So, I guess you can make some rules about rectangles and squares.

1. A rectangle has to have four equal angles and four sides.

2. A square is a rectangle with four equal sides and four equal angles.

3. A rectangle has two sets of equal sides.

One more thing, what's the sum of the angles of a rectangle? Where have you seen that number before?

You'll explore the Rule of 360 and lots of other shapes in the later chapters of this book. In the meantime, let's get some practice using what you're just learned.

Drawing Shapes Around the Center

Here's a challenge for you. Suppose you had to draw a rectangle around a spot somewhere on the screen. How would you do that?

The first thing you need to know is the size of the rectangle. Then you need to know where to put it.

- Draw a rectangle that is 50 turtle steps wide and 120 turtle steps high.

- Put the center of the rectangle 100 turtle steps from HOME and 100 turtle steps to the left.

Now let's figure out how to do this.

The command to draw the rectangle looks easy enough. From the lower right corner of the rectangle, tell the turtle to

    REPEAT 2 [FD 120 RT 90 FD 50 RT 90]

That will work, won't it?

Next, finding the center of the rectangle seems easy enough, also. How about this:

    PU HOME FD 100 LT 100

This is the center of the rectangle.

Looking at the picture should give you an idea for drawing the rectangle around that spot. Do you see how to do it?

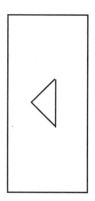

Sure! You go FD half the width of the rectangle, turn RT 90, and then go FD half the length of the rectangle. Turn around and your set to draw. Remember to put the pen down first.

```
FD 50 / 2
RT 90
FD 120 / 2
RT 180
PD
```

Now draw your rectangle.

```
REPEAT 2 [FD 120 RT 90 FD 50 RT 90]
```

There you are, a rectangle drawn around a center spot somewhere on the screen. You'll see more of this type of thing as you move through the book.

What's a Parallelogram?

"Logy, there's something strange here? You've got a rectangle that looks like it's falling over."

"You're right, you know. I never thought of a parallelogram like that," said Logy.

"Para-who?"

"That's another shape, a parallelogram. You might call that the granddaddy of a square," Logy answered.

"I don't get it? What do you mean, granddaddy?"

"Take a look at this command. It's a bit different from the one in the rectangle procedure. Yet it also does the same thing."

```
REPEAT 2 [FD _____ RT _____ FD _____ ~
        RT 180 - _____]
```

"Whoa! What's that little squiggly thing?"

That's a tilde. In MSW Logo, it tells Ernestine to look on the next line for the rest of the command. You'll see lots more of these in this book. Right now, go ahead and fill in the blanks of the REPEAT command above and then press Enter.

Look familiar? It's draws a parallelogram something like the one on the previous page. What would happen if I changed the angles to RT 90?

"Hey, that would be a rectangle," said Morf, jumping up and down excitedly.

"So, you can say that a rectangle is sort of like the 'child' of a parallelogram. A parallelogram can take many shapes, one of which is a rectangle."

"Now look at the sides. What would happen if both FD commands used the same number?"

"Well, let's see. You'd have two sets of sides that are all the same."

"And if all the angles are RT 90, what's that?"

"Hey, that's a square!"

"OK, then. Is it fair to say that a square is the child of a rectangle?"

"Seems that way."

"Right! So now we can add a new shape rule."

- A square has four equal sides and four equal angles.

- A rectangle has two sets of equal sides and four equal angles.

- A parallelogram has two sets of equal sides and two sets of equal angles.

Rules for Parallel Lines

There's something else important that we need to look into before we leave parallelograms. This is a project you can do on your own.

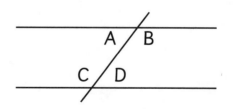

1. Draw two parallel lines like those shown in the drawing above. You know what parallel lines are by now, don't you? They're lines that are always the same distance apart no matter how long they are.

2. Next, draw a line at an angle. You pick the angle.

3. Now what are the relationships between all these angles?

   Which angles are equal?

What's the total of angles C and D? A and B?

4. Try the same thing using a different angle, two parallel lines with a different angle.

    Did you discover some new rules here about parallel lines and angles?

Sure there are! You discovered some things on your own. So write them down in your Logo journal. They may come in handy later on.

Morf's Oneliners

OK, so this one isn't really a Rabbit Trail. It's all about having some fun with your new shape commands on the computer rather than off the computer.

Think about all the things you know how to do now. You can move Ernestine around the screen. You can draw squares, rectangles, and triangles using the REPEAT command. Why not put them all together in one Big, Fantastic, Gorgeous "oneliner?"

What's a "oneliner?" Well, why not start with this one. It uses a square.

REPEAT 12 [REPEAT 4 [FD 100 RT 90] RT 30]

Add a stem and it looks like a flower, doesn't it?

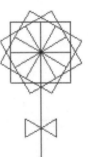 

What do these look like?

    REPEAT 6 [FD 100 REPEAT 6 [FD 10 BK 10 RT 60]~
      BK 100 RT 60]
    REPEAT 6 [FD 100 REPEAT 60 [FD 20 BK 20 RT 6]~
      RT 60]
    REPEAT 8 [RT 45 REPEAT 6 [REPEAT 90 [FD 2 RT 2] ~
      RT 90]]
    REPEAT 8 [REPEAT 4 [RT 90 FD 100] BK 100 LT 45]

Try changing the REPEATs to see what other designs you can produce.

Don't forget your pen commands. They can add some interesting variations to your creations. Here's one from some Logo friends in Israel. It sort of looks like a radar screen.

PX REPEAT 10000 [FD 200 RT 179]

Here's a real puzzler to think about.

PX REPEAT 1000000[FD 40 FD 40 BK 80 RT 1]

Now try it this way. After all, 40 + 40 = 80, right? Does it do the same thing?

PX REPEAT 1000000 [FD 80 BK 80 RT 1]

We'll look at this one again when we talk about bitmaps and graphics. For now, why not see who can come up the prettiest or the fanciest "one-liner."

Try It on Paper

Dreaming up one-liners can be tough sometimes. So why not try it on paper first?

Draw a design or a picture using just one shape. Earlier in this chapter, you saw a caterpillar made from squares. You also saw stacks of boxes, flowers, bowties, hourglasses, and other things made from just one shape.

What can you do with triangles or rectangles?

A young lady in the third grade drew a cat using just triangles. Then she drew it on the computer so she could print it to show to her family.

Think of what you can do with just one shape.

Reading Oneliners

When you have very long oneliners or other long and complicated commands, it can be tough to keep things straight. That's OK. Logo lets you get as complicated as you want. But Logo is really very straight forward. It operates one command at a time, from left to right. To understand a command, all you have to do is read it.

Let's take a look at one of Morf's one-liners as an example.

REPEAT 12 [REPEAT 4 [FD 100 RT 90] RT 30]

Is this right? Let's see.

Logo starts from the left and reads the first word, the command REPEAT. To run correctly, REPEAT needs a number to tell it how many times to repeat, followed by a list of the instructions to be repeated.

So, Logo reads to the right. Yes, there's the number 12. So the next step is to look for a list that will tell REPEAT what it is going to repeat twelve times.

The brackets — those are the things that look like square parentheses [ ] — tell you that the things inside them are a Logo list. In Logo, lists can be groups of words, numbers, letters, or even other lists. Among other things, lists can include spaces. You'll see lots of lists in this book.

And that's just what you find after REPEAT 12, another list.

There's that REPEAT command again. And, yes, it is followed by the number 4 and a list. The list tells the turtle to do what's inside the brackets — go forward 100 steps and turn 90-degrees to the right.

That's OK. This list is followed by the command RT 30. So it seems that there's a perfectly good list for the first REPEAT command. This is what Logo repeats 12 times.

        [REPEAT 4 [FD 100 RT 90] RT 30]

Now let's try something. Type the REPEAT command shown next and press Enter.

        REPEAT 12 [REPEAT 4 [FD 100 RT 90 RT 30]

What happened? What's that tell you about brackets?

For every left bracket, there has to be a right bracket.

You'll see long, complicated command lines in this book and in the procedures on the CD. To understand them, just remember to read from left to right, one command at a time. You'll learn more about tracing and stepping through commands in the next chapter.

Time to Experiment

Here's an experiment to try using brackets and parentheses — quotation marks, too.

You know how Morf loves experiments. So·let's experiment with something new, the PRINT command.

Type this in the Input Box:

PRINT "HELLO, "LOGY!

What happened?

Now try this:

(PRINT "HELLO, "LOGY!)

What happened this time? Do you see what the parentheses did?

Now try this one:

SHOW "HELLO,\ LOGY!

What's the difference between the command above and this one?

SHOW "|HELLO, LOGY!|

One command uses the backslash and the other uses the big vertical lines. But what they show looks the same, doesn't it.

PRINT and SHOW are a lot alike as you'll see. Use either one, for now. Can you find the difference between the two commands?

What does that backslash do? It creates a space, right? See what happens with this one:

PRINT "HELLO,\ LOGY.\ \ MY\ NAME\ IS\ MORF.

OK, let's get back to brackets. Try this one:

PRINT [HELLO, LOGY!]

No quotation marks this time. Why not? What happens if you include parentheses or quotation marks inside the brackets?

PRINT ["HELLO, "LOGY!]

What does this tell you about quotation marks? Think about that. We'll talk about quotes, words, lists, brackets, and parentheses lots more.

But, before we go, what else can you do with the PRINT command? How about this!

You guessed it, I bet. PR is a shortcut for PRINT. But we're getting off track. Brackets and parentheses are very important but we need to get back to what we were doing.

Rabbit Trail
9

Clocks, String, and Other Stuff

Do you need some help understanding angles, degrees, and things?

Well, here are some off-the-computer activities you can use to make some sense out of this. In these activities, you'll be looking at angles, degrees, shapes, and planes — using clocks, string boards, balls of string, or colored yarn.

The Turtle's Clock

Let's start with a clock. If you can tell time, you can understand angles and degrees.

You'll need some help from your friends or the others in your class. You'll also need a large room or a big space outside. The last thing you'll need is a long piece of string or rope at least as wide as your circle will be.

The first thing to do is draw a large chalk circle on the floor. Here's an easy way to do it.

1. Have one person hold the string down on the floor in the center of the room.

2. Stretch the string out to where you want the edge of the circle to be.

3. At the edge of the circle, wrap the string around the chalk a few times.

4. With the chalk on the floor, keep the string tight and walk in a circle around the person in the middle. Make sure the middle person turns with you so the string doesn't get wrapped around them.

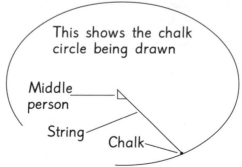

This shows the chalk circle being drawn

Middle person

String

Chalk

5. When your circle is complete, stretch your string across the middle of the circle from top to bottom.

6. Mark the top and bottom positions on the circle as 12:00 o'clock and 6:00 o'clock.

7. Stretch the string across the middle of the circle from side to side. This should divide the circle into four equal parts. Mark the side positions as 3:00 o'clock to the right of 12:00 o'clock and 9:00 o'clock to the left.

8. With the string stretched across the center of the circle, mark off the positions for 1:00 o'clock and 7:00 o'clock, 2:00 o'clock and 8:00 o'clock, 4:00 o'clock and 10:00 o'clock, 5:00 o'clock and 11:00 o'clock.

Now you have a clock face on the floor.

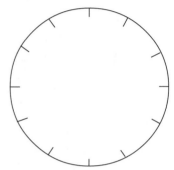

If you're at HOME facing 12:00 o'clock, what time will it be if you turn RIGHT 90? It will be 3:00 o'clock, right?

If you turn RIGHT 90 again, what time is it? 6:00 o'clock, right?

Turn RIGHT 90 again and it's 9:00 o'clock.
Turn RIGHT 90 once more and you're back at 12:00 o'clock again.

You turned RIGHT 90 four times for a total of 360° or 360 turtle turns.

There's that number again, 360!

Standing at HOME and looking at 12:00 o'clock, turn to 1:00 o'clock. If it's 90 turns to 3:00 o'clock, how many is it to 1:00 o'clock? To 2:00 o'clock?

Turn back to 12:00 o'clock. How far will you have to turn to look at 6:00 o'clock? How far is it if you turn right? If you turn left? It's the same, isn't it. It's 180 turns each way.

Let someone else have a turn playing turtle. If that person faces 6:00 o'clock and turns RIGHT 90, where are they facing? Remember the turtle turns from the direction she is facing, so it's 9:00 o'clock.

Don't play using just RIGHT or LEFT 90.

What's the turn from 4:00 o'clock to 8:00 o'clock? From 1:00 o'clock to 10:00 o'clock? Try out all sorts of turns in both directions. Here's your chance to get used to working with many different angles.

There's a clock face with hands on the next page that you can use for practice. There's also a file on your CD called CLOCK.BMP. Print it and then cut out the hands.

Rabbit Trail

10

Clocks On and Off the Computer

Write the numbers 1 through 12 on small stickers. Start with the turtle at HOME and have one of your friends type FD 100 BK 100. Put the 12:00 o'clock sticker at the top of the first line. Have the next friend type RT 30 FD 100 BK 100. Put the 1:00 o'clock sticker at the end of this line. Continue like this all the way around the circle until you have all twelve numbers on the screen. Does this look like a clock?

Now you can play "Simon Sez" or "Mother, May I" on and off the computer using times instead of distances.

Simon Sez turn to 4:30 o'clock.
Simon Sez turn to 11:00 o'clock.
Turn to 9:00 o'clock.

Rabbit Trail

11

Learning With a Ball of String

You're going to need a piece of wood from which you can cut a square that is about 12 inches on each side. Use a piece of shelf board or a piece of plywood.

You're also going to need at least thirteen small nails about 1-$\frac{1}{2}$ inches long, a hammer, a pencil, and about 12 feet of yarn. String will do.

1. Hammer a nail into the center of the board, just part way so that you have an inch or more sticking up from the board.

2. Tie the string to the nail in the center. Now you're going to make a circle around the center nail.

3. Stretch the string out to the edge of the board.

4. Put your pencil out near the edge of the board. (Hold it up straight.) Then wrap the string around the pencil.

5. Hold the pencil up straight and stretch the string out from the nail. Make sure you hold the string so that it doesn't come off the pencil. Then draw a circle around the center nail.

Now we're ready to hammer the other twelve nails into the board. But first, do you have a printer that can print pictures? If so, the turtle can make you a pattern for your string board.

Do you remember how to draw a triangle with three equal sides?

REPEAT 3 [FORWARD 100 RIGHT 120]

Now let's use that in a one-liner to make a pattern.

REPEAT 12 [REPEAT 3 [FORWARD 100 RIGHT 120] RIGHT 30]

Wow! There's a pattern with twelve points, just like the numbers on a clock. Print the screen.

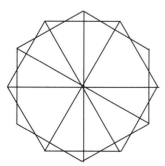

Now carefully push the pattern over the nail in the center of the board. Hold or tape the pattern in place. Then draw a line along each of the pattern lines to the circle you drew before. Where each line crosses the circle, hammer in a nail.

Looks like a clock, doesn't it? Well, now you and the string can play turtle graphics.

Take the string from the center nail (that's HOME on the screen) and stretch it up to the nail at 12 o'clock.

Rockin' Around the Clock

Go around the 12:00 o'clock nail and take the string around the 3:00 o'clock nail. Then take the string HOME.

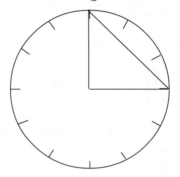

Now do the same thing, only go around the 1:00 o'clock nail and the 4:00 o'clock nail.

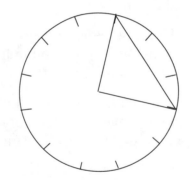

What's really going on here?

You're moving a triangle through space, turning it on a vertical axis that passes through HOME. Can you think of a better way to demonstrate how things move through space?

"You're moving around a what?"

"The circle is on a vertical axis. Vertical means it goes up and down or top to bottom. It's the opposite of horizontal, which means it's lying flat or going from side to side.

"It looks something like this."

The line is the center is the axis. As you draw triangles on the circle, it's like they are moving through space on the circle. That's the plane or surface.

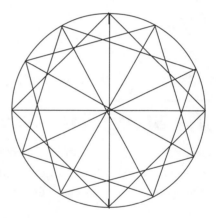

But let's not get too complicated. You're supposed to be having fun, remember?

Yeah, but how do you draw a circle to look like that? You'll learn more about that in Chapter 8.

Now, go around the 2:00 o'clock nail and the 5:00 o'clock nail, the 3:00 o'clock nail and the 6:00 o'clock nail, the 4:00 o'clock nail and the 7:00 o'clock nail. Continue on all the way around.

What pattern has the string made? It looks just like the one you printed, doesn't it? Only this one's inside a circle.

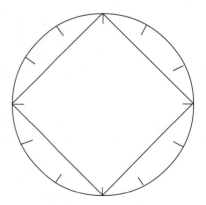

Your hand acted like the turtle as it moved around the string board, didn't it? But instead of drawing lines on the screen, you made a line of string.

Take a close look at this drawing. We've been talking about and using triangles to create this. But do you see some other shapes here? Do you see the squares? Can you find the one shown in the picture below?

How many squares can you find?

Now look carefully at the command that made the pattern.

REPEAT 12 [REPEAT 3 [FORWARD 100 RIGHT 120] RIGHT 30]

Your first REPEAT 3 [FORWARD 100 RIGHT 120] went from HOME, around the 12:00 o'clock nail, around the 3:00 o'clock nail, and then HOME. Then did you turn RIGHT 30 turtle turns?

Guess so, right?

If you turn back to the beginning of this Rabbit Trail, you'll find that you can do all the clock activities you did on the floor on your new string board.

How about doing your string board activities on the floor, too!

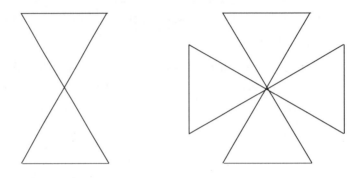

Rabbit Trail

12

The String Toss Game

This can be a great game with a group of friends. It gives you the chance to act out Logo commands by drawing with a ball of string or, better yet, a ball of colored yarn.

Have one person stand in the middle of your chalk circle. Then put other friends at each of the twelve points at the edge of the circle. You can also have one friend write down commands. Another can do the commands on the computer.

The person in the middle is like the turtle. The turtle always starts facing 12:00 o'clock.

LEFT 30

Toss the string to 11:00 o'clock, then to 1:00 o'clock. Then toss it HOME.

What shape is this?

Sure, it's a triangle. See how this works? It's even more fun when you make crazy shapes. Try it.

Finding Shapes All Over

One more thing!

Now that you've had some fun working with different shapes, why not go outside and see if you can find any of them in your neighborhood?

Look at your house. Can you find a rectangle there? A square? A triangle? Do you see any trees that look like circles? Triangles?

There are lots of basic shapes in nature and in the things we build. That's why it's important to know how to work with them.

Morf loves flowers.

```
TO DAISY
CS HT
REPEAT 30 [TRI 120 RT 12]
REPEAT 30 [TRI 80 RT 12]
REPEAT 30 [TRI 40 RT 12]
END
```

How about a tree?

Why not draw some fancy ornaments? Print them out and then color them for a holiday.

Why not decorate your room?

There are all sorts of things you can do!

"But what about the other kinds of shapes?"

You really need to learn more about writing procedures first. You'll see lots of different shapes in later chapters. In the meantime, you've got enough to enjoy for a while.

Have fun! In fact, have lots of fun!

Writing Procedures

4

Have you been getting all wrapped up in typing all those commands over and over and over again?

It's the only way you can tell the turtle what to do, right?

Maybe not! Think about this for a minute.

Did you have to tell the turtle how to move? Of course not! She already knew that. FORWARD, BACK, LEFT, RIGHT are all Logo primitives, remember? Primitives are the instructions, or procedures, the turtle already knows.

Now think about this. What if there was a way to teach the turtle how to draw squares, rectangles, triangles, flowers, snowflakes, and other things — and she wouldn't forget?

That's just what this chapter is all about. You can teach the turtle to do all sorts of things — lots more than just drawing shapes. However, since drawing shapes is what we've been doing so far, let's start with shape procedures. Then we can use them to do lots more things.

What is a Procedure

First of all, just what is a procedure?

Look at it this way. What procedure do you follow when you wake up in the morning?

You get out of bed. Morf has a lot of trouble with that sometimes.

You get cleaned up, put on your clothes, eat your breakfast, brush your teeth, go to school – or something like that.

Procedures are what you do. They are the steps you take to make something happen.

Logo procedures are things you teach Logo to do. They include all the steps Logo must take to make something happen.

Writing Your Own Procedures

When you write a procedure to draw a shape, you teach Ernestine, the turtle, how *to* draw it. This is why you always start a procedure with the word, TO. You want the turtle or Logo TO do something. What would call your procedure for getting up in the morning?

You could call it

> TO GET.UP

Then you could add procedures for all the things you do when you get up.

> TO GET.UP
> GET.OUT.OF.BED
> WASH.YOUR.FACE
> GET.DRESSED
> EAT.BREAKFAST
> BRUSH.YOUR.TEETH
> END

Naming Procedures

What's with all the periods between the words?

That's one of the rules about naming procedures. You can name a procedure anything you want. You can call it SUPERCALIFRAGILISTICEXPIALIDOCIOUS if you want, or maybe just GET, or even G.

Name your procedure whatever you want it to be, just as long as the name

- has no spaces. TO GET is fine. TO GET UP is not.

- is not just a number. TO SEVEN is OK. TO 7 is not. TO 7A or TO A7 is OK. A procedure name must have a least one letter.

- is not a symbol that Logo uses such as: (:) \ # " | [or] You can use all the others. TO GET.UP or TO GET_UP are OK.

To get started writing procedures, why not teach the turtle how to make the shapes you made in Chapter 3?

Defining a Corner

The simplest shape you made was the corner: FORWARD so many steps and then turn RIGHT or LEFT 90. So let's teach the turtle

TO CORNER

When you type TO CORNER in the MSW Logo Input Box and press Enter, a little dialog box pops up on the screen.

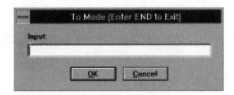

If you type a command on the same line as TO – for example:

TO CORNER FD 100

you will get a message telling you that [] doesn't like FD as an input. That's just another way of saying that you can't have blank spaces in the name of a procedure.

You'll hear more about Inputs when we talk about variables. For now, just remember that TO and the name you give the procedure have to go on a line all by themselves.

Using the To Mode Dialog

Type the first line of what you want the turtle to do in that little box right below the word Input: Left-click on OK or press Enter after each line that you type. If you don't like what you typed, you can delete a word or two. Or left-click on Cancel. That erases the whole procedure so you can start all over again.

When you have typed the last command of your procedure, type the word END on a line by itself so Logo will know this is the end of your procedure.

"Hey, I want to be able to see my procedure as I type them," Morf moaned.

"Can't I do that?"

Yes, you can. You can use the Editor window, which we talk about shortly. All you need to do is go to the Input Box and type

>   EDIT "CORNER

MSW Logo and some other Logo packages let you type ED "CORNER for short.

The Editor window is displayed showing

>   TO CORNER
>   END

in the upper left corner. Start typing your procedure in between the first line and END. When you have finished typing, left-click on File/ Exit to define your procedure. Then you can check it out.

More on using the Editor in just a little bit.

Writing the Corner Procedure

Whether you are working in the Mode dialog box or in the Editor window, here's how to write the Corner procedure. Type

>   FD _____ RT 90

Fill in any number you want. You can change it later.

When writing procedures, you can have more than one action command on a line if you want. You can have either

>   FD 100 RT 90

or

>   FD 100
>   RT 90

Now type END on a separate line. After you press Enter, Logo then sends you a message that says corner defined.

This only happens if you're working in the Mode dialog box. The editor sends you a different message, as you will see.

OK! You've defined your first procedure for the turtle. It's like a new command, so give it a try. Type

CORNER

How 'bout that!

Now, can you use your new procedure to make a square?

Writing a Square Procedure

Sure you can. Go ahead and type CORNER again and press Enter. What happened? What would happened if you did that again? And again? Well, why not just type

REPEAT 4 [CORNER]

Now we're getting some where. So let's write a procedure for a square.

TO SQUARE
REPEAT 4 [CORNER]
END

Now type SQUARE to run your new procedure.

Hey, we're on a roll!

Using Your Square

Now let's put that square to good use. Where are some of the places that you see squares in action? How about a checkerboard?

That shouldn't be too hard. You're going to need eight columns of eight squares each. All you have to do is just think through each step the turtle has to take.

First things first. Erase what you've done so far by typing ERALL — ERASE ALL for some other Logo packages. Still others tell you to REMOVE the procedures. Do whatever it takes so that everything is erased from your Logo screen.

79

Your workspace is the active part of the computer's memory where your procedures and things stay while your are working on them, and while Logo is up and running.

You'll see later on that a lot more goes on in the computer's memory than just holding procedures.

The first step is to draw a column of small squares. Start your checkerboard with squares that have a side length of 20. If you make the side much bigger, the checkerboard won't fit on the screen.

```
TO SQUARE
REPEAT 4 [FD 20 RT 90]
END
```

When you run the SQUARE procedure, the turtle ends up at the lower left corner of the square. To put another square on top of the first one, you have to move up the side and then draw the next square. Try this:

```
SQUARE FD 20
```

Where's the turtle? Does it look OK? What would happen if you tried the same commands again? And again?

Seems to work doesn't it. What about this?

```
REPEAT 8 [SQUARE FD 20]
```

Works for me. However, how are you going to draw the second and other columns?

You could pick the pen up, go HOME, move to the right, and then draw another column. However, that seems awfully complicated.

How about this? Turn right at the top of the first column, move over, and then draw the second column moving from top to bottom.

Would this work?

```
REPEAT 8 [FD 20 RT 90]
RT 90 FD 20 RT 90
```

Think about it – before you try it on the computer. Use your pencil turtle to draw it if you need to.

Here's what we ended up with.

```
TO CHECKERS
REPEAT 4 [COLUMNS]
END

TO COLUMNS
REPEAT 8 [SQUARE FD 20]
RT 90 FD 40 RT 90
REPEAT 8 [SQUARE FD 20]
LT 180
END
```

Works for me! You'll learn how to fill in the squares in the next chapter.

Saving Procedures

Saving your procedures is easy. Just type

SAVE "CHECKERS.LGO

or whatever you want to call it.

Now all the procedures in your workspace are saved under that name. Let's see how this works.

Type ERALL (or ERASE ALL) so that all your procedures are erased from your Logo workspace.

Now what happens when you type CHECKERS. Logo comes back and says

I don't know how to checkers.

Procedures are saved in your MSW Logo directory. You can, of course, save procedures to whatever directory you want. Remember, you have to use double backslashes like this:

SAVE "C:\\<pathname>\\CHECKERS.LGO

The backslash is a special character in Logo. The easiest way to explain it is to say that Logo reads the first backslash as a special character and gets ready to print whatever the next character is, even if it's a space.

As you will see later on, it's a way to include spaces in Logo words.

If this is too much typing, you can always use File/Save or File/Save As… to save your procedures to whatever name you want.

Loading Procedures

If you want to see your checkerboard, all you have to do is load it back into the workspace, right? Well, don't just sit there, go ahead and do it!

Type LOAD "CHECKERS.LGO

or

LOAD "C:\\<pathname>\\CHECKERS.LGO

where <pathname> is the directory in which your Logo files are stored.

You can also use your mouse. Open the File menu and left-click on Load. A menu appears from which you can pick the procedure you want to load.

Defining Other Shapes

Now let's get back to writing procedures. Do you remember the commands you wrote for a triangle with equal sides?

REPEAT 3 [FD 100 RT 120]

Now we can make that a procedure, too! Since TRIANGLE is a long title for such a short procedure, why not call it TRI for short.

TO TRI
REPEAT 3 [FD 100 RT 120]
END

Building Houses

What do you think would happen if we put the triangle on top of the square? You remember the SQUARE procedure, don't you?

TO SQUARE
REPEAT 4 [CORNER]
END

TO CORNER
FD 100 RT 90
END

Want to make it a bit shorter? Just one procedure? Try this:

```
TO SQUARE
REPEAT 4 [FD 100 RT 90]
END
```

OK, now add the triangle. Don't worry about getting it right the first time. Play around and see what you can come up with. Morf came up with a shape that looks like a house.

So he wrote a procedure.

```
TO HOUSE
SQUARE
FD 100 RT 30
TRI
END
```

Isn't it easier using procedures as commands? Not only do you save yourself a lot of typing, you make things easier for other people to understand. They can look at your set of procedures and know right away what it's supposed to do.

How would you ever know what the NYC procedure, shown later in this chapter, is supposed to do if you didn't see the picture?

Since you're getting so good at this, why not do some things on your own?

Why not add a door to your house? Add a window. Add a chimney. How about a TV antenna?   Maybe a walkway?

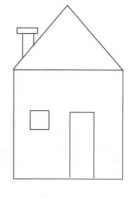

Just don't add the sore fingers!

Other Houses

If you don't like the standard house that most people start out with, why not make your own HOUSE procedure?

Tell you what, how about a native hut? You can use a square block, a smaller rectangle, and some straws or sticks for the roof.

```
TO HUT
REPEAT 4 [FD 60 RT 90]
FD 60 RT 30 FD 60 RT 120
REPEAT 20 [BK 6 FD 66 BK 60 RT 3]
END
```

Maybe this procedure will give you some other ideas. MYHOME.LGO on the CD that came with this book draws the entire yard. Color the picture after you've read the next chapter. By the time you get through, you'll be adding flying birds, passing cars, the setting sun and rising moon.

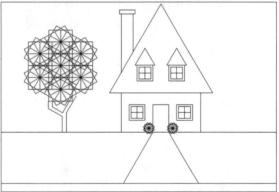

Why not write one procedure to draw several houses? Or, why not try a 2-story house – or something other than a house? Morf has some ideas for you in his next Rabbit Trail.

Rabbit Trail

13

Exploring With Blocks

You started out working with squares, triangles, and rectangles. Now let's put them to work.

One of the things that will help you get some ideas is to use blocks of different shapes. Sometimes seeing real things on the table top or on the floor can give you some good ideas to work with on the computer. Also, working with real shapes gives you a better idea of how things fit together.

Get some large sheets of paper. Then place the blocks on the paper to make a figure that you like. Now, carefully trace each shape with your pencil. You'll end up with a picture of your figure on the paper.

Get yourself a ruler and measure each side of each block. Write each measurement by each side on your picture.

Unless you're using very small blocks, the drawing you just made is much larger than the screen. Therefore, you're going to have to "scale" your drawing to fit the screen.

Scaling Your Drawings

What does it mean to scale a drawing?

Take a look at a map. Down at the bottom, there is usually a box that describes the map. This section also gives the scale. For example, one inch could equal ten miles. That means that one inch on the paper map equals ten miles of real distance.

You can do the same thing. You can draw your block figure on the screen using a scale such as one inch equals ten turtle steps.

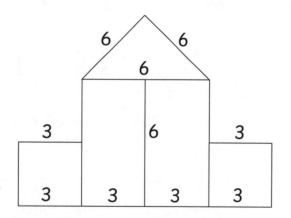

In the picture, the small square block is 3 inches on each side. To recreate that picture, you can write a procedure that says

```
TO SCALE
CS HT
REPEAT 2 [FD 6 * 10 RT 90 FD 3 * 10 RT 90]
REPEAT 2 [FD 6 * 10 LT 90 FD 3 * 10 LT 90]
RT 90 FD 3 * 10
REPEAT 4 [FD 3 * 10 LT 90]
BK 9 * 10
REPEAT 4 [FD 3 * 10 LT 90]
FD 3 * 10 LT 90 FD 6 * 10 RT 30
REPEAT 3 [FD 6 * 10 RT 120]
END
```

FD 3 * 10 means go FORWARD 3 times 10, or FD 30.

Do this with your other shapes, using the dimensions that you measured instead of the FD 3 that Morf measured. Now try these new procedures on the screen. You can draw a small version of your block figures as a Logo procedure.

But what if *10 is too small? You'll find a way to change that in the *Editing Your Procedures* section later in this chapter.

Houses, Squares, Wheels, and Things

If you don't have any blocks available, why not just explore what you can do with the shapes you've made. One young lady made a wheel out of the HOUSE procedure. How do you suppose she did that?

Well, let's take a look at the house procedure.

```
TO HOUSE
SQUARE
FD 100 RT 30
TRI
END
```

Before you run the HOUSE procedure, hide the turtle. Do you remember how to do that? If not, turn back to Chapter 2 and check it out.

After you hide the turtle, type HOUSE. Then type HOUSE again.

What happened?

Try it again. What happened this time?

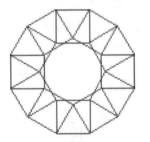

What number do you add to the WHEEL procedure to make our friend's wheel?

```
TO WHEEL
HT
REPEAT _____ [HOUSE]
END
```

Here's a car our young friend designed. We'll talk more about circles and curves later on. In the meantime, what can you dream up?

Write down all the things you can think of that use squares, triangles, rectangles – maybe even wheels.

How about a rocket ship?

Maybe the Space Shuttle?

Take a look. Here are some NASA rejects.

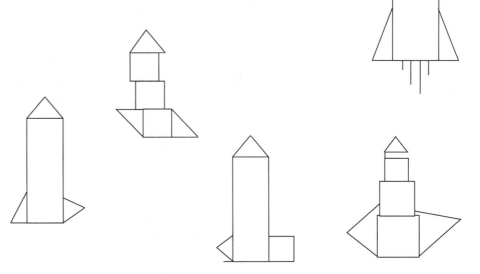

If you prefer to stay on Earth, how about a Logo castle?

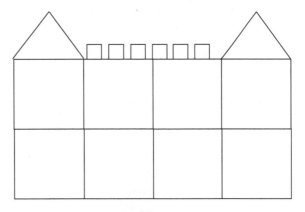

To see how the Castle was built, look at the CASTLE.LGO procedure on the CD that came with this book.

Bet you can make a much better looking castle. Why not give it a try? Go ahead, explore a bit. You can discover all sorts of things that way.

Snowflakes

Here's a fun project to help you get practice writing procedures.

Know what a snowflake is? It's an ice crystal. They say that no two snowflakes are alike. But they all have something in common. They are all crystals that have six sides or six points.

They're really pretty easy to create. All you have to do is use REPEAT 6. Add whatever works for you after that.

Why not get some friends together to see who can draw the fanciest snowflake. There are some sample Snowflake procedures on the CD than came with this book. Here's a look at some of them.

```
TO STARFLAKE
HT  REPEAT 6 [SNOW RT 60]
END

TO SNOW
SNF FD 30 RT 45 SNF SNF
FD 10 BK 50 LT 90 SNF
SNF FD 10 BK 50 RT 45
FD 50 LT 45 S RT 45 BK 100
END

TO SNF
FD 20 RT 45 S LT 180  S RT 135
END

TO S
REPEAT 5 [FD 10 RT 144]
END
```

Here's another one called SPIKE.LGO.

```
TO SPIKEFLAKE
SNOWFLAKE
PR [BY MEGAN HANKINS]
PR [2ND GRADE]
END

TO SNOWFLAKE
HT REPEAT 6 [SPIKE RT 60]
END

TO SPIKE
FD 50 BK 30 RT 30 FD 30 BK 30 LT 60
FD 30 BK 30 RT 30 BK 20
END
```

Michelle wrote procedures for a Snowflake show. It's on your CD as FLAKES.LGO.

Does it give you any ideas?

Maybe this will get you started.

1. Draw a snowflake.

2. Pick up the pen and move the turtle to another part of the screen.

3. Draw another snowflake and then move again.

4. Do this several times and the screen will look like a snow storm.

But remember! Since no two snowflakes are alike, each of yours should be different. You didn't think this was going to be easy, did you?

What's In Your Workspace

If you have been working through this chapter, you may have all sorts of things in your workspace by now. Maybe you want to save some of this, maybe not.

Logo offers you a set of commands that let you see what's in your workspace so that you can keep things organized. These are the Print Out commands, PO for short.

To list the titles of the procedures you have stored in your workspace, type

POTS   (That's short for Print Out TitleS)

Presto! There are the titles of all the procedures in your workspace.

To list all the procedures you have stored in your workspace, including all the commands, type

POPS   (That's short for Printout ProcedureS)

Presto! There are the names of all the procedures in your workspace. This is handy when you are working on lots of different procedures.

To see everything in your workspace – procedures, property lists, variable names, and other stuff you haven't read about yet – you have a choice. Use the command POALL. You can also use PO CONTENTS.

To get a preview of these and other PO commands, select Help/Index. Select Help Topics and then type PO in the box that is displayed.

PO and all the other Print Out commands are listed. You can look at any or all of these that you want.

Erasing Procedures

OK, now that you've displayed all the procedures, how do you get rid of the procedures you don't want to save?

There are actually several things you can do. You can erase the procedures you do not want to save one at a time using the ERASE command. Just type

ERASE "*<procedure name>*

For example, suppose you have these procedures in your workspace:

HOUSE
SQUARE
CORNER
TRI
DOOR
WINDOW
CHIMNEY
ANTENNA

Since lots of people get cable these days, you don't really need an antenna. So type

ERASE "ANTENNA

Let's say that you're going to remodel your house. You're going to replace the door, window, and chimney. To erase those procedures, type

ERASE [DOOR WINDOW CHIMNEY]

Get the idea?

Saving Lots of Procedures

But what if you don't want to erase the procedures? You just want to save them in different files.

Well, that's easy enough. Use the SAVEL command.

Here's an example:

SAVEL [HOUSE SQUARE TRI CORNER DOOR] "HOUSE.LGO

SAVEL [CHECKERS COLUMNS] "CHECKER.LGO
SAVEL [STARFLAKE SNOW SNF] "STARFLAK.LGO

SAVEL lets you save a list of procedures in a file that you name. It's a real handy way to straighten out a mess you may have made in your workspace.

Printing Procedures

Scrolling back and forth in the Editor to see whats in your workspace can be something of a hassle. It's easier to look at a printout.

You already learned about printing pictures. Well, how about printing procedures? There are actually several ways to print out procedures on your printer. The method you select depends on your printer and just what you want to print.

Here are two procedures that work with dot matrix printers and those printers set to text mode. They may work on a laser or inkjet printer depending on the printer settings.

To print procedures, open the Editor window. Open the File menu and select Print. The procedures displayed in the editor window are then printed on your Windows printer.

```
TO DUMP              TO DUMP
DRIBBLE "LPT1        OPENWRITE "LPT1
POALL                SETWRITE "LPT1
NODRIBBLE            POALL
END                  SETWRITE []
                     CLOSE
                     END
```

DRIBBLE and the OPENWRITE/SETWRITE combination send what ever follows to the file name or device to type after the command. In this case, you type the name of the printer port to send the procedure to be printed. There are some examples of these commands in the \projects\chpt4 directory on the CD that came with this book. You can also read more about these commands in the Help file.

You can also use the Edit or Notepad programs that come with Microsoft Windows to print your Logo procedures. Morf likes this idea because it doesn't matter what's in his workspace. He can print whatever he wants.

To print your procedure from Windows 95:

1. Click on Start and open the Accessories folder.

2. Select Notepad.

3. Select File/Open.

4. Open the directory where your Logo procedures are stored.

5. Select the procedure to print.

6. After it is displayed in Notepad, you can print it.

Instructions for Windows 3.1 are similar. Minimize MSW Logo temporarily. Open the Accessories Group and select Notepad. Select and print your procedure as described above.

Awfully simple? Or simply awful?

Editing Your Procedures

So far you've learned about loading, saving, erasing, and printing procedures. But what if you want to change them? Sometimes your procedures don't do exactly what you want them to do. So you have to change them. In Logo, we call this "editing." Guess how you do that?

Give yourself a Gold Star and double-dip ice cream cone if you said go to the "Editor."

To edit the House procedure, type

EDIT "HOUSE or ED "HOUSE for short. PC logo, as an example, uses EDIT HOUSE with no quotes.

Presto! The Editor window appears. This is where you can make any changes you want to make to your procedure.

The Editor Window

There are six menus in the Editor window. Here's a brief description of each. This is a good time to explore these choices to see just what each does.

File: This menu offers you just one choice. You can select Exit to close the Editor window.

Edit: The Edit menu offers you six selections that do the same thing that they do in other windows programs.

Undo: If you edit a line and then change your mind, Undo changes things back to the way they were.

Cut: This lets you cut things from one place so you can paste them somewhere else.

Copy: This lets you copy things from one place and paste them somewhere else.

Paste: Things you cut or copy stay on the clipboard until you paste them where you want them.

Delete: Use Delete to erase things from your procedures.

Clear All: This clears everything from the Editor.

Search: This menu gives you three standard Windows choices: Find, Replace, and Next.

Find: This helps you find a word or phrase in your procedures.

Replace: This allows you to replace words or phrases. For example, in the Rabbit Trail on blocks, if you want to change the * 10 to * 20 or something else. Try it.

Next: This is used with Find. Left-click on Next or press the F3 key to find the next use of a word or phrase.

Test: This lets you test a portion of your procedure to see if it does what you want it to do. More about this later.

Why not try some of the Editor menu options on the CASTLE procedures?

Opening More Than One Editor

MSW Logo lets you open as many Editor windows as you want. Take a look.

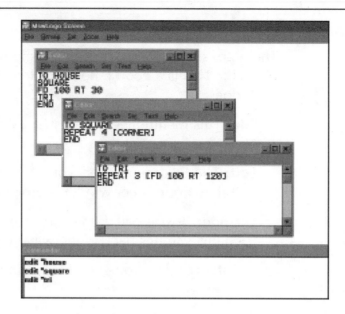

Look at the Commander window in the picture above. That shows you how three windows were made to appear on the MSW Logo Screen.

When you have lots of windows to chose from like this, it's easy to copy procedures from one window to another. In this way, Morf can keep his House procedure. You can make a copy of it to build a new two-story house.

Now Let's Edit

There are a couple of ways to build a two story house. First you can try the easy way. Later we'll get tricky and create new procedures where the only thing we'll type is the name. Watch and see!

The first thing to do is erase everything and then load the HOUSE procedures back into your workspace.

The Easy Way

Now you're ready to try the easy way of changing a house into a two-story building.

Type EDALL, EDIT ALL in some versions. You can also open the File menu, left-click on Edit, and select All.

The Editor window opens displaying all the House procedures.

Now you're ready to add a procedure to make a two story apartment. Type the following in the Editor window.

```
TO APT
SQUARE
FD 100 HOUSE
END
```

To close the MSW Logo Editor window, select File/Exit. If you have changed the file – you edited something – a box is displayed telling you just that. It says

You have the choice of selecting Yes, No, or Cancel. Left-click on Yes. The edited file is saved in your workspace. If you select No, your editing is not saved and you go back to the Commander window. To go back to the Editor, left-click on Cancel.

Editing Errors

If there is an error in your procedure, you get the message shown below.

You have the choice of selecting Yes, No, or Cancel. Left-click on Yes. The edited file is saved in your workspace. If you select No, your editing is not saved and you go back to the Commander window. To go back to the Editor, left-click on Cancel.

Select Yes to go back to the Editor where the procedure displays the definition causing the problem. Once you have corrected the problem, select File/Exit from the Editor window to get back to the Commander window.

To save this as a new procedure, left-click on File/Save as… Name the procedure APT or whatever you want and select OK to save it.

What would happen if you clicked on Save? Your new APT procedure would be saved over your HOUSE procedure. So be careful when saving procedures. You don't want to loose valuable work.

Let's Get Tricky

Erase your workspace. You remember how to do that, don't you? Sure you do. The command is ERALL. Then load the HOUSE procedures again.

The first thing we're going to do is copy the HOUSE procedure to a new Editor window. To open that new window, type

EDIT "APT

A new Editor window opens displaying two lines:

to apt
end

Now, left-click your mouse in the Editor Title Bar. Hold the button down and drag this Editor window out of the way so you can see the window with the HOUSE procedures in it.

1. Put the cursor to the left of the words TO HOUSE.

2. Drag the mouse over all the HOUSE procedures.

The text you highlighted changes color.

3. Left-click on the Edit menu and select Copy.

4. Now go over to the APT procedure. Put the cursor below the APT procedure. Left-click on the Edit Menu and select Paste.

Presto! You now have an APT procedure.

Copying and Pasting

Left-click to the left of the word SQUARE in the HOUSE procedure and drag the cursor over these commands:

SQUARE
FD 100

Select Edit/Copy. Now go to the APT procedure in the other Editor window and paste those commands into the APT procedure. Put the cursor to the left of the word END. Open the Edit menu and select Paste.

Now go back to the HOUSE procedure. Copy the word HOUSE from the procedure name and paste it to right after FD 100 in the APT procedure. Make sure that END is on a line by itself.

Your procedure should look like this:

```
TO APT
SQUARE
FD 100 HOUSE
END
```

Yes, this is a bit complicated. However, you did save yourself some typing. More importantly – and this is the point of the whole thing – you saw how you can copy all or parts of procedures from one Editor window to another.

Pretty cool! Open the File menu and select Exit to close the House Editor window and then we can get to more editing.

Now, put the cursor in front of the word SQUARE in the first line of the APT procedure.

Type CS HT and leave a space. The first line of your procedure should now look like this:

```
CS HT SQUARE
```

 It's always a good idea to clear the screen and bring the turtle HOME before you begin any procedure. In this case, you know your house will be on the ground and not tilted up in the air somewhere. Hide the turtle if you want.

Tracing Procedures

So far, we've talked about writing procedures, saving them, loading them, printing them, and editing them. What do you do when a set of procedure just doesn't do what you want them to do? Sometimes it can be tough finding these mistakes.

That's where "tracing" comes in. This lets you see just how your procedures work. MSW Logo offers you a TRACE command and a TRACE button. You can use either one. To turn tracing on, press the Trace button or type

```
TRACE <procedure(s) to be traced>
```

The list below shows you what happens when you trace the HOUSE procedure. You can trace a single procedure.

```
trace "house
house
 (house)
  house stops
```

Or you can trace a list of procedures.

```
trace [house square corner tri]
house
(house)
 (SQUARE)
 (CORNER)
   CORNER stops
 (CORNER)
   CORNER stops
 (CORNER)
   CORNER stops
 (CORNER)
   CORNER stops
 SQUARE stops
 (TRI)
  TRI stops
house stops
```

Do you see how it works? Some versions of Logo simply turn tracing on. Then everything you run is traced whether you want to see it or not. In MSW Logo, only the procedures you list are traced.

To turn TRACE off, type UNTRACE or press the UNTRACE button.

Stepping Through Your Procedures

"But what if I want to see how each line in a procedure works?"

That's when you need to use the STEP command. It is similar to the TRACE command except there is no STEP button. When run a stepped procedure, each instruction line in the procedure is displayed in a box like you see below.

Logo waits for you to say OK before moving to the next line. You might say that STEP is a detailed TRACE. To STEP through a procedure, type

STEP <procedure list>

To turn STEP off, type UNSTEP.

Why not try STEP on the some of the procedures you have written? This will give you a good idea of how it works.

Organizing Your Procedures

"Enough of this boring stuff. It's time to move on to some fun," Morf said, banging away at the computer.

"But wait a minute, Morf! There's lots more to writing procedures than just this. So far, we've been talking about short, easy procedures. What are you going to do when you want to make a really complicated procedure? How are you going to know what's supposed to happen if you don't organize your what you're doing?"

"You mean like this humongous procedure of New York City? Now this took a lot of organizing!"

"How do you like that picture? Pretty cool, huh!"

"Morf, I looked at that procedure – NYC.LGO on the CD that came with this book. It must be at least four pages long. How could you ever hope to edit something like that?"

When you're writing procedures, you do much better when you divide your procedures into chunks that are easy to work with, and easy to understand.

Take a look at this skyline of Dallas.

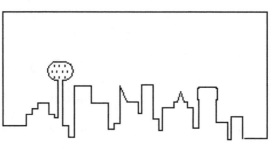

You can see how our friend, Larry, organized his procedures by looking at DALLAS.LGO on the CD.

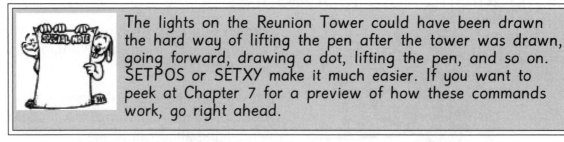

The lights on the Reunion Tower could have been drawn the hard way of lifting the pen after the tower was drawn, going forward, drawing a dot, lifting the pen, and so on. SETPOS or SETXY make it much easier. If you want to peek at Chapter 7 for a preview of how these commands work, go right ahead.

Do you see the difference between the NYC and the DALLAS procedures? NYC may be the biggest single procedure you will ever see. DALLAS makes a lot more sense. Each building is a separate procedure. If you ever want to change the drawing, you can simply change one procedure. If you ever wanted to change the NYC procedure, where would you start?

These two skylines actually came from a contest that Logy and Morf conducted to see who could draw the most creative skyline for their city? They got some really creative procedures.

Why not give it a try? You can use pictures from magazines, or photographs from the travel section of your newspaper. Go for it! Get creative!

Something else to think about. Do these very different procedures give you any ideas about superprocedures and subprocedures? Let's look at some other examples.

Tessellations and Optical Illusions

Let's tessellate!

Tessellations can be lots of fun, real brain teasers. They can also be great examples of superprocedures and subprocedures. But before we think about super and subprocedures, what's a tessellation?

You see tessellations all over the place. They're the patterns you see in wallpaper, in tile floors, in blankets – even in clothes. Strictly speaking, tessellations are patterns made by repeating one or more shapes over and over again in what seems like an endless pattern.

There are lots of books on tessellations. You can find them in your library and then try them on the computer.

Some tessellations are optical illusions. That means they look like something they are not. For example, if you look at the picture below, it looks like it is a stack of blocks.

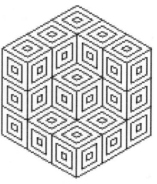

You can also find lots of books on optical illusions that can be lots of fun on the computer.

There's a long procedure that uses diamond shapes to make what looks like a stack of blocks. It's long, but it makes an interesting picture. It's on the CD as TESSEL.LGO.

To see what it's all about, type TESSELLATE. Pretty neat, huh?

Compare TESSELLATE with NYC. TESSELLATE almost uses too many procedures compared to the one humongous thing used to draw the NYC skyline.

Here's a challenge. Can you simplify TESSELLATE by combining two or more procedures?

What the difference between TESSELLATE and DALLAS?

These show you two different programming styles. You'll see many more different programming styles before you're done.

Rabbit Trail

14

Playing With Diamonds

TESSELLATE uses 27 diamond shapes to create the optical illusion. To see more of what you can do with these shapes, why not cut out 27 diamonds like the one shown below and then piece them together in different patterns?

When making your diamond designs, try stacking diamonds on top of each other, like the TESSELLATE procedure does. Or maybe you can discover an entirely new TESSELLATION all on your own.

Most importantly, have fun exploring.

Superprocedures and Subprocedures

The DALLAS and TESSELLATE procedures are good examples of different types of superprocedures. But what's a superprocedure?

Superprocedures don't do anything by themselves. But they do make a lot happen. That's because they call tell the subprocedures when it's time for them to do their jobs.

Take a look at the DALLAS procedures.

This superprocedure tells the other subprocedures when to do their jobs, when to execute their commands. In this case, each subprocedure in DALLAS is run, one after the other.

```
TO DALLAS
HOTEL
REUNION
BUILDING
BANK
BUILDING2
SPIRE
BUILDING3
BUILDING4
LIGHTS
BORDER
END
```

TESSELLATE uses a bunch of superprocedures to create that complicated pattern. Think what it would be like if you had to type in every move the turtle made to draw that optical illusion? That would sure be a lot of typing. It might even be worse than the NYC procedure!

More importantly, how would you ever organize your thoughts?

Let's take a closer look at TESSELLATE. Maybe there's more to learn from it. Start with a basic diamond.

```
TO DIAMOND
REPEAT 2 [FD 8 RT 60 FD 8 RT 120]
END
```

This draws the smallest diamond. Then you MOVE outside of that diamond to draw the next one.

```
TO MOVE
PU RT 60 BK 8 LT 60 BK 8 PD
END
```

DIAMOND1 has sides that are three times longer than the first one. How do you know? Why three times longer? Why not two? Or four?

Why not try FD 16 and FD 32 to see what happens? Does it look right to you?

```
TO DIAMOND1
REPEAT 2 [FD 24 RT 60 FD 24 RT 120]
END
```

Now look at DIAMOND2. Why do you think it uses FD 40? Why not some other number?

The answer is that the sequence of FD 8, FD 8 * 3, and FD 8 * 5 gives you the nice even appearance of the diamonds, each nested inside another.

Now, see what you can dream up. If you need a little help getting started, see what kind of vines you can grow.

```
TO VINE
REPEAT 12 [HALFVINE OTHERHALF.VINE FD 20]
END

TO HALFVINE
FD 6 RT 30 REPEAT 6 [FD 4 RT 20]
RT 60 REPEAT 6 [FD 4 RT 20] RT 30
END

TO OTHERHALF.VINE
FD 6 LT 30 REPEAT 6 [FD 4 LT 20]
LT 60 REPEAT 6 [FD 4 LT 20]
END
```

This vine grows in a circle. Can you make it grow up a wall? What would you have to change?

Here's another thing to think about. Did you ever see a black and white vine? How about adding some pizzazz to it?

That's coming up in the next chapter.

103

Color, Music, and Pizzazz

5

Drawing thin black lines on a dull white screen gets very boring very fast, doesn't it? So before we go any further, let's add some pizzazz to your Logo procedures.

Add color to your procedures! Add music. Animate the turtle. Change its shape. Make flashing signs. There are all sorts of things you can do in Logo – far too many to describe here.

Exactly how you add pizazz depends on the computer system you're using.

- What type of computer are you using? How much memory does it have?

- What type of monitor do you have? What is the resolution of your screen? 640x480, 800x600, or 1024x768?

- What type of video card are you using?

- What type of sound card are you using, if any?

These are among the things that can make a difference in how multimedia works for you.

Time to get started!

Adding Some Color

You can change the color of the background, the color used to fill shapes, and the color of the turtle's pen. You can even change the size of the turtle's pen in most versions of Logo.

Using Primary Colors

When you draw in color on the computer screen, your monitor mixes the three primary colors of light: red, green, and blue. Inside your monitor, there are electronic circuits that act something like "electronic flashlights," one for each primary color. These shine on your monitor screen, which has hundreds of rows on tiny dots called pixels. Your software tells each "flashlight" on which pixel it needs to shine its primary color to display your colored pictures

What's a primary color? Simple – it's a color that you cannot make by mixing two or more colors together. For example, yellow light is the mix of equal parts of red and green light. White is the combination of all colors. Black is the absence of light or no mix of anything.

These mixes work great with colored light. But don't try the same mixes with paint or crayons. That's another set of primary colors: red. blue, and yellow. Where green is a primary color of light, you mix yellow and blue paints together to make green. Make sense?

Didn't think so. So let's just focus on light for now.

Let's say that your color monitor displays 256 colors. That means it can mix 256 shades of red, of green, and of blue.

Now let's put those colors in a list of numbers. Each number represents a different shade.

Red = [255 0 0] (256 Red, 0 Green, 0 Blue)

Green = [0 255 0] (0 Red, 256 Green, 0 Blue)

Blue = [0 0 255] (0 Red, 0 Green, 256 Blue)

Each of these examples says that there is all of one color, but none of the other two. This also tells you that 100% yellow, for example, can't be made from just one color. You have to mix red and green together to get yellow.

Yellow = [255 255 0] (255 Red, 255 Green, 0 Blue)

We said that white is the mixture of all colors. So what would be the list of numbers to display white?

White = [? ? ?]

You probably know already. But let's see if we can prove what it is supposed to be.

If white is the mixture of all colors, let's first take a look at some of the other common colors and the mix of primary colors that you use to create them. Maybe you can learn something from them.

Logo Color Commands

MSW Logo gives you far more than just the few colors that Logy is using at the beginning of this chapter. You've got thousands. MSW Logo color commands use a list of three numbers to mix of red, green, and blue light.

SETPENCOLOR [255 000 000] – SETPC, for short – tells Ernestine what color to use to draw a line.

SETFLOODCOLOR [0 0 0] – SETFC, for short – tells the turtle what color to use with the FILL command. It lets you "flood" a closed shape with color.

SETSCREENCOLOR [255 0 0] – SETSC, for short – sets the background color to whatever you want it to be. Some Logo packages call it SETBACKGROUND or SETBG.

Why So Many Numbers

UCB Logo – it's on the CD that came with this book – is among those Logo packages that use just one number to represent the mix of red, green, and blue light. Some Logos let you type the name of the color. While MSW Logo's list of numbers may mean you have more typing to do, it does give you a better idea of what's really going on in your computer.

For example, here are the basic colors in PC Logo.

0	Black	8	Dark Grey
1	Blue	9	Light Blue
2	Green	10	Light Green
3	Cyan	11	Light Cyan
4	Red	12	Light Red
5	Violet	13	Magenta
6	Brown	14	Yellow
7	Light Grey	15	White

You might think that the primary colors are numbers 1, 2, and 4. Actually, they are 9, 10, and 12. This system gives you no idea of how the colors are mixed or what colors to mix to get other colors.

Colors in the Set Menu

If typing all those numbers for all those colors is too much trouble, use the Set menu. Go to the Menu Bar and open the Set menu. In addition to Pensize and Font, you'll see three color options:

- PenColor

- FloodColor

- ScreenColor

These three options let you custom mix colors to get just the color you want for the pen, the fill, or the screen color. Here's the Pencolor window. The others are just like it.

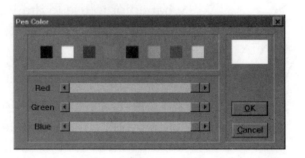

You can left-click on any of the eight choices shown across the top. If you want to make up your own color, you can slide each of the Red, Green, and Blue buttons (shown at the right of each color bar). The color is displayed in the larger box in the upper right corner. You can also press one of the arrow keys at each end of the color selection bars to slide the button back and forth.

Go ahead. Open the Set menu and select PenColor. Then experiment with the buttons and arrow keys. When you have the exact color you want, left-click on OK to set the pen to that color.

COLORS.LGO

Morf decided that writing some procedures would make life a bit easier. For example:

```
TO PINK
OP [255 200 255]
END
```

 OP is the shortcut for OUTPUT. This is a command that can only be used with another procedure. It does just what the name says, it outputs something to another procedure. In this case, it outputs the color to a color command. You'll hear lots more about this later. For now, let's keep it simple.

The color PINK tells you something about the colors you use with Logo. What do you think it is?

The higher the numbers in the list, the lighter the shade of the color being displayed. Make sense?

Try this:

SETSC [255 0 0]

The screen turns bright red.

What color do you think this is? SETSC [128 0 0] Try it and see. It's a darker shade of red, right?

As the numbers in the color list go down, the colors get darker. When you start adding other colors to red, like you did with PINK above, the colors get even lighter.

Take a look at the colors listed below. They're in the COLORS.LGO procedure on the CD that came with this book. The lighter colors all have higher numbers while the darker ones have lower numbers.

```
TO BLACK
OP [000 000 000]
END
```

```
TO BLUE
OP [000 000 255]
END

TO BROWN
OP [128 64 0]
END

TO CYAN
OP [0 255 255]
END

TO DKGREEN
OP [0 128 128]
END

TO GREEN
OP [000 255 000]
END

TO MAGENTA
OP [255 0 255]
END

TO OLIVE
OP [128 128 0]
END

TO ORANGE
OP [255 128 0]
END

TO PURPLE
OP [128 0 128]
END

TO RED
OP [255 0 0]
END

TO YELLOW
OP [255 255 0]
END
```

Look at the last two colors, red and yellow. Equal parts of red and green mix to give you yellow. Since orange has more red in it, it would seem that if you used less green, you just might get orange. Try it and see. Did you make your own orange color?

Now make some more of your own color procedures. You might also try experimenting to make white, if you haven't done it yet.

Now Morf doesn't need to remember all the different codes for colors. He simply adds the color name to his procedures.

Black and White

SETPC BLACK sets the pen color to [0 0 0] or black. The list [0 0 0] outputs to SETPC.

That tells you something about black, doesn't it? Black is the absence of all color, right? So there are no color values inside those brackets for black.

Try this:

SETSCREENCOLOR [0 0 0]

If [0 0 0] is the absence of all color, what would be the combination of all colors? How about

[255 255 255]

Go ahead. Set the pen color to [255 255 255]. Then give the turtle a command to see what color line is drawn. What's that tell you?

Since you can make any other color by combining red, green, and blue, the combination of 100% red, green, and blue must be the combination of all colors, right?

And that's white, isn't it? Guess we proved something, didn't we?

A Flood of Color

SETFC BLUE sets the flood, or fill color, to [0 0 255] or blue. Use it with the FILL command to fill closed shapes with color.

```
TO FILLIT
SETPC BLACK
REPEAT 4 [FD 100 RT 90]
PU RT 45 FD 40 PD
SETFC BLUE FILL
PU HOME PD
END
```

The first thing this procedure does is draw a square using a black pen color. Then the turtle picks the pen up, moves inside the square, and puts the pen down. The flood color is set to blue, and then the square is filled.

If FILL didn't work just right on your computer, don't be too surprised. It works differently on different computers. The same goes for setting the screen color.

One possible way to fix the screen is to left-click on the Zoom menu and then select "In." The picture gets twice as big as it was. And the square should look filled. If not, another way to fix it is to "minimize" your screen and then restore it again. You can also move the Commander window over the drawing and then put it back where it belongs.

Cyan is a light blue color. Let's set the screen to cyan, set the pen to red, and fill the square with yellow.

```
TO FILLIT2
SETSC CYAN
SETPC RED
REPEAT 4 [FD 100 RT 90]
PU RT 45 FD 40 PD
SETFC YELLOW FILL
PU HOME PD
END
```

That's not bad. But the red line is sorta thin.

Setting the Pen Size

Tired of skinny lines? Try colorful fat ones.

You can change the size of the lines that are drawn by using the SETPENSIZE command or by using the Set/PenSize menu option. Be sure to check that option out.

SETPENSIZE takes two inputs representing width and height. There's a long technical reason why there are two numbers. The easy thing is to just remember that both numbers must be the same.

The standard or default values are [1 1]. You can make those values just about anything you want. Try this:

```
SETPENSIZE [500 500] FD 100
```

Now that just about fills the screen, doesn't it? So you need to be careful not to get too carried away.

Try this:

```
TO FILLIT3
SETSC CYAN
```

```
SETPC RED
SETPENSIZE [5 5]
REPEAT 4 [FD 100 RT 90]
PU RT 45 FD 40 PD
SETFC YELLOW FILL
PU HOME PD
END
```

There! Now you can see a bold red line.

Want to try something really new? How about this one! First, write a simple triangle procedure.

```
TO TRI
RT 30 REPEAT 3 [FD 100 RT 120]
END
```

Now let's add some pizazz!

```
TO PIZZAZ
SETSC WHITE
SETPENSIZE [120 120] SETPC PURPLE TRI
SETPENSIZE [100 100] SETPC BLUE TRI
SETPENSIZE [80 80] SETPC MAGENTA TRI
SETPENSIZE [60 60] SETPC RED TRI
SETPENSIZE [40 40] SETPC ORANGE TRI
SETPENSIZE [20 20] SETPC YELLOW TRI
SETPENSIZE [5 5] SETPC GREEN TRI
END
```

Now that you have the pizazz, let's add some flash!

```
TO FLASH
REPEAT 20 [CS SETSC BLACK PIZZAZ]
END
```

Wow! Not bad, huh? Of course, what this looks like depends somewhat on the type of computer you are using. A 200 MHz Pentium is a lot faster than a 25 MHz 386 system.

Try something like this, maybe

```
TO TRI
REPEAT 3 [FD 100 RT 120]
END

TO PIZZAZZ
SETSC CYAN CS HT
PU LT 45 FD 100 RT 45 PD
```

```
SETPENSIZE [120 120] SETPC PURPLE RT 30 TRI
PU HOME LT 45 FD 80 RT 45 PD
SETPC BLUE RT 30 TRI
PU HOME LT 45 FD 60 RT 45 PD
SETPC MAGENTA RT 30 TRI
PU HOME LT 45 FD 40 RT 45 PD
SETPC RED RT 30 TRI
PU HOME LT 45 FD 20 RT 45 PD
SETPC ORANGE RT 30 TRI
PU HOME PD
SETPC YELLOW RT 30 TRI
PU HOME RT 135 FD 20 LT 135 PD
SETPC GREEN RT 30 TRI
END
```

This gives you another idea or two of what you can do with the basic color commands. We'll use these more as we go on. But for now, why not explore what you can do with color and the shapes that you know?

- Make a neon sign that flashes your name.

- Do you remember the Logo sports activities? Why not make a flashing home run or touchdown sign?

- Create a scene and color it in. Draw houses of different colors. Add lawns and flowers, a sky with clouds.

- Make a colorful map of your town or your neighborhood.

Colors and PX

If you want to explore some interesting effects with color, try PX, or PENREVERSE. This is another place where the three-number color list helps you see what's going on. Try this:

```
CS HT
SETPENSIZE [20 20] (You want a nice wide pen.)
SETPC [255 0 0]
FD 100
```

You now have a nice, wide red line on the screen, right? Well, now try this one:

```
PX BK 100
```

What happened? The pen color changed, didn't it? Now try

```
FD 100
```

Hmmmmmm. Changed back again, didn't it? Now here's a tough one. If the pen color was set to red, or [255 0 0], what was the color after the PX command?

[255 0 0] is 100% red and nothing else. So the reverse of that should be Cyan, or [0 255 255]. What about this one?

[200 150 50] What's this color in reverse?

[255 - 200 = 55 255 - 150 = 105 255 - 50 = 205] or

[55 105 205]

Now doesn't this make more sense than trying to guess what's going to happen when using single color numbers? Using the three-number code, you can plan your drawings to do exactly what you want them to do – and in just the right color.

What's the Color

"With all that flashy stuff, how can you ever remember what color you're using?"

That's easy. Type

SHOW PENCOLOR (Some use SHOW COLOR.)

The color mix is displayed in the Commander window; for example, [0 255 0]

You can also look in the Status window. Go ahead. Look over in the box of Commander Buttons. Left-click on the Status button.

The Status window is displayed and the button changes to NoStatus.

The Status window tells you a lot about what's happening on the screen, about the turtle, the pen, and other stuff. There's a box there that tells you the pencolor, the flood color, and the screen color. Left-click on NoStatus to close the window.

Bitblock

Here's a sneak preview of what you'll meet in the next chapter. We use them to show you another command that can add pizzazz to your drawings.

The BITBLOCK command uses SETFLOODCOLOR to put a block of color on the screen.

Just type

> BITBLOCK <width><height>

You don't have to draw a block and fill it. Just tell Logo what size block you want. Take a look.

Here's the procedure that created this picture:

```
TO COLOR :A :B :C
IF :A > 240 [STOP]
SETFLOODCOLOR (LIST :A :B :C)
PU FD 15 RT 90 FD 15 LT 90 PD
BITBLOCK 100 100
COLOR :A + 15 :B + 15 :C + 15
END

TO BLOCKS
PU CS HT
MAKE "A 0
MAKE "B 0
MAKE "C 0
COLOR :A :B :C
END
```

Hm-m-m-m! This procedure has a bunch of new stuff. There's the LIST command. It tells SETFLOODCOLOR to make a list from the variables :A, :B, and :C. Variables are a type of substitute; in this case, letters substituted for numbers. You'll get into Variables in the next chapter. Right now, let's just focus on the BITBLOCK command.

Try creating a few blocks to see how to use BITBLOCK. First tell Logo what color to use to fill the block. Type BITBLOCK followed by the number of steps wide the block is to be and the number of steps high. Make them anything you want.

Here's a procedure that tells you a few things about BITBLOCK. What can you discover?

```
TO BLOCKSQ
SETFC [255 0 0]
BITBLOCK 200 20
SETFC [0 255 0]
BITBLOCK 20 200
PU RT 90 FD 200 RT 90
SETFC [0 0 255]
BITBLOCK 20 200
```

```
PU HOME FD 200 PD
SETFC [128 128 128]
BITBLOCK 220 20
END
```

Hiding the Commander

Does the Commander window ever get in the way of your graphics, especially now as you start adding pizzazz?

Well, why not hide it? MSW Logo has an ICON command that will do just that for you. For example, ICON "COMMANDER changes the Commander window into a small icon in the lower left corner of the screen. UNICON "COMMANDER brings it back again. To see how these commands work, let's play with the BLOCKS procedure again.

```
TO BLOCKS
PU CS HT ICON "COMMANDER
LT 90 FD 400 LT 90 FD 320
MAKE "A 0
MAKE "B 0
MAKE "C 0
COLOR :A :B :C
WAIT 600
UNICON "COMMANDER
END

TO COLOR :A :B :C
IF :A > 240 [STOP]
SETFLOODCOLOR (LIST :A :B :C)
PU FD 15 RT 90 FD 15 LT 90 PD
BITBLOCK 100 100
COLOR :A + 7 :B + 7 :C + 7
END
```

Not bad! We threw in another command you'll find useful, the WAIT command. This command causes Logo to pause for as many 1/60ths of a second as you select. WAIT 600, for example, means to wait 10 seconds before doing the next command.

One more thing! You can also hide the MSW Logo screen, just as you can hide the Commander window. Commander is a single word so you use the command

ICON "COMMANDER

MswLogo Screen is two words. That's a list to Logo and lists go inside brackets.

ICON [MSWLOGO SCREEN]
UNICON [MSWLOGO SCREEN]

Adding Pizzazz to Text

You can't have a sign — even a flashing sign — without some words written on it, right? You may have already tried to draw your name using turtle commands. That's one way to write text on the graphics screen.

Is there another way to put some fancy text in one of the turtle's signs?

Sure is. Actually, there are a couple of ways to do it. The easiest way is to use Set/Font option. Remember? Font is one of the boxes in the Status window.

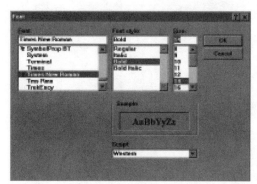

Open the Set Menu and select the Font option.

The Font window is displayed.

The three small windows list the fonts that are available on your computer, the style that is currently being used such as:

- regular, which is like this

- *italic*, which means the type is at an angle list this

- bold **like this**

- ***bold italic*** like this.

The last column lists the type sizes that are available. The sizes are listed in points.

There are 72 points to the inch. That will give you some idea of what the size you select will look like. A sample of your selection is displayed down below to give you an even better idea of what it will look like.

If you want to doctor up the font so that it looks just how you want it to look, you can use the SETTEXTFONT command. SETTEXTFONT can get very complicated. That's because of all the options it gives you. But it really isn't so bad. Here's how you use it.

SETTEXTFONT [*font*]

[*font*] is a list that shows the following information:

```
[[Name of the typeface]
Height
Width
Orientation
Weight
Italic
Underline
StrikeOut
CharSet
OutPrecision
ClipPrecision
Quality
PitchAndFamily].
```

"Logy, how do you expect anyone to remember all that stuff. I don't know what most of it means."

"I don't either, Morf. But for those who know lots about fonts and typefaces, this is important stuff."

Let's try something. It'll show you how to use SETTEXTFONT. Type

SETTEXTFONT [HELV]

Now, to add text to the graphics screen, use the LABEL command. LABEL prints the word or list that you type after it on the screen. For example, type

LABEL "HELLO

What happened?

There's the word HELLO reading up and down. That's because the turtle is facing toward the top of the screen. Try this one:

CS RT 120 LABEL "Graphics by Morf

Look better? You can write text at any angle you want. Why not try this:

CS RT 45 LABEL [HELLO, ERNESTINE.]

Now let's take a look at all those options. To see what options Logo is using, type

SHOW TEXTFONT

The TEXTFONT options are displayed:

[[Helv] 143 67 0 400 0 0 0 0 2 0 2 34]

Now you can start comparing these with the list of options on the previous page. Try this as an example:

[[Helv] 72 67 0 900 1 1 0 0 2 0 2 34]

What changes did this example make? You can read all about SETTEXTFONT and TEXTFONT in the MSW Logo On-line Help file.

Why not go ahead and explore some other possible changes? If yours look a bit crazy, just type CS and no one will ever know.

After that, how about some sound?

Add Some Sound Effects

MSW Logo allows you to do lots of different things with sounds including music. You also have a number of multimedia commands

available for controlling sound cards, CD-ROM players, and more. The MCI commands let you add sounds to your procedures. You can even narrate your own Logo show in your own voice if your computer lets you do that. Multimedia is a big subject for a whole new book. You'll get an introduction to multimedia a bit later. We'll just deal with the Logo commands for now, the one's that let you make sounds that will play through the speakers on your PC.

SOUND is the command for making music in MSW Logo. Some use Logo packages use NOTE. Others use TONE. Each of these commands takes a list of the frequency of the sound and the length of time it is to play. The length of time, or duration, is based on the speed of your computer. So you'll have to do some experimenting to make it sound the way you want.

Frequency is the number of sound waves or sound vibrations per second.

So what's a sound wave you ask?

When you drop a pebble into a pool of water, you see the waves move out from where the pebble hit the water. Sound acts the same way. It travels in waves out in all directions from the source of the sound.

Think of that line through the middle as the surface of pond when there are no waves. When you make a wave, part of it rises above the level of the pond. Part of it sinks below the level of the pond.

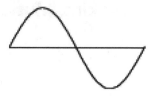

When you make lots of sound waves in each second, the sound is higher — fewer waves per second gives a lower sound. For example, when a piano wire vibrates 262 times each second, you get the note Middle C. When it vibrates 440 times each second, you get the note A above middle C. At 220 vibrations per second, you get the note A below C.

Here are two octaves of sounds you can use to play music.

FREQUENCY	NOTE
220	A (below Middle C)
223	A# (the # stands for Sharp)
247	B
262	C (Middle C)
277	C#
294	D
311	D#
330	E
349	F
370	F#
392	G
415	G#
440	A
466	A#
494	B
523	C
554	C#
587	D
622	D#
659	E
698	F
740	F#
784	G
831	G#

Making Music

Time to put all this good sound stuff to use. First let's write procedures for the basic scale, Middle C to High C (CC).

```
TO C
SOUND [262 100]
END

TO D
SOUND [294 100]
END

TO E
SOUND [330 100]
END

TO F
SOUND [349 100]
END

TO G
SOUND [392 100]
END

TO A
SOUND [440 100]
END

TO B
SOUND [494 100]
END

TO CC
SOUND [523 100]
END
```

Now you can start playing music from the keyboard. Just press the letter for the note you want to hear and press ENTER.

There's another way also. You can write a song procedure.

```
TO SAINTS
SOUND [262 50]
SOUND [330 50]
SOUND [349 50]
SOUND [392 150]
WAIT 50
SOUND [262 50]
```

```
SOUND [330 50]
SOUND [349 50]
SOUND [392 150]
WAIT 50
SOUND [262 50]
SOUND [330 50]
SOUND [349 50]
SOUND [392 100]
SOUND [330 100]
SOUND [262 100]
SOUND [330 100]
SOUND [294 100]
END
```

SAINTS is a song popular in New Orleans. It's part of "When the Saints Go Marching In."

Rabbit Trail

15

Musical Fractions

Do you have trouble with fractions? Well, don't feel lonely. Everyone has trouble with fractions. Thousands of years ago when people first started to think about numbers, they had trouble with fractions.

A few years ago, we learned about a neat way to understand fractions from Judi Harris, O.L.E. That's short for Official Logo Enthusiast. She wrote an article for a Logo newspaper that is included on the CD that comes with this book. It's called MUSIC.PDF. Teachers and parents will be particularly interested in this article.

As Judi says, people have had an easy way to deal with fractions from the very beginning, ever since they began to play music. So let's use her example. Only we'll show it to you in MSW Logo.

```
TO ROW
SOUND [262 40]
SOUND [262 40]
SOUND [262 30]
SOUND [294 10]
SOUND [330 40]
SOUND [330 30]
SOUND [294 10]
SOUND [330 30]
SOUND [349 10]
SOUND [392 80]
END
```

This exercise is a lot easier if you draw the actual musical notes on music paper. If you don't have actual music paper, draw five lines on a piece of paper. Or maybe you can just used regular lined paper.

The first note in the song procedure is called a quarter note. The last note is called a half note. If you look at the length (duration) numbers, an interesting idea begins to appear. Look at the lengths of the first and last notes:

$$40 + 40 = 80$$

Strangely enough, one-quarter plus one-quarter equals one-half. What else can you think of?

$$\frac{1}{4} + \frac{1}{4} = \frac{1}{2}$$

$$25 \text{ cents} + 25 \text{ cents} = 50 \text{ cents}$$

What about the other notes and their lengths? The length of 10 is one-quarter of the length of the quarter note. What does that equal?

$$\frac{1}{4} * \frac{1}{4} = \frac{1}{16}$$

A sixteenth note is a quarter note with two flags flying from the top. An eighth note has one flag and a quarter note has none. When you play two sixteenth notes close together, the two flags stretch from one note to the next.

The third note in ROW (SOUND [262 30]) would be written as an eighth note with a period next to it. The period is musical shorthand, meaning to add half the length of an eighth note or a sixteenth note, to the eighth note. If that sounds confusing, look at the lengths in the Logo procedure.

If a length of 10 is one-quarter that of a quarter note, then a length of 30 should be three-quarters that of the quarter note:

$$3/4 * 1/4 = 3/16$$

When you have an eighth note linked with a period followed by a sixteenth note, this is the same as a 3/16th and a 1/16th note played together.

What is this equal to?

$$\frac{3}{16} + \frac{1}{16} = \frac{4}{16} = \frac{1}{4}$$

In one simple ten-note phrase, you have played with all sorts of things that have to do with fractions. But there's a lot more in Judi's article. Check it out!

Some More Ideas

You've added color and sound to your procedures. Before you go too far, why not see what you can do with these new commands.

What can you do with shapes now? Can you color them?

Why not draw a colorful birthday cake and then play Happy Birthday? How about drawing colorful lines that streak across the screen, like a rock concert laser show? Remember the FLASH procedure? That gives you an idea on how to get started.

Starting Procedures Automatically

Here's a problem everyone gets caught in once in a while. Someone gives you a great set of procedures but you can't figure out how to start it.

Wouldn't it be great if procedures could start by themselves when they're loaded?

Take a look.

There are a couple of different ways to start procedures without typing the commands.

An easy way is simply to add instructions in the Editor window like this:

```
TO HUT
REPEAT 4 [FD 60 RT 90]
FD 60 RT 30 FD 60 RT 120
REPEAT 20 [BK 6 FD 66 BK 60 RT 3]
PU HOME PD
END

HT PU LT 90 FD 200 RT 90 PD
HUT
PU LT 90 FD 120 RT 90 PD
HUT
PU LT 90 FD 40 RT 90 PD
HUT
PU RT 90 FD 40 LT 90 PD
HUT
PU RT 90 FD 120 LT 90 PD
HUT
PU RT 90 FD 200 LT 90 PD
HUT
```

When you load the HUT procedure, you'll get a row of huts across the screen.

You can also use STARTUP. This gives you an introduction to the variables you'll meet in the next chapter. You want to

```
MAKE "STARTUP [HUTS]

TO HUT
REPEAT 4 [FD 60 RT 90]
FD 60 RT 30 FD 60 RT 120
REPEAT 20 [BK 6 FD 66 BK 60 RT 3]
PU HOME PD
END

TO HUTS
HT PU LT 90 FD 200 RT 90 PD
HUT
PU LT 90 FD 120 RT 90 PD
HUT
PU LT 90 FD 40 RT 90 PD
HUT
PU RT 90 FD 40 LT 90 PD
HUT
PU RT 90 FD 120 LT 90 PD
HUT
PU RT 90 FD 200 LT 90 PD
HUT
END
```

When you load any MSW Logo procedure, the first thing that Ernestine does is search for the STARTUP variable. If she finds it, she does what the variable is set to do. In this case, you said

MAKE the STARTUP variable [HUTS]

which tells Ernestine to run the HUTS procedure as soon as it is loaded into your workspace.

Varying Variables

How many people are in your family? In your class? Are they all the same? Or are they **variable**?

Got one in on you, didn't I? There's that word, "Variable."

How many of your friends have the same color hair? The same color eyes? How many are the same age? How many were born in the same month as you? Anyone born on the same day?

How many things about you and your group are the same? How many are "variable?"

Variables in Logo

Now let's talk about Logo.

By now, you should know what this procedure will look like after it's been run. What do you think?

```
TO BOXES
REPEAT 4 [FD 100 RT 90]
RT 90 PU FD 120 PD LT 90
REPEAT 4 [FD 100 RT 90]
END
```

Sure, that's a procedure to draw two boxes side by side.

But what if you wanted to draw 20 boxes? What if you want each box to be bigger than the last?

What if you want them smaller? In other words, what if you want to vary the size or the number of boxes?

No problem! This is where those things called "variables" come in. A variable is something you put into a procedure so you can change the procedure every time you run it.

Yes, that does sound confusing, doesn't it?

To help explain it, let's take another look at the experiment you did creating pictures using just one shape. Find a big sheet of paper and draw a picture using your favorite shape. Use triangles, squares, or rectangles – or even circles, if you've peeked ahead in this book.

Remember, you can only use one type of shape. But you can vary the size of the shape all you want.

There's that word again, "vary."

Remember the caterpillar example? That's a picture drawn using just squares (and a little piece of a straight line). And don't forget the cat.

OK, got your drawing done? Before you try to put your picture on the computer, let's take a look at the new BOXES procedure below. It may give you some ideas.

```
TO BOXES :SIZE
REPEAT 4 [FD :SIZE RT 90]
RT 90 PU FD :SIZE + 20 PD LT 90
REPEAT 4 [FD :SIZE RT 90]
END
```

You probably know what the variable is, don't you? It's the :SIZE. That's right.

Now when you type BOXES to run the procedure, you have to provide something new, an input.

Try it out. Type...

BOXES 20

BOXES 40

BOXES 60

BOXES 100

When you type BOXES 20, you tell the :SIZE variable to use the :SIZE of 20. What about BOXES 60. What will :SIZE be then?

Variables must always have an input, or value. And they must also have the two dots in front so Logo knows it's a variable.

Yes, that's a colon. But in Logo, we call them "dots." You'll find they can save you a lot of time and typing.

Take a look. Remember the TRI procedure? Let's add a variable.

```
TO TRI :N
REPEAT 3 [FD :N RT 120]
END
```

See! You can name variables just about anything you want. Rather than call this one :SIZE, call it :N. The :N can stand for number. Of course, you could call it :X, :Z, or :WHATEVER.

But you still have to use the dots.

Here are some examples that a 7-year-old had fun dreaming up. They use this SQUARE procedure.

```
TO SQUARE :N
REPEAT 4 [FD :N RT 90]
END
```

It started as a simple exercise to see what different squares would look like.

```
TO SQUARES
SQUARE 60
SQUARE 80
SQUARE 100
SQUARE 120
END
```

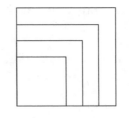

Then she added a left turn, and that reminded her of her mom's stacking tables.

```
TO TABLES
SQUARES
LT 90
SQUARES
END
```

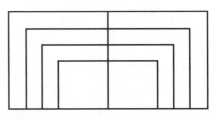

The more she looked at the tables, the more it looked like half of a decorative mirror.

```
TO MIRROR
TABLES
LT 90
TABLES
END
```

And what would happen if you stacked mirrors?

```
TO MIRRORS
MIRROR
LT 45
MIRROR
END
```

This is a lot to think about. So why not stop for a while and experiment using one shape in a design.

After you've had fun with one shape, try doing something with two shapes.

You've already seen what you can do with a square and a triangle. These were combined to make a house. Then they were used to make a wheel.

Since you've also made some flowers, maybe you can "plant another garden?"

Polygons and Things

Polygon? Now there's a new word for you. Do you know what it means? No, it doesn't mean that Poly flew away.

We'll talk lots more about polygons. But for now, think about this for a moment.

Squares, triangles, and rectangles are polygons. So are pentagons, hexagons, and octagons.

All of these shapes have one thing in common. They all enclose an area that has at least three sides. (You can't enclose anything with two sides, can you?)

Triangles have three sides, squares and rectangles have four, pentagons have five, and octagons have eight. Seems like there's a rule for polygons in there somewhere.

A polygon is a closed shape with at least three sides.

Rabbit Trail

16

Variable String Toss

Here's something else to explore. How about trying a variation of the game String Toss? It's called FD :N. (We're sneaking the variables in here, too.) The idea is to create a design by passing the ball of string back and forth. The :N variable can equal one step or as many as you want.

Let's say you want to create a square of string. That's really easy. One person plays the Turtle starting at Home. The Turtle holds one end of the string, gives the ball of string to the first person, and says FD :N times 5. The first person takes 5 steps.

The first person then turns RT 90, holds the string to make a corner, and gives the ball of string to the second person. That person goes FD :N * 5 and RT 90. A third person takes the ball of string and goes FD :N * 5 RT 90. And finally a fourth person takes the string and brings it HOME.

See how this works? The string is now in the shape of a variable square. Now try a hexagon, why don't you?

Then maybe you can connect six triangles to make a fancy hexagon.

It's more fun when you make crazy shapes. Try it.

If you find it hard to see the shapes, have everyone carefully put the string on the floor and then step back. Can you see the shape now?

Hexagons and Spiderwebs

To make that String Toss Game design on the computer, you can use the TRI :N procedure you wrote earlier in this chapter.

```
TO TRI :N
REPEAT 3 [FD :N RT 120]
END
```

What would happen if you repeated the TRI :N procedure, turning after each triangle?

```
REPEAT 6 [TRI :N RT 60]
```

What do you call a shape that has six sides like this? That's a hexagon, right?

Hmmmm? That sort of looks like a see-through box — one of those optical illusions.

But back to hexagons for now.

```
TO HEXAGON :N
REPEAT 6 [TRI :N RT 60]
END
```

Be sure to tell the turtle how big to make the hexagon. Try this:

```
HEXAGON 60
HEXAGON 80
HEXAGON 100
```

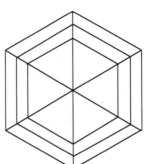

What does this look like? Of course, it's a spiderweb!

Can you think of another way to write this procedure so that the turtle will do the same thing? How about this!

```
TO SPIDERWEB :N
HEXAGON :N
HEXAGON :N + 20
HEXAGON :N + 40
END
```

Go ahead. Type the SPIDERWEB :N procedure and then try

SPIDERWEB 40

Play around with this idea to see what it can do. Make up some other shape procedures using variables.

Adding More Variables

Can you think of a way to use more variables in the SPIDERWEB procedure? What about substituting a variable for 10? For 20? For both?

```
TO SPIDERWEB :N :X :Y
HEXAGON :N
HEXAGON :N + :X
HEXAGON :N + :X * :Y
END
```

This is getting complicated.

:N gives you the size of each side.
:X tells you how much to add to :N
:Y tells you to multiply :X by this number

After you've typed in this procedure, see what happens when you try

SPIDERWEB 60 20 2

Does this look like the first spiderweb the turtle drew? It should. Let's change the variables to numbers and take a look.

```
TO SPIDERWEB 60 20 2
HEXAGON 60
HEXAGON 60 + 20
HEXAGON 60 + 20 * 2
END
```

Changing a Variable

Typing SPIDERWEB 60 20 2 is fine when you want to make three hexagons that have sides of 60, 80, and 100. But what if you want to do five hexagons? Seven hexagons? Seventy hexagons?

Let's try something! When you write a procedure, it becomes another command you can use, right?

OK. Then let's make the most of it. Tell SPIDERWEB to draw a hexagon using the variable :N. Then tell SPIDERWEB to add 10 to itself and do the same thing again.

133

```
TO SPIDERWEB :N
HEXAGON :N
SPIDERWEB :N + 10
END
```

Try it! What happens?

Wait a minute!

The last line of the SPIDERWEB procedure has the procedure using itself. That's strange!

No, that isn't strange, that's recursion. There's a whole chapter on what you can do with recursion. For now, let's just stick with the variables.

Local and Global Variables

Most versions of Logo use two types of variables: local and global. Global variables are used by any procedure. Take a look.

```
TO SHAPES :N
TRI :N
SQUARE :N
RECTANGLE :N
END
```

How about it? Can you write procedures for a triangle, a square, and a rectangle using :N to represent the distance forward.

```
TO TRI :N
REPEAT 3 [FD :N RT 120]
END
```

```
TO SQUARE :N
REPEAT 4 [FD :N RT 90]
END
```

```
TO RECTANGLE :N
REPEAT 2 [FD :N RT 90 FD :N * 2 RT 90]
END
```

Now, when you type SHAPES 100, each of the procedures will use 100 wherever there is an :N. The :N is a global variable. It's available to anyone who wants to use it.

Global variables tend to be a nuisance. Logo has to keep track of which procedures uses which global variable, what the value of the variable is, has it changed? This takes up valuable memory.

Of course, sometimes you have to use global variables. But it keeps things neater if you can use local variables.

Local variables are "local" to the one procedure where it is used. So there isn't nearly as much record-keeping required, making it easier on Logo.

You write them like this:

```
TO TRI
LOCAL "X
MAKE "X 100
REPEAT 3 [FD :X RT 120]
END
```

Hey, there's a new command, MAKE. You'll learn more about that on the next page. In the meantime, go ahead. Change your TRI procedure. Change the TRI :N in the SHAPES procedure to just TRI. Now run the SHAPES procedure using SHAPES 100 again. What does the picture look like? Why?

You'll see lots more examples of local variables as you move through the rest of this book.

Outputting Variables

OK, local variables are good. Global variables are not so good. Is there another way to pass information between procedures without using global variables?

Sure is!

You can OUTPUT them. You remember, OUTPUT sends information to another procedure. Let's use the TRI procedure as an example. Here's what you need to do.

```
TO TRI
REPEAT 3 [FD X RT 120]
END

TO X
OUTPUT 100
END
```

In this example, X isn't really a variable. It's a procedure. So how would you add a local variable to this so that X would pass information to TRI?

How about this?

```
TO X
LOCAL "Z
MAKE "Z READWORD
OUTPUT :Z
END
```

Is this really the best way to run the TRI procedure? Of course not. The important lesson here is

Don't ever close your mind to new possibilities!

In other words, never say "Never."

Making Variables

LOCAL "X is easy enough to figure out in the TRI procedure. But what's with the MAKE "X 100?

MAKE is a command that gives a value to the variable named <name>. The <name> given to a variable must always be what Logo sees as a word. That means it can be a letter, such as "X, or a word such as "variable.

MAKE "<name> <value>
The <value> can be a character, number, word, or a list.

In the TRI example, the goal was to MAKE the variable X have the value of 100. Then you can use the variable :X within that procedure whenever you want something to be equal to (have the value of) 100. In the TRI procedure, the variable :N was used as the side of the triangle, which in this case is 100 turtle steps long.

More Ways to Make Variables

You just got introduced to MAKE. Well, Logo gives you lots of other ways to vary your variables. Let's start with another look at MAKE.

MAKE "JOE 2
MAKE "TOM 4
MAKE "SAM :JOE + :TOM

So what does :SAM equal? If you said six, you get a Gold Star.

You can also NAME :JOE + :TOM "SAM

This does the same thing as MAKE "SAM :JOE + :TOM except that you NAME <value> "<name>.

If you want to see what :SAM equals, you can tell the computer to

PRINT :SAM

or

SHOW :SAM

You can also tell Logo to

SHOW THING "SAM

or

PRINT THING "SAM

THING does the same thing as the dots. It outputs the value of the variable named in the word that follows THING. Sure, that sounds confusing. Try it a few times and it will begin to make sense. That's why Morf likes to experiment so much.

Conditional Things

Remember the SPIDERWEB procedure?

```
TO SPIDERWEB :N
HEXAGON :N
SPIDERWEB :N + 10
END
```

The problem with this procedure is that it just keeps running, filling your screen with spiderwebs. Is there no way to stop it other than pressing the HALT button?

Well, there is a way. You just tell the turtle that IF the last hexagon that it drew was as big as you want the spiderweb to be, THEN stop drawing.

Here's how you use IF. Since IF knows what you mean, you don't have to use the word THEN.

```
TO SPIDERWEB :N
IF :N > 100  [STOP]
HEXAGON :N
SPIDERWEB :N + 10
END
```

Look at that first line in this new procedure. When the turtle reads this line, it learns that IF :N is greater than 100, then stop drawing.

Greater Than, Less Than

That thing that looks like an arrowhead after the :N > is the symbol for "greater than." It means that if the value of :N is greater than 100, then STOP.

If > means "greater than," what does that other arrow symbol [<] mean?

You guessed it. It means "less than." An easy way to remember which symbol is which is that the arrow always points to the smaller value.

- IF :N > 100 means that the value of :N must be larger than 100, at least 101.

- IF :N < 100 means that the value of :N must be less than 100, no more than 99.

For our example, we picked 100 as a place to stop. You can select your own stopping point. Or you can make the stopping point another variable. How would you do that?

Go ahead. Give it a try. But remember, if you're going to use a variable like this, you have to add it to the procedure name.

```
TO SPIDERWEB :N _____
IF :N > _____ [STOP]
HEXAGON :N
SPIDERWEB :N + 10 _____
END
```

"OK, I understand IF. IF something is true, then Logo will carry out the next instruction. And that sits inside brackets. But what if that something is not true? What if I want Ernestine to do something if the answer is false?"

TEST

Actually, there are two ways to handle that. Look at how SPIDERWEB has been changed below.

```
TO SPIDERWEB :N
TEST :N > 100
IFTRUE [CS CT PR [SORRY!] STOP]
IFFALSE [HEX :N]
SPIDERWEB :N + 10 _____
END
```

The first lines says to test :N to see if it is greater than 100. The next line says that if the test is true, clear the screen, clear the text, print SORRY!, and stop. The third line says that if :N is not greater than 100, go ahead and run HEX :N. (HEX :N is a new short name for HEXAGON :N.)

What do you think would happen if you left out IFFALSE? Then you'd have

```
TEST :N > 100
IFTRUE [CS CT PR [SORRY!] STOP]
HEX :N
```

Would that work? Try it and see. What did you learn from that?

You don't always have to have both IFTRUE (IFT for short) and IFFALSE (IFF for short) in your procedures.

IFELSE

Another way is to use the IFELSE command. Let's change the SPIDERWEB procedures and try it out.

```
TO SPIDERWEB :N
IFELSE :N > 100 [CS CT PR [SORRY!]STOP][HEX :N]
SPIDERWEB :N
END
```

The first line says that if :N is greater than 100

- clear the screen

- clear the text

- print SORRY!

- Stop

If not, run the HEX procedure and move on the next line. You can think of IFELSE as IF a condition is true, THEN do this or ELSE do this. Actually, this is just what some Logo packages let you do. For example:

```
TO L.OR.R
PR [SHOULD THE TURTLE GO LEFT OR RIGHT?]
IF RC = "L THEN LT 90 FD 100 ELSE RT 90 FD 100
END
```

139

You can also write the IF line as

IF RC = "L [LT 90 FD 100][RT 90 FD 100]

This works just fine in some versions of Logo — but not in MSW Logo. You need IFELSE.

Go ahead and explore. You'll see more of IFELSE.

When you've finished with spiderwebs, why not add variables to your procedures for drawing other shapes? See what you can do with squares, rectangles and things.

Remember, this is your own *Great Logo Adventure!*

More on Tessellations

Tessellations are really great places to use variables. These repeating patterns usually start with a basic shape that is repeated in varying sizes.

Do you remember the tessellation from Chapter 4 that used Diamonds? This gets a bit tricky so think this one through carefully. Can you combine DIAMOND, DIAMOND1, and DIAMOND2 to make one procedure using variables? How would this change the other procedures?

Here are the Diamond procedures.

```
TO DIAMOND
REPEAT 2 [FD 8 RT 60 FD 8 RT 120]
END

TO DIAMOND1
REPEAT 2 [FD 24 RT 60 FD 24 RT 120]
END

TO DIAMOND2
REPEAT 2 [FD 40 RT 60 FD 40 RT 120]
END
```

Look at the distances the turtle moves. Can you write one procedure for these that uses a distance variable?

```
TO DIAMOND :DIST
REPEAT 2 [FD :DIST RT 60 FD :DIST RT 120]
END
```

Now, rather than use DIAMOND, DIAMOND1, or DIAMOND2, you can use DIAMOND 8, DIAMOND 24, or DIAMOND 40.

More Fun With Squares

Let's try a tessellation with squares. The first thing to do is draw a tower of squares, each square smaller than the last.

```
TO SQUARES :S
IF :S < 0 [ STOP]
REPEAT 4 [FD :S RT 90]
FD :S
SQUARES :S - 5
END
```

Try SQUARES now using different inputs. This is going to be the basic pattern in the tessellation. The picture above was made using 30 as the input to SQUARES.

Next, let's make a TOWER of SQUARES.

TOWER takes two inputs: one that says how big the SQUARES are, and the second to tell the turtle how many times to repeat the SQUARES pattern.

```
TO TOWER :S :T
IF :T = 0 [STOP]
SQUARES :S
TOWER :S :T - 1
END
```

Here's the pattern made by using TOWER 15 5.

And this raises a question. Are you just going to make a tall, skinny tessellation? Or can you make the TOWER procedure turn the corner, maybe like a picture frame?

```
TO FRAME
PU LT 90 FD 100 RT 90 BK 40 PD
REPEAT 4 [TOWER 15 4 RT 90]
END
```

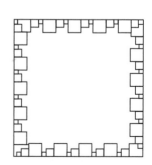

The first thing the FRAME procedure does is move the turtle over to the left. Then it draws the FRAME using the REPEAT command.

REPEAT 4 [TOWER 15 4 RT 90]

Now we're getting some where. Try different inputs. TOWER 15 4 seems to work pretty good.

To make this into an interesting tessellation, why not just fill up a frame with the SQUARES pattern? How are you going to do that?

Rabbit Trail

17

Tessellating Squares

Here's a quick and easy Rabbit Trail for you. It's a great way to discover what you can do with your SQUARES pattern. You can either use squares of different sizes or better yet, print a page full of the SQUARES pattern and cut them out.

Now move the patterns around to see what kind of patterns you can make.

Can you make the FRAME pattern using squares or your cutouts?

Once you figure that one out, then figure out what the turtle would have to do to fill the FRAME pattern after it draws the first TOWER pattern?

More Towers

When the turtle draws TOWER 15 4, it can't just turn around a draw the pattern again, can it? What would happen? Why not try it and see?

After the turtle gets to the top of the first pattern, it is going to have to move over a bit to draw the TOWER pattern coming down the screen. But how far?

You know that the pattern is :S steps wide. In TOWER 15 4, :S is 15, right? So let's write a procedure for the turtle to move at the top of the TOWER.

```
TO MOVE1
RT 90 FD _____ RT 90
END
```

When the turtle gets to the top of the TOWER, she'll turn right, move over, and then turn right again. What happens if we use the value of :S or 15? Does that work?

No. The turtle ends up drawing the pattern over the original drawing. When the turtle turns at the top, it starts drawing the SQUARES pattern by moving to the right. This means the turtle has to move twice as far, or :S * 2.

Try it. See what happens.

```
TO MOVE1 :S
RT 90 FD :S * 2 RT 90
END
```

Try this:

        TOWER 15 4
        MOVE1 15

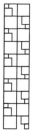

It seems to work, doesn't it!

You're not out of the woods yet. Do you see that blank space at the bottom — to the right?

How are you going to fill that in? Also, what is the turtle going to have to do to draw the next TOWER?

How about this?

```
TO MOVE2 :S
RT 90 FD :S BK :S RT 90
END
```

The turtle turns right, fills in the gap, backs up, turns right again (that's 180 degrees), and is ready to start again.

You didn't know this was going to be this complicated, did you?

There's one more thing to do now. That's to write a procedure that will create the repeating tessellation.

We'll call it COVER.

```
TO COVER :S :T :X
IF :X = 0 [STOP]
TOWER :S :T
MOVE1 :S
TOWER :S :T
MOVE2 :S
COVER :S :T :X - 1
END
```

You already know what the :S and :T variables are. What about the :X?

That's easy enough. Just like the :T variable, :X tells COVER the number of times to repeat itself.

Musical Variables

In the last chapter, we talked about making music. Now that you've read about variables, how about some musical variables?

Do you want to turn your keyboard into musical keys? Here's one way to do it.

143

```
TO MUSIC
MAKE "KEY RC
IF :KEY = "C [SOUND [262 100]]
IF :KEY = "D [SOUND [294 100]]
IF :KEY = "E [SOUND [330 100]]
IF :KEY = "F [SOUND [349 100]]
IF :KEY = "G [SOUND [392 100]]
IF :KEY = "A [SOUND [440 100]]
IF :KEY = "B [SOUND [494 100]]
IF :KEY = "S [STOP]
MUSIC
END
```

There's another new command, RC. That's short for READCHAR.
When Logo sees the READCHAR or RC command, it stops and waits
for you to type a character. In this case, the letter you type becomes
the variable :KEY.

If you type one of the keys – A, B, C, D, E, F, G – you hear a note.
Just make sure you use a capital letter. Otherwise Logo just runs the
MUSIC procedure again and again until you hit one of the sound keys
and press Enter.

Rabbit Trail

18

Tangrams

The Tangram is an Oriental puzzle with seven shapes of different sizes.

The puzzle is to use these shapes to make lots of different things.
Here's my pup tent.

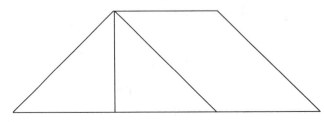

Why not visit your local library or bookstore? You'll find there are a number of books on tangrams that will give you lots of ideas of what to do with your new puzzle pieces.

There's a BMP file on the CD that came with this book called TANGRAM.BMP.

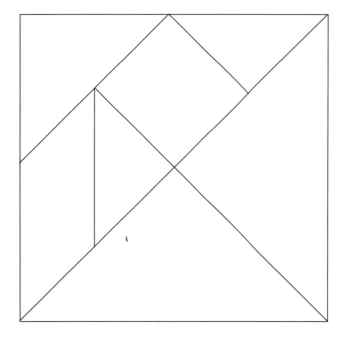

1. Print the picture and paste it to a piece of cardboard.

2. Carefully cut out the pieces.

3. Now you can play with the pieces to create interesting shapes: birds, ships, dragons, and other interesting designs. Here's some to get you started.

4. Now draw them on the computer.

There's a procedure on the CD that came with this book called TANGRAM.LGO. You can use that to create your Tangram shapes. We talk about it in *The Great Math Adventure* chapter.

Now, why not see what you can do with Tangrams?

Adding Borders

Morf just loves to put borders around things, even the graphics window. Take a look!

Joe Power, a friend from California, taught Morf how to do that. It comes in real handy when you want to do a pretty card or announcement.

Here's the procedure.

```
TO BORDER
CS HT
PU LT 90 FD 200 LT 90 FD 100
LT 180 PD
BRAID
END
```

You can change this procedure to make the border larger or smaller. You also have to change the last line of the BRAID procedure.

```
TO BRAID
MAKE "SQR2 1.4          ;Square root of 2
MAKE "HFSQ2 0.7         ;Half the square root of 2
MAKE "S2 8.5            ;Square root of 2 * 6
MAKE "H2 4.2            ;(Square root of 2 * 0.5) * 6
MAKE "S2H2 12.7         ; :S2 + :H2
PU FD 24 RT 45 FD 4.2 SETH 0 PD
REPEAT 2 [STRIP 20 CORNER STRIP 30 CORNER]
END
```

What's that stuff out to the side?

Adding Comments

Those are comments. Programmers usually "annotate" their code, or programs. That means that they leave explanations written in their programs so that users will know what the program or procedure is supposed to do. In this case, the notes tell you what the variables mean.

You can add notes to your MSW Logo procedures by typing a semicolon followed by your notes. Logo doesn't pay any attention to anything that follows the semicolon. If your version of Logo does not recognize the semicolon, use this procedure. It does the same thing.

```
TO ; :comment
END
```

As to the "square roots" in the comments, don't worry about them right now. You'll get into them in The *Great Math Adventure* chapter. You've got enough to think about just trying to figure out what the BORDER procedure is doing.

Varying the Border

To change the size of the BORDER, change the number of times that STRIP is repeated. Change it from STRIP 20 to STRIP 15, for example. Go ahead. Give it a try.

```
TO CORNER
LT 45 FD :H2 RT 45 FD 6
RT 45 FD :S2 RT 45 FD 18
RT 45 FD :S2H2 PU
RT 90 FD :H2 PD RT 90 FD :S2
LT 45 FD 18 LT 90 FD 6 PU
LT 45 FD :S2 PD LT 90 FD 17 PU
RT 90 FD :H2 PD RT 90 FD 17 PU
RT 45 FD 6 RT 90 FD 12 PD
RT 45 FD :H2 RT 45 FD 6
RT 45 FD :H2 PU RT 90 FD :H2 PD
RT 45 FD 6 PU BK 15 RT 90 FD 9 RT 90 PD
END
```

```
TO START
; Here's a simple procedure that puts a braided border
; around the edge of the screen.  Morf likes frames
; for his pictures.
; You can change the size of the border by changing the
; variable used by STRIP in the BRAID procedure.
BORDER
END
```

```
TO STRIP :N
REPEAT :N ~
    [
    LT 45 FD :H2 RT 45 FD 6 RT 45 FD :S2H2
    PU RT 90 FD :H2 PD RT 90 FD :S2 LT 45 FD 6 PU
    LT 45 FD :S2H2 PD LT 135 RT 45 FD :H2 LT 45
    FD 6 LT 45 FD :S2H2 PU LT 90 FD :H2 PD LT 90
    FD :S2 RT 45 FD 6 PU RT 135 FD :S2H2 RT 45
    FD 6 PD
    ]
END
```

Using the Tilde

The Strip procedure is actually one long line. But look how it's written.

REPEAT :N ~

What's that symbol after :N?

It's a tilde. In MSW Logo, that means that the instruction list is continued on the next line. There you find a single bracket:

[

When you have long lines and lists inside other lists, they can get confusing — very difficult to read. MSW Logo gives you some help. When MSW Logo sees a single bracket like that, it knows to look on the next line for the rest of the list.

The rest of the line in STRIP is simply a long list of commands. But what if you had lists within lists. Here's a simple example.

```
TO HEX
REPEAT 6 ~
   [
    REPEAT 3 ~
       [
         FD 100 RT 120
       ]
    RT 60
   ]
END
```

This is the same as

```
TO HEX
REPEAT 6 [REPEAT 3 [FD 100 RT 120] RT 60]
END
```

When procedures begin to get long and complex, you need a system that allows you to read and understand what's going on. As you will see in coming chapters, this can come in real handy.

Check out the procedures in the MSW Logo "Examples" directory for some other examples of multi-line procedures.

From Two to Three Dimensions

"Morf, do you remember Jamie, the six-year-old from that kindergarten class we worked with a few years ago?"

"The name's familiar. What did she do?"

"She was the one who told that newspaper reporter that she was smarter than the computer — because she could roller skate!"

Jamie was among the children at a private school near Dallas who enjoyed learning with Logo on and off the computer. What made her kindergarten class so special was the way they quickly and easily learned to visualize the differences between their three-dimensional world and Logo's two dimensional world.

Here's a challenge for you. Draw pattern of a soccer ball on the screen.

The first thing you see, looking at a soccer ball, is a bunch of hexagon shapes. When some 3rd and 4th grade computer club members were asked to draw this pattern on the screen, they thought it would be easy.

```
TO SOCCER.BALL :DIS
REPEAT 6 [REPEAT 6 [FD :DIS RT 60] FD :DIS LT 60]
END
```

The boy's team thought that all they had to do was draw a series of hexagons. But the center was a pentagon, not a hexagon. So their procedure didn't quite work, did it.

The girl's team was the first to figure out that they could not make the soccer pattern on the screen as it appears on the ball. They had to flatten it out. At first, they thought this procedure was wrong. But then they discovered it was really correct.

```
TO SOCCER :DIS
REPEAT 5 [REPEAT 6 [FD :DIS RT 60] FD :DIS LT 72]
END
```

The girls printed twelve of their patterns, colored them, cut them out, taped them together, and made their own soccer ball. When they were finished, they decided it made a better pinata.

So they filled it with candy and had a party.

149

Adam's Soccer Ball

One young man decided to see if he could produce the entire soccer ball pattern in just one printout. Two was the best he could do.

Here's a picture of Adam's soccer ball. The procedure is on the CD that came with this book as SOCCERM.LGO. Maybe you can figure out a way do it all at once.

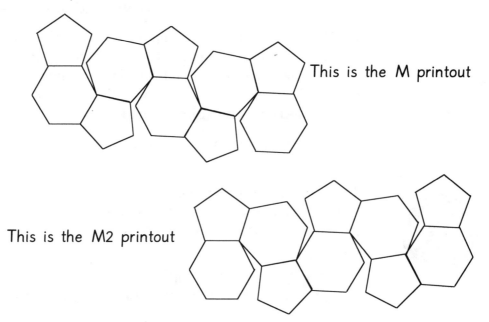

This is the M printout

This is the M2 printout

Rabbit Trail

19

Folded Paper Fun

Making the soccer ball out of paper is just one of many things you can do with Logo and folded paper. The computer club that made the first flattened soccer ball pattern found that you can make all sorts of three dimensional objects from folded paper.

How about a simple cube? This takes you from the two dimensional square to a three dimensional cube.

```
TO CUBE :D
CS HT
REPEAT 4 [SQUARE :D RT 90 FD :D LT 90]
PU HOME REPEAT 2 [RT 90 FD :D] RT 180 PD
REPEAT 3 [SQUARE :D FD :D]
END

TO SQUARE :D
REPEAT 4 [FD :D RT 90]
END
```

The group first cut out a number of cardboard squares. Then they taped them together to see what kind of shapes they could make. The next step was to transfer the pattern to the computer.

Making 3-D shapes from triangles really got interesting

```
TO TETRAHEDRON  :D
RT 30 TRI :D MOVER :D TRI :D
MOVEL :D TRI :D
END

TO MOVER  :D
RT 60 FD :D LT 60
END

TO MOVEL  :D
LT 60 FD :D RT 60
END

TO TRIR  :D
RT 60 FD :D TRI :D
END

TO TRI  :D
REPEAT 3 [FD :D RT 120]
END

TO OCTAHEDRON  :D
LT 30 TRI :D RT 30 TETRAHEDRON :D
LT 60 TRI :D TRIR :D TRIF :D
END

TO TRIF  :D
FD :D RT 60 TRI :D
END
```

TETRAHEDRON and OCTAHEDRON are just the beginning of what you can do with Logo and a printer.

Go ahead. Try these. Print them. Fold them up. And then design your own 3-D figures.

The whole idea is to explore, to discover what you don't know and then go find the answers.

FOR

"No, Morf, this isn't a golf match. FOR is a new command to explore. It can be a big help sometimes. Here, watch what this one-liner does."

```
FOR [N 0 2200] [FD 3 RT (:N * :N)]
```

That's not nearly as bad as it looks. There's just a bunch of stuff to remember. Maybe it would help to look at the procedure below. It does the same thing.

```
TO CRAZY.CIRC :N
IF :N > 2200 [STOP]
FD 3 RT (:N * :N)
CRAZY.CIRC :N + 1
END
```

Here's another look at it as a different kind of one-liner.

```
MAKE "N 0 REPEAT 2200 [FD 3 RT (:N * :N) ~
    MAKE "N :N+1]
```

This tells you exactly how it works.

```
N is the name of the variable used in the crazy circle.
0 is the starting value of :N
2200 is the final value of :N
[FD 3 RT (:N * :N)] The list of instructions to carry out.
```

In MSW Logo, FOR looks for two lists. The first list "sets the rules" for what's supposed to happen. The second is a list of what is going to happen.

Logo looks for a word as the first element in the first list. Yes, N is a word in Logo even though it's only one letter. The rest of the list includes two or three numbers.

The first number is the starting value for the variable, N. The second number is the final value for :N. There can be a third number that tells Logo how to count from the first value to the final value of the variable. Normally Logo will count by 1 as it did in CRAZY.CIRCLE. How about this one:

```
FOR [N 0 100 5] [SHOW :N]
```

In this case, Logo counts by five. This line says:

For the variable :N, start at 0 and go to 100, making each step 5. Now show (or print) :N.

Here's some other examples to play with. These came from an on-line contest to find the prettiest one-liner.

```
FOR [X 1 150] [FD :X RT 89]
FOR [I 0.01 4 0.05] [REPEAT 180 [FD :I RT 1]]
FOR [X 10 200] [SETPENSIZE SE :X :X REPEAT 36 [FD 20 RT 15]]
FOR [I 0.01 4 0.05] [REPEAT 180 [FD :I RT 1]]
```

DEFINE Your Procedures

Speaking of oneliners, here's another way to define procedures and variables. Use the DEFINE command.

```
DEFINE "SQUARE [[SIDE] [REPEAT 4 [FD :SIDE RT 90]]]
```

Try it. You'll see that this line is the same as:

```
TO SQUARE :SIDE
REPEAT 4 [FD :SIDE RT 90]
END
```

Keep in mind that DEFINE does what it says it's going to do: define a procedure. It doesn't run the procedure. You have to tell Logo to do that.

The nice thing about it is that DEFINE can be used as a command within another Logo procedure, whereas TO requires you to use the Mode window or the editor.

The first thing that DEFINE looks for is a word that says what the name of the procedure is to be. In this case, the name of the procedure is SQUARE. Next, DEFINE looks for a list that includes any variable inputs followed by lists of instructions. Each line of instructions is put inside brackets.

You don't have to use variables to use the DEFINE command. Both of these examples work just fine.

```
DEFINE "SQUARE [[][REPEAT 4 [FD 50 RT 90]]]
DEFINE "HELLO [[][PR "|I'M LOGY!|][PR "|I'M MORF!|]]
```

Remember the SHAPES procedure? Here's another way to write the shapes procedures using DEFINE within a superprocedure.

```
TO SHAPES
DEFINE "SQUARE [[][REPEAT 4 [FD 50 RT 90]]]
DEFINE "TRI [[][REPEAT 3 [FD 50 RT 120]]]
DEFINE "REC [[][REPEAT 2 [FD 50 RT 90 FD 100 RT 90]]]
SQUARE TRI REC
END
```

Here's one to have some fun with:

DEFINE "FRAC [[N] [IF :N > 1 [FRAC :N RT 60 FRAC :N FD :N]]

is the same as defining this procedure like this:

```
TO FRAC :N
IF :N > 1 [FRAC :N * .6 RT 60 FRAC :N  *.6 FD :N]
END
```

Now that's weird! You've got a procedure calling itself — not just once, but twice. That's recursion, which is discussed in the *Recursion* chapter.

This little monstrosity is a fractal procedure. To really understand what's going on, you'll have read the *Recursion* chapter and *The Great Math Adventure* chapter. In the meantime, why not have some fun with it.

Try FRAC 100

Try different numbers to see what it does. Then change .6 to another number, like .7 or .4. Change RT 60 to RT 90 or RT 72. What happens?

Copying Definitions

Hey, do you want to play a trick on your parents? Maybe on your teacher? I just love playing tricks on Logy.

COPYDEF and REDEFP are commands that let you rename your own procedures as well as your Logo primitives. Don't worry, these new names are not saved. And while these commands can be useful at times, they sure can be fun. They use variables, too!

Let's start with COPYDEF. This one's easy.

COPYDEF "FRACTAL "FRAC

This copies the new name FRACTAL to the old name FRAC.

Now type

EDIT "FRACTAL

You get

```
TO FRAC :N
IF :N > 1 [FRAC :N * .6 RT 60 FRAC :N  *.6 FD :N]
END
```

What happened to the new name FRACTAL? Actually, it's buried, something you'll read about in the next section. Some versions of Logo copy the whole procedure with the new name. Then you'll get:

```
TO FRACTAL :N
IF :N > 1 [FRAC :N * .6 RT 60 FRAC :N  *.6 FD :N]
END
```

This shows you that you have to be careful using COPYDEF. What would happen if you erased the FRAC procedure?

You'd be in big trouble, that's what.   So what good is this new command?

Suppose you wanted to run a procedure that uses the SETPOS command but your version uses the SETXY command. One of the ways to get around this difference is to simply type

```
COPYDEF "SETPOS "SETXY
```

Now you've got a SETPOS command that acts the same as the SETXY command. Get the idea?

Redefining Primitives

Now that you know how to copy a new name to a procedure, let's try it on a Logo primitive. To do that, you have to make REDEFP true. That means to turn it on. Here's how:

```
MAKE "REDEFP "TRUE
```

Now you can go ahead and change the Logo primitives.

```
ERASE "FD
```

Now try FD 100. What happens? You get

I don't know how to FD

Now try this one.

```
COPYDEF "FD "BK
FD 100
```

Remember, you COPYDEF *<new name><old name>*. So what happened? Does this give you any ideas?

Bury and Unbury

When you COPYDEF a new name over an old name, the old name stays around just as you saw above. The new name gets buried.

BURY is one of those Logo primitives that is often ignored. But it can be very useful.

Let's try something.

1. Load any procedure.

2. Type BURYALL and press Enter.

3. Type POALL and press Enter.

   Where'd the procedures go?

4. Try to run the buried procedure. What happened?

5. Now load another procedure.

6. Type UNBURYALL and press Enter.

7. Type EDALL and press Enter.

Both the procedures are now visible in the Editor, aren't they?

What this means is that when you bury something, it moves from your workspace into another part of the computer's memory. It's like it's buried!

Why not bury the color procedures from the last chapter? First load the color procedures. Then type

   BURY "COLORS

If you type POTS, nothing is displayed, right? Now type

   SETSC BLACK

   The screen color turns black.

You don't have to remember color numbers anymore. Use the names.

If you ever want to see what's buried, just say

   UNBURY "COLORS or

   UNBURYALL

This "digs up" everything that's buried.

Planting Another Garden

Early in this chapter, you had the chance to "plant another garden." Before you leave this chapter on variables, how about planting another garden by adding a twist to the Anyshape procedure. This also adds a twist to running procedures automatically and shows you something else about variables.

In the FLOWERS procedure, you run procedures from within another procedure. Take a look.

```
TO FLOWERS :REPEATS :LIST
REPEAT :REPEATS [RUN :LIST RT 360 / :REPEATS ]
END
```

RUN is a command that tells Logo to run a list of commands. Your remember what a list is, don't you? The GARDEN procedure gives you a pretty good idea. Lists can contain words, commands, or other lists.

Take a look at the first line of GARDENS. After you clean the screen, you have FLOWERS 5. That means that the :REPEATS variable has a value of 5. Then you have a list [FD 50].

```
TO GARDEN
CS FLOWERS 5 [FD 50] WAIT 60
CS FLOWERS 5 [FD 60 SHAPE 50 5] WAIT 60
CS FLOWERS 5 [FD 50 LT 30] WAIT 60
CS FLOWERS 7 [FD 50 LT 60 FD 50 RT 120 FD 50 LT 60 FD 50]
WAIT 60 CS FLOWERS 8 [SHAPE 100 5] WAIT 60
CS FLOWERS 8 [SHAPE 100 3] WAIT 60
CS FLOWERS 8 [SHAPE 100 4] WAIT 60
CS FLOWERS 8 [SHAPE 80 6] WAIT 60
CS FLOWERS 5 [FD 80 FLOWERS 8 [SHAPE 80 3] BK 80]
END
TO SHAPE :SIZE :REPEATS
REPEAT :REPEATS [FD :SIZE RT 360 / :REPEATS]
END
```

Waiting

Do you remember when we mentioned "waiting" before? There are times that you want to slow down the computer so you can see what's going on, or when you just want it to wait a few seconds. That's where the WAIT command comes in.

WAIT <time in 60ths of a second>

There's another way to slow the computer down or to have it take a pause. Write your own WAIT command. Because WAIT is a primitive already, call your new procedure TIME or TIMER.

```
TO TIMER :T
IF :T = 0 [STOP]
TIME :T - 1
END
```

You can make this procedure as precise a timer as you need because you can make :T whatever you want. After all, it is a variable. You can also change :T - 1 to :T - 0.25 or whatever. It's another way to get Logo to do exactly what you want it to do. You can get it to wait in hundreths or even thousandsth of a second.

"What if I just want to pause for a moment while running a procedure? Can I do that?"

Sure, you can. That's what the Pause button is for; the one over to the right in the Commander Box. Try it and see what happens.

Last Minute Ideas

The GARDEN procedure is OK. But have you ever seen a black and white garden? Try adding some color to it.

GARDEN shows you a number of individual flower shapes. Maybe you want to change those shapes. Or maybe you want them to stay on the screen for a longer time. Add a WAIT command.

Remember the last FLOWER picture that is displayed?

FLOWERS 5 [FD 80 FLOWERS 8 [SHAPE 80 3] BK 80]

Why not add some variations of this to the GARDEN procedure so you have different groups of flowers in your garden. Here's one idea:

FLOWERS 12 [SHAPE 30 8]

Also, why not have your flower garden "grow" when it loads.

Make "startup [GARDEN]

Whatever you do, have fun with your new garden.

158

Polygons, Circles, Stars and Stuff

"Now it's time for the magic!"

"Magic?" asked Morf. "What do you mean, magic? You've never talked about Logo magic before."

"We've talked about shapes, and how you can put two or more together to make a picture. We've talked about writing procedures and adding variables and things to those procedures. But this is all pretty ordinary stuff. Now it's time to discover some of the magic – not just Logo magic, but math magic too."

What's the relationship between a square and a circle, for example? Is there a relationship? And why have it? What rules fit for the square, the circle, and other shapes? How can you prove that those rules are true?

There's a lot to look at here, more than we can cover in just one chapter. However, we'll tell you where to explore to discover all sorts of new things.

Playing With Polygons

You've worked with three, four, and six-sided polygons so far. By the way, can you write a procedure for a two-sided polygon?

You had better say NO. Polygons are closed shapes with at least three sides.

Seems to me that we missed one above. Three, four, and six-sided polygons? What about a five-sided polygon? What do you call that?

That's a pentagon, just like that big building near Washington, D.C.

Pentagon Power

Pentagon   REPEAT 5 [FD :SIDE RT _____]

How do you know how far the turtle should turn for the pentagon?

You can try a few numbers to see what works. But before you waste a lot of time, let's see if there is something to be learned from the other shape procedures you already know.

Look at the triangle. 3 repeats times 120 turns = _____

How about the square? 4 repeats times 90 turns = _____

The hexagon? 6 repeats times 60 turns = _____

The rectangle? 2 repeats times 90 + 90 = _____

What goes in the blanks? I bet it's 360 turns. (There's that number again.) So here's what you have:

For a triangle 3 repeats * 120 turns = 360

Another way of writing that is 360/3 repeats = 120 turns. Isn't that right? If you did that for a square and hexagon, what would you have?

For a square: 360/4 repeats = 90 turns

For a hexagon: 360/6 repeats = 60 turns

So, if you want to write a procedure for a pentagon, how about this?

REPEAT 5 [FD :SIDE RT 360/5]

Try it. What happens?

Any Number of Sides

If you can do that for a 5-sided shape, bet you can do that for any number of sides. Try that, too!

REPEAT 3 [FD :SIDE RT 360/3]
REPEAT 4 [FD :SIDE RT 360/4]
REPEAT 6 [FD :SIDE RT 360/6]
REPEAT 9 [FD :SIDE RT 360/9]
REPEAT 15 [FD :SIDE RT 360/15]

What happens as the number of repeats gets bigger? What does the shape look like?

Actually, before you can tell what it looks like, the shapes begin to go off the screen. When this happens, you can fix it by taking fewer steps.

REPEAT 30 [FD 15 RT 360/30]
REPEAT 60 [FD 10 RT 360/60]
REPEAT 90 [FD 5 RT 360/90]
REPEAT 180 [FD 2 RT 360/180]

The important news is that the larger the number of repeats, the more the shape begins to look like a circle. If that's true, what would the procedure for a circle be?

Playing With Circles

With all you've learned about the number 360, this one should be easy. How about this?

TO CIRCLE
REPEAT 360 [FD 2 RT 360/360]
END

That's the same as:

TO CIRCLE
REPEAT 360 [FD 2 RT 1]
END

Of course, circles don't have to go to the right. Why not try a circle to the left?

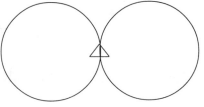

```
TO CIRCLES
REPEAT 360 [FD 2 LT 1]
REPEAT 360 [FD 2 RT 1]
END
```

Gee, it looks like cross-eyes, doesn't it?

A Circle Challenge

How would you put two smaller circles inside these big ones? Solving this challenge is like solving any problem.

1. Start with what you know.

   You know that the turtle just drew two large circles by first going FORWARD 2 steps, then RIGHT or LEFT 1 turtle turn 360 times.

2. Now, what do you need to know?

   You need to know how to change the procedure so the circles will be smaller.

   OK, what can you change?

   - You can change the number of repeats.

   - You can change the number of turtle steps.

   - You can change the number of turtle turns.

You have already learned that to draw a circle, you tell the turtle to

```
REPEAT 360 [FD :SIDE  RT or LT 1]
```

So, to draw a smaller circle, it seems as if you can make the number of steps smaller. So try this:

```
REPEAT 360 [FD 1 RT 1]
```

It looks all right, doesn't it? Next draw a circle to the left.

Now, that really does look like cross-eyes.

Why not create some other drawings using circles and the other shapes you've been using? Draw them on paper or in your journal. Then draw them on the screen.

More About Circles

What else do you know about drawing a circle?

You know that the number of repeats times the number of turtle turns equals 360. You used 360 times 1. What happens if you change that to 180 times 2? Would that make a smaller circle or a larger one? Go ahead. Try it out.

Earlier, you started with the familiar shapes of square, triangle, rectangle, and hexagon, and increased the number of REPEATS and the number of turns. Now let's turn this around and go the other way — just for the fun of it.

REPEAT 360 [FD 2 RT 1]

REPEAT 180 [FD 2 RT 2]

REPEAT 120 [FD 2 RT 3]

Now make up shapes of your own. It soon stops looking like a circle

Defining a Circle

Just what is a circle, really? You made up some rules about other shapes. So what is the rule for circles?

If you ask a math teacher, you'll find that a circle is a closed curve where every point on the curve is the same distance from a fixed point. On the Logo screen, you can use HOME as the fixed point. (That fixed point is really the center.) Then a circle is a closed curve where every point on that curve is the same distance from HOME.

Make sense? Sure! Now, can you write a procedure to draw a circle like this?

Let's make HOME our fixed point, the center of our circle. Next you have to draw a line so that every point on that line is the same distance from HOME.

How can you do that?

You'll have to pick the pen up, go out to where you want your circle to be, draw a point, come back, turn a little bit, go out the same distance, draw another point, come back, turn a little, and so on.

Before you start drawing the line, let's first write a procedure to draw a point.

```
TO POINT
PD RT 90 FD 1
BK 1 LT 90 PU
END
```

See what that does? Now let's put this procedure to good use.

```
TO CIRCLE :SIDE
HOME CS PU
REPEAT 360 [FD :SIDE POINT BK :SIDE RT 1]
END
```

The procedure starts from HOME with a clear screen. Now, rather than go FD 1 and RT 1 like you did before, the turtle goes FD :SIDE, draws a point, goes back HOME, and turns RT 1 turtle turn, goes out, draws a point, comes back, and starts all over again. You end up drawing a line where every point on that line is the same distance from the center.

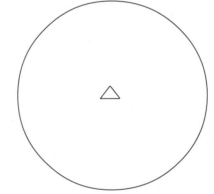

What do you call that distance from the center of the circle, the fixed point, to the edge?

That's the radius of the circle.

What do you call that edge, the line around the fixed point? Right, that's the circumference of the circle.

Here's another one. What do you call the distance from one side of the circle to the other, the line that goes through the center of the circle?

Give yourself a Gold Star if you said that's the diameter of the circle.

One more: what's the relationship between the diameter of the circle and the circumference? Hmmm? That's a tough one, isn't it?

The diameter times Pi equals the circumference. But what's Pi?

Pi is the 16th letter in the Greek alphabet. It is also one of those strange mathematical numbers that will keep your computer busy for hours. They call it a "transcendental" number because it has no set value The computer will keep on dividing for hours. Pi will never come out even.

PICALC.LGO is a procedure on the CD that comes with this book that calculates Pi to as many decimal places as you want. Load the procedure. Then type PICALC and the number of decimal places to which you want Pi calculated. For example, PICALC 50.

Here's Pi calculated to 50 places.

3.14159265358979323846264338327950288419716939937510 5

It takes some time for your computer to figure that one out. Why not try an even larger number and see how long that takes?

The Rule of 360

Now, do you remember all that you learned about that number 360? It keeps popping up doesn't it. Well, there's another rule in there somewhere. Actually, there are two.

- It seems that when you add up the angles you need to draw any closed shape that is made from straight lines, the answer is 360.

- Another interesting thing is that when the turtle travels through 360 degrees, she always ends up where she started.

Try it. Add the same number to both blanks in this procedure.

REPEAT_____[FD :SIDE RT 360/_____]

Take a look at these commands again. How would you write one procedure that would draw all of them?

Triangle: REPEAT 3 [FD :SIDE RT 360 / 3]

Square: REPEAT 4 [FD :SIDE RT 360 / 4]

Pentagon: REPEAT 5 [FD :SIDE RT 360 / 5]

Hexagon: REPEAT 6 [FD :SIDE RT 360 / 6]

Octagon: REPEAT 8 [FD :SIDE RT 360 / 8]

In these procedures you use the variable :SIDE for the length of one side of the shape.

How about this:

```
TO POLYGON :SIDE :REPEATS
REPEAT :REPEATS [FD :SIDE RT 360/ :REPEATS]
END
```

Once you've played with this procedure a bit, write one to draw all of the shapes up to a circle.

```
TO POLYGONS :SIDE :REPEATS
IF :REPEATS = 360 [STOP]
REPEAT :REPEATS [FD :SIDE RT 360 / :REPEATS]
POLYGONS :SIDE :REPEATS + 1
END
```

You can make the :SIDE anything you want. But what would you start :REPEATS at? Think about the definition of a polygon. That will tell you.

Here's what the procedure looks like when it's run. We had to stop it before it got to big for the screen.

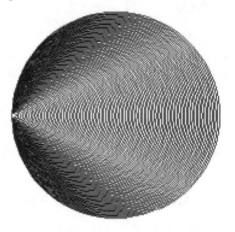

Rule of 360 Worksheet

Fill in the correct numbers in the following chart and draw a picture of what happens on the screen. A few have been filled in to get you started.

The numbers at the top of each column in the table are the number of repeats. The numbers down the left column are the number of turtle turns.

For the first row across the top of the table, the number at the top of each column equals the number of sides for the shape.

Number of Turtle Turns (TT)	Number of Repeats						
	3	4	5	6	8	10	12
TT * 1	120	90	72	60			
TT * 2			144	120			
TT * 3	360						
TT * 4		360					
TT * 5			360				

More Playing With Polygons

Do you remember how we got started developing shapes? The first thing you did was create a corner.

```
TO CORNER
FD 100 RT 90
END
```

Then you used the corner to make a square. But what if you changed that procedure? What if you added variables?

```
TO CORNER :SIDE :ANGLE
FD :SIDE RT :ANGLE
END
```

Now you can make just about any shape. What's this one?

```
REPEAT 3 [CORNER 100 120]
```

Or this one?

```
REPEAT5 [CORNER 100 72]
```

Since you've already used CORNER before, let's find another name. Since this procedure is used to draw polygons, why not call it POLY?

```
TO POLY :SIDE :ANGLE
FD :SIDE RT :ANGLE
END
```

Now let's see what you can do with POLY. The procedures shown on the next page can be found on the CD that came with this book as POLYS.LGO.

For one thing, you can improve on your "Any Shape" procedure.

```
TO POLYGON :SIDE :ANGLE
REPEAT 360/:ANGLE [POLY :SIDE :ANGLE]
END
```

Here's a few other variations you'll find in the POLYS.LGO file.

```
TO DUOPOLY :SIDE1 :SIDE2 :ANGLE
REPEAT 50 ~
 [
    POLY :SIDE1 :ANGLE
       POLY :SIDE2 :ANGLE
 ]
END

TO RANDPOLY :SIDE :ANGLE
REPEAT 100~
 [
    IFELSE (RANDOM 10) = 0 [PD] [PU]
    POLY :SIDE :ANGLE
 ]
END
```

Random and Rerandom

There's another new command for you — RANDOM. RANDOM picks an integer between 0 and the input you give it. If you don't know what an integer is, it's a whole number — a number without any fractions or decimals after it.

15 is an integer or whole number. It doesn't include any parts of a number such as a fraction ($1\text{-}\frac{1}{2}$) or decimal (1.5). You'll read more about integers and whole numbers in *The Great Math Adventure* chapter.

To see what RANDOM does, try this:

REPEAT 10 [SHOW RANDOM 10]

What happened? You got a list of 10 numbers selected randomly from the numbers 0 - 9. Now try it again. And again.

You get a different list each time, right? But what if you want to use that same list again and again? That's where RERANDOM comes in.

RERANDOM takes what they call a seed number. This seed number identifies a particular sequence of random numbers. Take a look.

When you want to select a sequence of random numbers to use over and over again, use the RERANDOM command followed by the RANDOM command. Take a look.

```
(RERANDOM 15)
REPEAT 2 [SHOW RANDOM 5]
4
2
```

To repeat that sequence, type

```
(RERANDOM 15)
REPEAT 2 [SHOW RANDOM 5]
4
2
```

If you want to add another sequence of numbers randomly selected from 0 - 4, just change the seed number.

```
(RERANDOM 25)
REPEAT 2 [SHOW RANDOM 5]
1
0

(RERANDOM 25)
REPEAT 2 [SHOW RANDOM 5]
1
0
```

To demonstrate the value of RERANDOM, try this one again.

```
(RERANDOM 15)
REPEAT 2 [SHOW RANDOM 5]
```

What happened?

There's another thing to consider. What if you want to select a random number but not zero? How about this.

SHOW (RANDOM :INPUT) + 1

Some versions of Logo pick a number between 1 and your input, rather than from 0. So if you ever want Logo to pick 0 as the input, use

(RANDOM :INPUT) - 1

Dressing Up Poly

These procedures are rather ordinary by themselves. To dress them up a bit, why not add a small turn at the end of each list. For example:

```
TO DUOPOLY :SIDE1 :SIDE2 :ANGLE
REPEAT 50~
  [
    POLY :SIDE1 :ANGLE
    POLY :SIDE2 :ANGLE
    RT 10
  ]
END
```

or

```
TO RANDPOLY :SIDE :ANGLE
REPEAT 100 ~
  [
    IFELSE (RANDOM 10) = 0 [PD] [PU]~
    POLY :SIDE :ANGLE RT 10
  ]
END
```

Play around with different numbers to see just what these procedures can do.

Here's a set of procedures that draws with dots. What type of variations can you dream up for this procedure?

```
TO POLYSPI :ANG
MAKE "SIDE 0
REPEAT 100 ~
  [
    POLY :SIDE :ANGLE
    PD FD 1 BK 1 PU
```

```
            MAKE "SIDE :SIDE + 2
      ]
      END
```

Finally, what can you do with this inward spiral?

```
      TO INSPI :SIDE :ANGLE :INC.
      FD :SIDE RT :ANGLE
      INSPI :SIDE :ANGLE + :INC :INC
      END
```

If you really want a challenge, try digging into this procedure. Can you predict what different values for the variables will be produced?

If this seems too easy, try this one.

```
      TO INSPI_1 :SIDE :ANGLE :INC
      REPEAT 360 * :ANGLE ~
         [
         FD :SIDE
         RT REPCOUNT + (2 * :INC - :ANGLE)/ ~
            (2 * :ANGLE)
         ]
      END
```

There's another new command REPCOUNT. It outputs the number of repeats called for by the REPEAT command. Here's a very simple demonstration of what REPCOUNT does.

```
      REPEAT 3 [(PR "|THIS IS REPCOUNT| REPCOUNT)]
```

```
      THIS IS REPCOUNT 1
      THIS IS REPCOUNT 2
      THIS IS REPCOUNT 3
```

As shown in the INSPI_1 procedure, you can use the output of REPCOUNT to calculate other values.

You can spend a very long time studying the mathematics of the INSP and INSPI_1 figures. Here's some inputs to get you started.

This figure was created using inputs of 8 8 5. Why not try

```
      INSPI_1 10 7 3
      INSPI_1 10 10 7
      INSPI_1 10 12 5
```

Have fun with these!

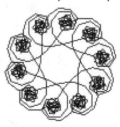

Arcs, Circles, Hoops, and Things

By now, you should have a pretty good idea of how to work with shapes such as the square, rectangle, triangle, circle, and such.

Now it's time to start making Logo jump through some hoops! In the rest of this book, you'll find there's a lot more to turtle graphics than just drawing shapes.

You already know that you can draw a circle using an instruction like this one.

REPEAT 360 [FD 1 RT 1]

How would you draw a curve – just part of a circle?

If there are 360 degrees in a circle, part of a circle would be something less than that. So let's try

REPEAT 90 [FD 1 RT 1]

Hmmm?

Think about this. You already know that RT or LT 180 makes the turtle turn around and go the opposite direction. So what would happen if she "did a 180" here?

REPEAT 4 [REPEAT 90 [FD 1 RT 1] RT 180]

That's interesting. But what happens when you try this one?

REPEAT 6 [REPEAT 60 [FD 1 RT 1] RT 240]

Does this one remind you of a snowflake?

REPEAT 2 [REPEAT 90 [FD 1 RT 1] RT 90]

I don't know about you, but that looks like a leaf to me.

What would happen if you just continued around the circle?

Here's the leaf:

TO LEAF
REPEAT 2 [REPEAT 90 [FD 1 RT 1] RT 90]
END

Now try this:

TO LEAVES
REPEAT 4 [LEAF LT 90]
END

You know, with a little bit of work, that could be all sorts of things. Why not see what you can do with this shape before you move along? Maybe it could be a butterfly.

Or maybe a Indian headdress. That's made from feathers, right?

How about a chrysanthemum?

How about making a whole flower bed using different sizes of arcs for different sizes of leaves?

What other types of flowers can you draw?

How about three-dimensional flowers?

```
TO DAHLIA
CS HT CLEARPALETTE SETPENSIZE [2 2]
REPEAT 16 ~
   [
   SETPC (LIST REPCOUNT*256/16 0 0)
   REPEAT 8 [RT 45 REPEAT 4~
         [
         REPEAT 90 [FD 2 RT 2] RT 90]
         ]
   RT .4
   ]
PR [ISN'T IT PRETTY!]
END
```

There's another new command here that you can read about in the MSW Logo on-line help file – CLEARPALETTE.

Arc and Circle Tools

There are lots of times when you want to use ARC and CIRCLE procedures. So we made up a set of tools you can use at any time. These are on the CD that came with this book as ARCTOOLS.LGO. Just load them into your own procedures and you're ready to go.

Before you do that, however, there are a few things to note.

ARCL and ARCR start from the edge and draw arcs to the left and right. CIRCLEL and CIRCLER also start from the edge and draw circles to the left and right. The variable :RADIUS tells the computer how big to make the arc or circle. Do you remember, the radius of a circle is the distance from the center to the outside rim or circumference?

The variable :DEGREES tells the computer how big to make the arc. ARCR 100 60 tells the turtle to draw an arc that is 60 degrees long and with a radius of 100.

What is that number 3.14159? That's Pi, remember. Some people use 3.14. Some use 3.1416. In some versions of Logo, you can use the Logo primitive, Pi.

```
TO ARCL :RADIUS :DEGREES
LOCAL "AMT
MAKE "AMT 2 * :RADIUS * 3.14159 / 36
REPEAT :DEGREES / 10 [LT 5 FD :AMT LT 5]
END

TO ARCR  :RADIUS :DEGREES
LOCAL "AMT
MAKE "AMT 2 * :RADIUS * 3.14159 / 36
REPEAT :DEGREES / 10 [RT 5 FD :AMT RT 5]
END

TO CIRCLEL  :RADIUS
LOCAL "AMT
MAKE "AMT 2 * :RADIUS * 3.14159 / 36
REPEAT 36 [LT 5 FD :AMT LT 5]
END

TO CIRCLER  :RADIUS
LOCAL "AMT
MAKE "AMT 2 * :RADIUS * 3.14159 / 36
REPEAT 36 [RT 5 FD :AMT RT 5]
END
```

What's that :AMT variable?

That's part of the mathematical formula for drawing a circle or part of a circle. It calculates the size of the circle based on the size of the radius you give it.

Have some fun with these procedures. They are useful tools to keep handy.

There's a lot more to do with polygons and things, especially when you start digging into recursion. But first, let's take a look at turtle positions.

174

ARC, ARC2, CIRCLE, and CIRCLE2

Now that you've learned the hard way to develop arc and circle tools, it's time to tell you about the easy way. There are tools in the Logolib directory that will draw arcs and circles from either the center of the circle or from the edge.

ARC and CIRCLE draw from the center. ARC2 and CIRCLE2 draw from the edge.

The ARC procedures take two inputs:

> ARC *<angle><radius>*

The CIRCLE procedures only take one input, the radius. Why not try these commands?

Rabbit Trail
20

Star Gazing

Draw a big pentagon on the screen. Do you remember how to do that?

> REPEAT 5 [FD 100 RT 360 / 5]

Now print the screen. Take a pencil and a ruler and draw a diagonal line to each corner. In this way, every corner is connected to every other corner by a line.

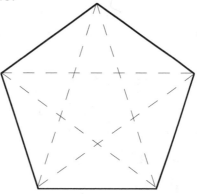

What do you see inside the pentagon? I see a big star; how about you?

Now draw a big hexagon on the screen.

> REPEAT 6 [FD 100 RT 360 / 6]

Draw diagonal lines to connect all the corners. What do you see? There's a Star of David, right? That's a six-pointed star.

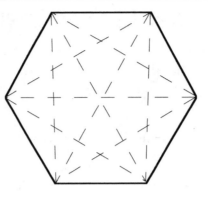

Try this with an octagon. Now that's a lot of lines to draw.

How would you draw these stars on the screen? Do the drawings you did on paper help you figure it out?

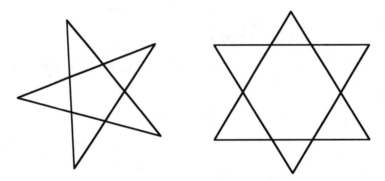

You drew a shape first. Then you drew diagonals to each of the corners. So let's explore the shapes first and see what can be learned there.

Take a look at the pentagon.

To draw the pentagon shape below, the turtle first turns LT 18, then goes FD 100 RT 360 / 5 (that's the same as RT 72).

Why turn LT 18?

    90 - 72 = 18.

You should be able to figure that out by looking at the drawing below.

The angle outside the pentagon is 72. What's the angle inside the pentagon?

Let's find out. This is going to get a bit complicated, so hang in there. Just follow along at the computer.

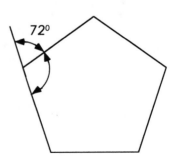

Clear the screen and draw another pentagon like the previous one. Make sure you can see the turtle.

Then type:

FD 100

The turtle has now moved up the first side of the pentagon, right? Now what's the command to make the turtle turn around and head back to HOME? It's not BACK 100. The turtle doesn't turn around using the BACK command.

The command to turn around is RT or LT 180, isn't it? That turns you in the opposite direction from where you were headed. Go ahead, try it.

RT 180 FD 100

Now where's the turtle? Type HOME and see what happens.

All the turtle does is turn around. She's back home. So let's try something else. Turn LT 18 and head up to left side of the Pentagon.

FD 100 RT 72

Now the turtle is set to move up the second side of the pentagon.

Now the big question? How far do you have to turn to send the turtle HOME?

That's not that hard, really. You turned 180 the first time when you wanted to face home, when you did not turn RT 72. So what's 180 - 72? I get 108. What do you get? Try it:

RT 108 FD 100 HOME

There you are! Ernestine is right where she was before.

Believe it or not, you're actually getting somewhere. Don't believe me? Well, try this:

LT 18 REPEAT 5 [FD 150 BK 50 RT 72]

Wow! That's a pretty weird pentagon! But it shows you what you've been doing. It clearly shows the five 72-degree angles Ernestine turns at each corner.

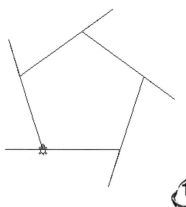

This highlights something that a lot of people get confused about, even Logy and Morf.

When we think about the angles the turtle moves through to make a polygon, we usually think about the angles inside the shape.

Well, don't you?

Compare the angles inside a shape with the angles outside a shape.

- The angles inside a triangle: 180°
- The angles inside a rectangle (or square):   360°
- The angles inside a pentagon: 540°
- The angles inside a hexagon: 720°

You can figure what the other shapes total yourself. Now what about the outside angles of each shape? What do they total?

Is that a familiar number?

Now where were we. Try the same thing with the hexagon that you did with the pentagon.

   REPEAT 6 [FD 150 BK 50 RT 60]

When drawing a hexagon, Ernestine goes FD 150, BACK 50, and turns RT 60 on the outside. That leaves an angle of what on the inside?

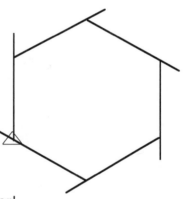

If you said 120, let's make you a big Gold Star!

Look at the drawing of the pentagon with the diagonals below. How many angles do you see at each corner? I see three, how about you?

Are all the angles the same?

It sure looks that way. So if that inside angle is 108, what are each of the three angles? That's 108 divided by 3 or 36, right?

Now, take your pencil and ruler and draw along any one of the diagonal lines to make it go out beyond the pentagon – like Ernestine did when she went FD 150 BK 50.

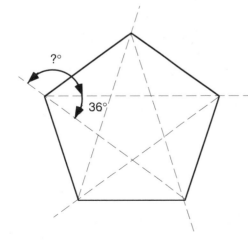

Here you have the large angle outside the star and the small angle inside. You already know the small angle is 36. So what's the big angle?

That's 180 - 36 or 144.

Now you're really getting somewhere! So what angle do you need to draw a star?

REPEAT 5 [FD 162 RT _____]

Now add this one:

LT 36 REPEAT 5 [FD 100 RT 72]

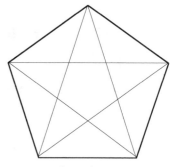

How about that! There's the star inside the pentagon, just like the picture you drew on paper. But how'd Ernestine know the distance was 162? Well, that's a lesson in trigonometry that you can read about in *The Great Math Adventure* chapter.

Why not see what you can do with the Star of David now? If you look closely, you'll see there are two triangles in the star.

Here's a hint. If the side of the hexagon is 100, try 172 for the side of the triangle.

```
TO PENTAGON
REPEAT 5 [FD 100 RT 72]
END

TO STAR
REPEAT 5 [FD 162 RT 144]
END

TO STAR.IN.PENT
RT 18 STAR
LT 36 PENTAGON
END

TO HEXAGON
REPEAT 6 [FD 100 RT 60]
END

TO STAR.OF.DAVID
RT 30 TRI PU
RT 90 FD 100 PD
LT 150 TRI
END
```

```
TO TRI
REPEAT 3 [FD 172 RT 120]
END

TO STAR.IN.HEX
STAR.OF.DAVID
LT 30 HEXAGON
END
```

Something Else to Think About

How would you draw a seven-pointed star?

A seven-sided polygon is easy!

REPEAT 7 [FD :SIDE RT 360 / 7]

Now turn that into a procedure for drawing a seven-pointed star.

Here's a picture of a seven-sided shape with all of its corners connected.

Can you see a seven-pointed star in this picture? How would you draw such a shape?

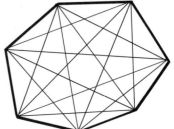

It's really pretty easy. However, to understand it, let's back up a bit.

The procedure to draw any polygon is

REPEAT :REPEATS [FD :SIZE RT 360 / :REPEATS]

The :REPEATS variable stands for the number of sides. Since you're going to be working with Stars now, let's change that to :POINTS.

REPEAT :POINTS [FD :SIZE RT 360 / :POINTS]

Now let's take a look at the total of the angles in some of the shapes this procedure draws.

- The angles inside a triangle: 180°
- The angles inside a rectangle (or square): 360°
- The angles inside a pentagon: 540°
- The angles inside a hexagon: 720°
- The angles inside a septagon (7 sides):   900°
- The angles inside an octagon: 1080°
- The angles inside a nanogon (9 sides):   1260°

Look at the triangle and rectangle. To draw each of these shapes, the turtle turns through 360 degrees. Remember, that's one of the rules for a polygon.

To draw a five-pointed star, the turtle actually turns around twice. It starts facing the top of the screen. After five turns, it has moved through 360 degrees twice. To see this clearly, try this:

```
REPEAT 5 [FD 100 RT 144 WAIT 60]
```

If that's true, what would happen if you wrote a procedure like this?

```
TO STAR
REPEAT 5 [FD 100 RT 360 / 5 * 2]
END
```

Would this work for a Star of David?

```
TO STAR.OF.DAVID
REPEAT 6 [FD 100 RT 360 / 6 * 2]
END
```

No, it won't work. Here's a challenge that will help explain the confusion. Try to draw a six-pointed star without lifting your pencil from the paper and without ever drawing over the same line again.

The Star of David is unique. It's actually two separate triangles linked together. It has been the symbol of Judaism for about 3000 years.

What about a seven-pointed star?

```
REPEAT 7 [FD 100 RT 360 / 7 * 2]
```

What's the difference between this star and the one created by this command?

```
REPEAT 7 [FD 100 RT 360 * 3 / 7]
```

Now see what you can do with 8, 9, 10, 11 points – and other star shapes. If you need help, try this procedure.

```
TO STARS :POINTS :SIZE :MULT
REPEAT :POINTS [FD :SIZE RT 360/:POINTS * :MULT]
END
```

What's that :MULT variable? Take another look at the inside angles.

To draw a pentagon: REPEAT 5 [FD 50 RT 360/5] The angles inside the polygon total 720 (360 * 2).

To draw a hexagon: REPEAT 6 [FD 50 RT 360/6]
The angles inside the polygon total 720 (360 * 2).

To draw an octagon: REPEAT 8 [FD 50 RT 360/8]
The angles inside an octagon total 1080 (360 * 3).

To draw a 10-sided shape: REPEAT 10 [FD 50 RT 360/10]
Angles total 1440 (360* 4).

To draw a 12-sided polygon: REPEAT 12 [FD 50 RT 360/12]
Angles inside the shape total 1800 degrees (360 * 5).

To draw a 360-sided shape: REPEAT 360 [FD 50 RT 360/360]
Angles inside total 64,440 (360 * 179).

Do some experimenting with different numbers to see what happens. Among other things, you'll find you have to change the Rule of 360 a little bit.

Before we said

"Another interesting thing is that when the turtle travels through 360 degrees, she always ends up where she started."

Now we have to change that to read

"Another interesting thing is that when the turtle travels through 360 degrees, or any multiple of 360, she always ends up where she started."

You can also say that whenever the turtle travels through any closed shape, then travels through 360 degrees or a multiple of 360 degrees.

Is that really true? What do you think? Have you proven that or not?

From the Center Again

Remember when you had to draw a rectangle around the center? How would you do that for other polygons? How would you find the center of a nine-sided polygon, for example?

Before you start worrying about nine-side shapes, let's start with the simple ones. When you drew a rectangle around the center, you started at the center and went FD Width / 2, LT 90, FD Length / 2. This put you in the lower left corner from which you could draw your rectangle.

To find the center of a rectangle or a square, you start at a corner and go FD Length / 2, RT (or LT) 90, FD Width / 2. It might be easier to read if it's written like this:

```
TO CENTER :SIDE
REPEAT 4 [FD :SIDE RT 90]
REPEAT 2 [FD :SIDE / 2 RT 90]
END
```

Now let's try this on a triangle.

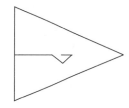

```
TO CENTER :SIDE
REPEAT 3 [FD :SIDE RT 120]
REPEAT 2 [FD :SIDE / 2 RT 90]
END
```

OK, the line doesn't end in the middle of the triangle. But from what you learned about triangles, you know that the center has to be somewhere along that line. What do you have to do to find that point?

First, let's write a procedure to draw that line that goes through the center.

```
TO FWD :SIDE
FD :SIDE/2
RT 90
FD 100 BK 100
LT 90
FD :SIDE/2
END
```

Now let's see what happens when you put that into your shape procedures.

```
TO CENTER :SIDE
REPEAT 3 [FWD :SIDE RT 120]
END
```

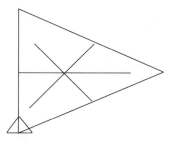

How about that? It seems as if we've stumbled onto something here.

Would this work for other polygons? Try it out.

```
TO POLY :REP :SIDE
REPEAT :REP [FWD :SIDE RT 360 / :REP]
END
```

Now for the acid test, the nine-sided polygon.

183

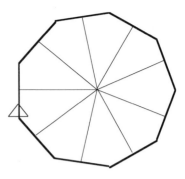

Works for me.

Your next challenge is to figure out how to measure the distance to the center.

There's much more to working with polygons, circles, stars, and stuff in coming chapters. But before you get there, there's some work to do with Turtle Positions and Coordinates.

Turtle Positions and Coordinates

So far, we've moved the turtle around the screen using the direction commands: FORWARD, BACK, LEFT, RIGHT. Well, there are two other ways to move the turtle around that give you all sorts of new things to do. These new choices are turtle headings and X-Y coordinates.

Turtle Headings

When you want the turtle to move from HOME up to the right, you can tell her go RIGHT 45 FD 100 LEFT 45.

Another way to do the same thing is to tell the turtle to set her heading to 45 and then go forward 100 steps and then set her heading back toward the top of the screen.

SETHEADING 45 FD 100 SETHEADING 0

Or you can use shorthand. Clear the screen and type

SETH 45 FD 100 SETH 0

When you typed SETH 45, what direction did the turtle turn? She turned the same direction as when you told her RIGHT 45, correct?

If you typed SETH -45 FD 100 SETH 0, what do you think would happen? Go ahead – try it and see. Remember to clear the screen first.

OK, now type SETH 45 FD 100 SETH 0 again, but without clearing the screen. What happened?

Hmmmm? This is interesting. Now type SETH 45 FD 100 SETH 0 again. What happened this time?

Well, it seems as if you can use the SETH command to turn the turtle. But it certainly doesn't act like the RIGHT and LEFT commands.

SHOW HEADING

If you ever want to know what heading the turtle is on, type

SHOW HEADING

HEADING is a new command. You can easily guess what it means.

SHOW, you may remember, is a command that is a lot like PRINT. The big difference is that PRINT shows lists of things without brackets. SHOW displays them with brackets.

PRINT [1 2 3 4 5]

The result is   1 2 3 4 5

SHOW [1 2 3 4 5]

The result is   [1 2 3 4 5]

OK? Back to HEADINGs. Remember the string clock you made a while ago, the one you made with a piece of board and some nails? This is a good tool for learning about headings. Well, let's look at that clock again.

What heading is at 12:00 o'clock? 3:00 o'clock? 6:00 o'clock? 9:00 o'clock?

Get the idea? Turtle headings follow the hands of the clock. The heading at 12:00 o'clock is zero. At 3:00 o'clock, it's 90. At 6:00 o'clock, it's 180, and at 9:00 o'clock, it's 270.

This isn't to say that you can't move counter clockwise, to the left. You've already seen what happens when you typed

    SETH -45.

What time would it be at SETH -90?

What about SETH -180?   SETH -270?

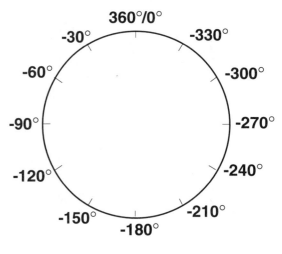

The Turtle's Compass

When you look at a clock like this, with all the hours marked off in degrees, what does it make you think of?

How about a compass?

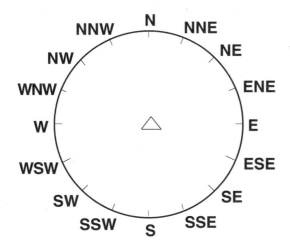

Yes, that's it. It's like a compass. Now, what do you think you can learn from a compass?

The compass needle always points to North. If North is at 12:00 o'clock or 360 degrees, where's East? South? West?

Now let's get tricky. Where's Northeast? How many degrees is that? What about Southwest?

Morf's got a great game that will help you out. You'll learn about the procedures to draw this marked-off circle a little later in this chapter.

The Turtle Rally

Have you ever heard of a car rally?

Well, car rallies are special types of races. Only this type of race doesn't depend on how fast you can drive. It depends on how well you can follow directions. Each car has a driver and a navigator. The team that can find its way through the course closest to the time limit is the winner.

In the Turtle Rally, you are given a compass and a list of directions. You'll need a digital watch that shows the seconds or a watch with a second hand so you can time yourself.

Here's how to play.

Have one person set up the course, maybe your teacher, your mom, or a person elected to be Rally Captain. This can be a course through the house, through the neighborhood, around the school yard, or anywhere you can set up a safe course to follow.

The directions will read something like this, only there should be many more.

1. You have 15 minutes to complete the race.

2. Start from Home. Set your heading to 0 and go forward for 40 seconds.

3. Set your heading to 90 and walk forward 120 steps.

4. Set your heading to 30 and run forward for 10 seconds.

You can make up any kind of directions you want. They can be simple. They can be silly. Or they can be tough. It makes the race more fun when you mix them up: walking, running, turning – and don't forget Back!

Another thing you can do is make a map for each team. Only maybe you leave off some names to make it tough. Maybe you change the names to make it silly.

Use compass directions, such as North, Southwest, Northeast. Maybe you can mix up compass directions with degrees and headings. There are all sorts of things you can do to get practice. And you can have a fun rally at the same time.

The Rally Captain times each team – the time each team starts and the time each team finishes. Each team starts a minute or two apart so that teams don't bump into each other along the path.

It is a good thing to have checkpoints along the path where teams have to pick up something like a piece of paper and return it to the finish line. Maybe the paper can have a question each player has to answer correctly. Use your imaginations. The main thing is to have some fun while practicing with headings and directions.

After you've run your Turtle Rally, why not try one on the computer? You'd be surprised what you can create using headings and directions. In fact, that's just what you'll do a little later in this chapter.

X - Y Coordinates

Imagine this screen with 1000 columns drawn on it and 1000 rows. All of these columns and rows may not show on your computer screen but they are there. You can change the numbers if you want. Read the instructions in the RELEASE.TXT file that was installed when you installed MSW Logo.

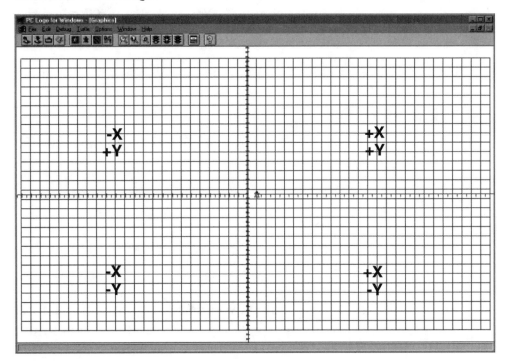

Columns go up and down. Rows go from side to side. To find a position, you'd have to know which column and which row to pick.

This is exactly what you do when using the X- and Y-coordinates. X-coordinates count the number of columns from side-to-side. Y-coordinates count the number of rows up and down.

There are two lines that divide the screen in half, one divides the screen from top to bottom and one divides the screen down the

189

middle, from side to side. Where these lines meet is HOME, where X is 0 and Y is 0.

> If you move up to the right, both the X-coordinate numbers and Y-coordinate numbers are positive (+).

> If you move up to the left, the X-coordinate becomes negative (-) but the Y-coordinate remains positive.

> If you move down to the left, both the X- and Y-coordinates become negative.

> If you move down to the right, the X-coordinate is positive and the Y-coordinate is negative.

If you'd like to put the same type of grid on your computer screen, use the GRID procedure (GRID.LGO on the CD that came with this book). Make sure you maximize the graphics screen to run this. Left-click on the button at the far left of the Graphics screen title bar. Then left-click on "Maximize." You can also use the command

ICON "COMMANDER

This reduces the Commander window to a small icon.

XCOR and YCOR

HOME is at X-coordinate 0 and Y-coordinate 0. In Logo, we use the shorthand names:

XCOR

YCOR

Clear the screen. Then type SHOW XCOR. What happened?

Hmmmmm. Very interesting.

What do you think you need to do to send the turtle to another X-coordinate? Give yourself a Gold Star if you said SETX, not SET XCOR.

Go ahead, try it. Type SETX and a number.

Now try moving the turtle up and down. What's the command? That one should be real easy.

I bet you've already guessed that you can combine these two commands. Sure!

SETXY _____ _____

That's right. It's SETXY.

Now, where were we?

Was the pen down when you typed the SETX, SETY, and SETXY commands? What happened? Did you end up with a crazy drawing on the screen?

If the pen was up, put it down and then do a few more SETXY commands to get some practice using the commands.

SETPOS

SETPOS is like SETXY except that it takes a list of x- and y-coordinates as inputs. It moves the turtle to the coordinates you put in the list.

SETPOS [_____ _____] or

SETPOS LIST :X :Y

POS and TOWARDS

There are times when you want to remember the turtle's position while she goes off and does something else. That's where POS comes in. This command remembers the coordinates of where the turtle was when you issued the command.

For example:

```
TO S
SETXY -100 50 SETH 0 FD 25 LT 90 FD 15
MAKE "A POS
RT 90 FD 200 SETH 135 FD 25
MAKE "B POS
PU SETPOS :A PD
SETH TOWARDS :B
FD DIST :A :B
END

TO DIST  :A :B
OP DIST1 (FIRST :A) - (FIRST :B) (LAST :A) - (LAST :B)
END

TO DIST1  :DX :DY
OP SQRT (:DX * :DX ) + (:DY * :DY )
END
```

The first and third lines of the S procedure are whatever you want them to be. The idea is to make the turtle off somewhere, make the variable A the POS or coordinates of the final location, and then go off to another location, which is named B.

PU SETPOS :A PD takes the turtle back to the coordinates of :A.

SETH TOWARDS :B tells the turtle to turn towards the coordinates that were remembered as position :B.

Finally, the procedure tells the turtle to go FD the DISTance to :B. You know that :A and :B are lists of coordinates. Then you should be able to figure out what this line does:

OP DIST1 (FIRST :A) - (FIRST :B) (LAST :A) - (LAST :B)

FIRST :A and FIRST :B are the first elements of :A and :B or the X-coordinates. So what's LAST :A and :B?

Remember these examples. POS, TOWARDS, and the DIST procedures can come in real handy.

Drawing an Ellipse

"Do you remember back in Chapter 3 when you were talking about that vertical axis thing?" Morf asked. "The axis was going through what looked like a circle on its side, sort of like it was flattened a bit. Can you show us more about that now?"

"Sure. I never really thought about it that way, but an ellipse does look like a flattened circle."

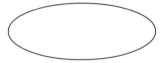

To get a more accurate picture of an ellipse, take a look at the Ellipse procedures in the Logolib directory that was setup when MSW Logo was installed. That will give you an idea of how complex ellipses are.

First of all, if you really want to know what the ELLIPSA2 procedure is doing, you have to know what an ellipse is.

An ellipse is a closed plane curve (something like a circle) that is made by a point moving in such a way that the sum of its distances from two fixed points is a constant.

"I knew I wasn't going to understand it." said Morf. "But what the heck. I can still use it to draw things."

"No, now wait a minute. Ellipses aren't that tough. Do you remember when we talked about a circle being a closed curve where all points on that curve were the same distance from the center?

"Do you remember when you drew the circle on the floor? You stretched a piece of string from the center and moved the chalk around the center. The length of the string remained the same, didn't it?

"That means it remained constant.

"Well, now it's my turn to give you a Turtle Trail to follow off the computer. It will help you make sense out of ellipses and that ellipse procedures."

Logy's Turtle Trail

Drawing an Ellipse

Find yourself a flat surface in which you can stick some tacks or pins. Of course, you have to find the tacks or pins, too. Small nails will also do just fine. You can use a wide piece of shelf board, a piece of plywood, or you can even use the side of a corrugated box.

Now tape a piece of paper on the flat surface. Stick the pins in the surface so you end up with something looking like this.

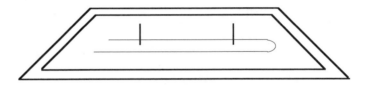

Now get yourself a piece of string about as long as the one shown in the picture above. Tie the two ends together to make a loop. Drop the loop over the two pins. Then put the tip of your pencil inside the loop and stretch it outward so that the loop of string is tight.

It should look something like this.

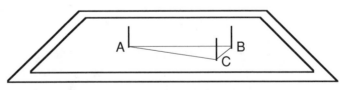

The two pins are at points A and B. That's your pencil at point C. Now move the pencil around the two pins keeping the string tight. What's the picture look like?

Looks like an ellipse, doesn't it?

It should. Because that's exactly what you've drawn. Go back and check the definition again to be sure. To draw a different shape of ellipse, just move the pins.

An ellipse is a curve that is made by a point — the point of your pencil — moving in such a way that the sum of its distances from two fixed points — the two tacks or pins — is a constant. That's another way of saying the sum of its distances remains the same.

Check it out. The pins are the two fixed points. So the distance from A to B is always the same, right?

The string doesn't change its length, does it? So the sum of the two distances, AC and CB, must also remain the same. The individual distances will change as the pencil moves around the pins. But the sum of the distances will always be the same.

Make sense? Sure it does. You just proved it.

The ELLIPSE Procedure

Now take a look at this ELLIPSE1 procedure.

```
TO ELLIPSE1 :A :B
ELL -:A :A :B 1
END

TO ELL :X :A :B :INC
IF (:X * :X) > (:A * :A) [STOP]
IF :X = :A [MAKE "INC -1]
SETPOS LIST :X :INC * :B * SQRT (1 - (:X * :X) / (:A * :A))
ELL :X + :INC :A :B :INC
END
```

This procedure draws an ellipse based on the position of the turtle. To run it, you enter the horizontal radius or X-coordinate of the ellipse, and the vertical radius or Y-coordinate. For example, try

ELLIPSE1 100 40

The turtle starts from the center of the ellipse, moves along the X-axis to the edge and then heads for the Y-axis, drawing an ellipse as it goes.

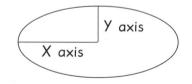

The ELLIPSE1 procedure is on the CD that came with this book, along with a second ELLIPSE2 procedure that draws an ellipse starting from the edge. If you want to see just how these procedures work, you can do some editing and test them from the MSW Logo Editor.

Here's the other procedure.

```
TO ELLIPSE2 :S :E
MAKE "N 0
REPEAT 120 [RIGHT :N FD :S LT :N LT :N ~
    FD :S * :E RT :N MAKE "N :N + 3]
END
```

Now let's see how these work. We'll start with this one since it's the easiest.

1. Load ELLIPSE2.LGO from the CD that came with this book.

2. Type EDALL in the Input Box.

    ELLIPSE2.LGO is displayed in the Editor Window.

3. Drag your mouse over REPEAT 120 [and press Delete.

    REPEAT 120 [is deleted.

4. Delete the closing bracket also.

5. Since you're not going to run the procedure, the variables don't get entered. So you'll have to enter them separately. Type

    ```
    MAKE "S 2
    MAKE "E 4
    MAKE "N 0
    ```

6. Left-click in the Editor window title bar and drag it out of the way so that you can watch the turtle.

7. Highlight the line in the procedure that begins, "RIGHT :N."

8. Left-click on Test on the Editor to start the procedure. At this point, the procedure should be easy to follow. Just keep on clicking on Test to watch the Ellipse being drawn.

    You can also left-click on any one or more commands in that line to watch each command be carried out. The main thing is to watch each line. Think about what happens to each variable as you left-click on Test.

9. To stop the procedure or to try different variables, simply type CS in the Input Box.

    The screen is cleared and you're ready to start again.

Type a negative number as the :E variable. What happens? Why does the turtle act that way? Carefully trace the procedure using Test to see how and why the procedure works the way it does.

Now for the other ELLIPSE procedure.

```
TO ELLIPSE1 :A :B
ELL -:A :A :B 1
END

TO ELL :X :A :B :INC
IF (:X * :X) > (:A * :A) [STOP]
IF :X = :A [MAKE "INC -1]
SETPOS LIST :X :INC * :B * SQRT (1 - (:X * :X) / (:A *   :A))
ELL :X + :INC :A :B :INC
END
```

This time we're going to do just about the same thing.

1. Load the ELLIPSE1 procedure.

2. Type EDALL to display the ELLIPSE1 procedure in the Editor window.

3. You have four variables to enter: X, A, B, and Inc.

```
MAKE "X -100
MAKE "A 100
MAKE "B 40
MAKE "INC 1
```

To check out this procedure properly, there's a couple of lines you need to add to the ELL procedure.

```
TO ELL :X :A :B :INC
IF (:X * :X) > (:A * :A) [STOP]
IF :X = :A [MAKE "INC -1]
SETPOS LIST :X :INC * :B * SQRT (1 - (:X * :X) / (:A *   :A))
MAKE "X :X + :INC
SHOW POS
ELL :X + :INC :A :B :INC
END
```

Now highlight the three lines that begin with SETPOS, MAKE "X, and SHOW.

Then left-click on Test and watch the turtle move.

While you can't break the procedure apart like you could with the previous one, you can display the changes in the variables as well as the changing coordinates.

Lessons Learned

"Gee, I think I just learned everything I never really wanted to know about ellipses," Morf commented.

"Yes, but look at the other lessons you learned along the way. You saw different ways to make ellipses including the use of the SETPOS command. You also got some practice breaking complex procedures apart and editing them to see how they work. That's something you can use in many situations.

"Now that's something worthwhile, isn't it?"

More Circles and Arcs

Remember the marked off circles you saw at the beginning of this chapter? Well, here are the procedures used to create those circles. They may look a bit familiar.

```
TO ARCR :CENTER :RADIUS :ANGLE
LOCAL "AMT
MAKE "AMT :RADIUS * PI / 180
PU SETXY :CENTER LT 90 FD :RADIUS RT 90 PD
REPEAT :ANGLE [FD :AMT RT 1]
END

TO CIRCLEM :CENTER :RADIUS :ANGLE
REPEAT 360 / :ANGLE [ARCR :CENTER :RADIUS :ANGLE MARK]
PU SETPOS :CENTER PD
END

TO MARK
RT 90 FD :RADIUS/10
BK :RADIUS/10 LT 90
END
```

CIRCLEM draws a circle as a series of arcs with a mark between each arc. To draw the individual arcs that are between the hours on the clock, type:

```
ARCR [100 20] 100 30
```

In this procedure, the variable :CENTER is a list representing the X- and Y-coordinates. The turtle moves to the X-coordinate of 100 and the Y-coordinate of 20. It then turns and moves to the edge of the arc and draws it one degree at a time.

197

This is a bit different from the circles you did before. With those, you simply started at the edge and drew a circle. You had to tell the turtle how far to go forward and how many degrees to turn.

In these new circle and arc procedures, you tell the turtle where the center of the circle is to be and what the radius is to be. You know what a radius is, don't you? It's the distance from the center of a circle to the edge. It's one-half the diameter of the circle. The diameter stretches from edge to edge through the middle of the circle.

What's that :AMT variable?

It's just like the variable you used in the arc and circle procedures in the last chapter. That's part of the mathematical formula for drawing a circle. It calculates the size of the circle based on the size of the radius you give it.

```
TO CIRCLE :CENTER :RADIUS
LOCAL "AMT
MAKE "AMT :RADIUS * PI/180
PU SETXY :CENTER
SETX XCOR - :RADIUS SETH 0 PD
REPEAT 360 [FD :AMT RT 1]
PU SETXY :CENTER PD
END
```

What does this line mean?

```
MAKE "AMT :RADIUS * PI/180
```

Change the PI / 180 to PI / 360. What happens? Do you remember the relationship between the diameter of the circle and PI?

Diameter * PI = Circumference

So, maybe :RADIUS * PI / 180 will make more sense if we write it as

```
(:RADIUS * 2) * PI / 360
```

Radius * 2 equals the diameter, right? Then we have the diameter * PI that equals the distance around the circle. That's divided by 360. How does this fit in the command:

```
REPEAT 360 [FD :AMT RT 1]
```

That makes :AMT equal to 1. You end up with the more familiar command for drawing a circle:

```
REPEAT 360 [FD 1 RT 1]
```

Awfully simple? Or simply awful?

Go ahead. Play with these procedures a bit. Make sure you understand how they work. Then we'll get creative.

Creative Coordinates

You saw how coordinates can be used to create pictures in the GRID procedure. Here's a simple procedure that uses the SETPOS command.

```
TO SAILBOAT
CS PU SETPOS [ 20 -40] PD
SETPOS [-160 -40]  SETPOS [ 20 160]
SETPOS [ 140 -40] SETPOS [ 20 -40]
PU SETPOS [ -120 -60] PD
SETPOS [ -80 -100]
SETPOS [ 80 -100]
SETPOS [ 120 -60]
SETPOS [ 20 -60]
SETPOS [ 20 -40]
SETPOS [ 20 -60]
SETPOS [ -120 -60]
END
```

Flower Gardens

Here's a picture that Olga created and sent to Logy and Morf. It's on the CD that came with this book as OLGA.LGO.

Some of the other procedures Logy and Morf received showed butterflies and birds flying around.

A Coordinate Challenge

Now, how about a challenge. Can you identify what the WHAT.LGO procedure will draw. It's on the CD that came with this book. START gets you started. WHAT1, WHAT2, and WHAT3 are simply subprocedures to break a large procedure into pieces.

Here's a hint – it's a circus animal. Want to make a guess as to what type of animal?

Erase your workspace and then load WHATISIT.LGO. What do you think this procedure will draw? You deserve First Prize if you said a row of circus animals. To draw our row of animals, we use variables with the SETXY command.

But, wait a minute. The X-coordinate is the only variable. Why?

The reason for this is that the X-coordinate is the only coordinate that changes as each animal is drawn. The Y-coordinates stay the same for each animal drawn.

Remember, Y-coordinates are the lines going up and down. If you changed them, some of the animals might end up walking in mid-air. And that would sure look funny!

A Target Game

Do you want to have some fun practicing with X- and Y- coordinates? Then try this target game. It's TARGET.LGO.

The turtle draws a small target on the screen. You are then asked to guess the X- and Y-coordinates of the target. If you guess correctly, the CHEERS procedure runs. If you don't guess right, you get another chance.

Go ahead. It's fun.

There are a lot of things to talk about in this game.

Defining the Target

Look at this line in the TARGET procedure. It starts with PU HT:

SETXY (RANDOM 900) - 450 (RANDOM 580) - 290

This seems complicated, doesn't it. Remember that RANDOM only picks numbers between 0 and the number you select. Since coordinates can be less than 1, we need random numbers that can put the target anywhere on the screen.

So let's read this line:

SETXY (RANDOM 900) - 450 (RANDOM 580) - 290

SETXY takes a list of two inputs, the X- and the Y-coordinate. First, Logo looks for the X-coordinate. You know the MSW Logo screen is 1000 turtle steps wide. So, the X-coordinates can be from -500 on the left of the screen, to 500 on the right.

But since we don't want our target right on the edge, we make the biggest number RANDOM can select a little smaller than 500.

(RANDOM 900) - 450

- If RANDOM selects the largest number [900] Logo subtracts 450 from it giving you an X-coordinate of 450.

- If RANDOM selects the smallest number [0] Logo subtracts 450 giving you an X-coordinate of -450.

NOTE: These coordinates are for an SVGA monitor set at 1024 x 768 resolution. You may have to adjust these coordinates to fit your screen.

Once Logo has the X-coordinate, it reads to the right to find the Y-coordinate.

(RANDOM 580) - 290

If we do the same arithmetic with the Y-coordinate as we did with the X-coordinate, we can have a Y-coordinate from 290 to -290. So, with this line, we can have a target just about anywhere on the screen.

Once the target position has been selected, a circle is drawn around that spot.

Testing Your Target Skills

There's the TEST command again. TEST is a conditional command that is a lot like IF, remember? TEST checks to see if something is true of false. IFTRUE, or IFT, then it does one thing. IFFALSE, or IFF, it does something else.

```
TEST OR (ABS :X1) > 450 (ABS :Y1) > 290
IFTRUE [PRINT [YOUR NUMBER IS TOO BIG.~
     TRY AGAIN.] WAIT 100 PLAY.GAME]
IFFALSE [PD ST SETXY :X1 :Y1]
```

If you want, you can use IF...THEN...ELSE instead.

```
IF OR (ABS :X1) > 450 (ABS :Y1) > 290  ~
     [[PR [YOUR NUMBER IS TOO BIG.  TRY AGAIN.]~
```

```
        WAIT 100 PLAY.GAME]] [PD ST SETXY :X1 :Y1]
```

I don't know about you, but that gets a bit tough to read. That's why TEST can be a handy alternative.

```
        TEST OR (ABS :X1) > 450 (ABS :Y1) > 290
```

This command tests your inputs for :X1 and :Y1 to find out if the coordinates you entered are within the target zone.

Reading from the left, Logo first reads the word TEST. To find out what needs to be tested, Logo continues reading.

```
        TEST OR
```

OR is what they call a logical operator. It asks if either of two conditions is true:

```
        (ABS :X1) > 450
        (ABS :Y1) > 290
```

ABS stands for absolute value, which means it is neither a positive or a negative number. What ABS says is that it doesn't care if the X-coordinate :X1 is a positive number or a negative number. It drops the positive or negative symbol and just tests the random number.

For example, (ABS :X1) > 450 tests to see if the coordinate you input is within the target zone, no more than 450 or less than -290.

There's an ABS procedure in the Logolib directory or you can use this procedure.

```
        TO ABS :NUM
        IFELSE :NUM < 0 [OP :NUM * -1] [OP :NUM]
        END
```

If :NUM is less than zero — if it is a negative number — then output :NUM times -1. Two negative numbers multiplied together give you a positive number. If :NUM is positive, then output :NUM. Does that help?

Let's get back to the game procedures.

```
        IFTRUE [PRINT [YOUR NUMBER IS TOO BIG.
            TRY AGAIN.] WAIT 20 PLAY.GAME]
```

If the test is true — the number you typed is too big — print "YOUR NUMBER IS TOO BIG. TRY AGAIN." If it is false, or within the proper range, then the turtle draws a line out to the coordinates you guessed.

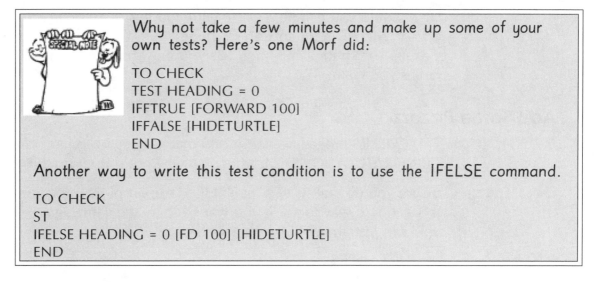

Why not take a few minutes and make up some of your own tests? Here's one Morf did:

```
TO CHECK
TEST HEADING = 0
IFFTRUE [FORWARD 100]
IFFALSE [HIDETURTLE]
END
```

Another way to write this test condition is to use the IFELSE command.

```
TO CHECK
ST
IFELSE HEADING = 0 [FD 100] [HIDETURTLE]
END
```

Hitting the Target

Did you hit the target or not?

Actually, in this game, you don't have to hit the target exactly. If you come within 12 steps of the target coordinates, you score a hit. If not, you start over again.

Here's how Logo checks.

```
IF OR (:X1 > (:X + 12 ) ) (:X1 < (:X - 12))~
    [PU HOME PD PLAY.GAME]
IF OR (:Y1 > (:Y + 12)) (:Y1 < (:Y - 12))~
    [PU HOME PD PLAY.GAME]
CHEERS
```

The first two lines check to see if the X coordinate you picked is greater than X + 12 or less than X - 12. If so, the turtle gets sent home to start again.

If your X coordinate is on target, Logo then moves to the next line to check the Y coordinate. If your Y coordinate is also on target – less than Y + 12 and less than Y - 12 – Logo moves to the CHEERS procedure.

But first, why use 12? Why not 10? Or 15?

No reason. It's just that the target CIRCLE has a diameter of 24. The center is at the halfway point or 12.

```
REPEAT 36 [FD 2 RT 12}
```

203

How would you handle a circle with a radius of 10 or 15? Check back to More Circles and Arcs. There you'll find a circle procedure that starts from the center and lets you draw a circle with whatever radius you want.

Add Some Pizzazz

This CHEERS procedure doesn't do much, does it? It just prints CONGRATULATIONS! 24 times. So why not soup it up a bit.

Before you do that, take a look at the last part of the procedure. This is a standard way to ask if you want to play the game again. This works in just about all versions of Logo.

```
TO CHEERS
CT REPEAT 24 [PRINT [CONGRATULATIONS!]]
WAIT 100
PRINT [WANT TO PLAY AGAIN?    (Y/N)]
MAKE "ANS READCHAR; Some use RQ or REQUEST
IF :ANS = "Y [GAME]
IF :ANS = "N [PRINT [BYE FOR NOW!]]
END
```

However, MSW Logo offers a rather special way to do the same thing. You can use the YESNOBOX. To check it out, run this simple procedure.

```
TO CHECK
MAKE "CHECK YESNOBOX [QUESTION] [PLAY AGAIN?]
IFELSE :CHECK = "TRUE [PR "GOOD][PR "BYE]
END
```

Now, why not change your CHEERS procedure.

```
TO CHEERS
<Add your own Pizzazz here.>
WAIT 100
MAKE "ANS YESNOBOX [TARGET][WANT TO PLAY AGAIN?]
IFELSE :ANS = "TRUE [GAME] [PRINT [BYE FOR NOW!]]
END
```

See how the YESNOBOX works? First you give the box a name. In this case, the box is called TARGET after the game. In the box, the question is asked, "WANT TO PLAY AGAIN?" YES outputs TRUE so you go back to the game. NO outputs FALSE which send you to the option.

BYE FOR NOW!

The YESNOBOX is just one of many useful windows commands you can discover using MSW Logo. You'll read more of these in Chapter 11.

From the Center One More Time

The target in the game is drawn around a center position. Do you remember drawing rectangles and things around a center point in Chapters 2 and 6? Now you have another way to look at that problem.

- Draw a rectangle that is 50 turtle steps wide and 120 turtle steps high.

- Put the center of the rectangle 100 turtle steps from HOME and 100 turtle steps to the left.

Rather than take turtle steps to find the center, you can use SETPOS.

```
TO RECTANGLE :CENTER :WIDTH :HEIGHT
PU SETPOS :CENTER FD :WIDTH / 2 RT 90
FD :HEIGHT / 2 RT 180 PD
REPEAT 2 [ FD :HEIGHT RT 90 FD :WIDTH RT 90]
END
```

This is like what you did before. But there's another way to draw that rectangle.

```
TO RECTANGLE :X :Y :WIDTH :HEIGHT
PU SETXY :X :Y
SETXY :X - :WIDTH / 2 :Y - :HEIGHT / 2 PD
SETY YCOR + ::HEIGHT SETX XCOR + :WIDTH
SETY YCOR - HEIGHT SETX XCOR - :WIDTH
END
```

Here's one more way to draw this rectangle.

```
TO RECTANGLE :X :Y :WIDTH :HEIGHT
PU SETXY :X :Y
SETXY :X - :WIDTH / 2 :Y - :HEIGHT / 2
MAKE "A POS
SETY YCOR + :HEIGHT MAKE "B POS
SETX XCOR + :WIDTH MAKE "C POS
SETY YCOR - :HEIGHT MAKE "D POS
SETPOS :A PD
SETPOS :B
SETPOS :C
SETPOS :D
```

205

```
SETPOS :A
END
```

Now you can even draw the diagonal lines between the corners.

```
TO DIAGONALS :X :Y :WIDTH :HEIGHT
RECTANGLE :X :Y :WIDTH :HEIGHT
SETPOS :C
SETPOS :B
SETPOS :D
END
```

This will give you something new to think about. Can you find an easier way to write these procedures? Surely you can do better than this. What about doing the same thing with other polygons?

Who's Who in the Zoo

Now let's take a look at what some other young people did with creative coordinates. These procedures were sent to Logy and Morf as entries into contests they used to run.

One of the contests they ran a few years ago was to find the best animal procedures. Some of them are pretty simple. Others get pretty complicated. The procedures are on the disk that comes with this book

You can start off with one of the simpler ones, MORPH.

Did you know that the scientific name for a rabbit is "lagomorph?"

That sounded a lot like Logomorph. So a young lady from Virginia just shortened the last part and came up with a new name for Logy's friend.

Some young friends from New Jersey worked on a series of animal drawings for the contest.

I bet this is one of the cutest crabs you ever saw. It comes from one of the Ron Ebberly books. Take a look at CRAB.LGO to see the procedures that created the crab.

The young people that designed the crab and the tiger cub (CUB.LGO) used a version of Logo that has no FILL command. So they wrote their own.

Here are two procedures they wrote to fill a curved area. They're a nice use of recursion to create a drawing.

```
TO FILL.ARCR :N :S
IF :N = 0 [STOP]
MAKE "SAVEX XCOR MAKE "SAVEY YCOR
MAKE "SAVEHEADING HEADING
ARCR :N :S
SETXY LIST :SAVEX :SAVEY
SETH :SAVEHEADING
FILL.ARCR :N - 1 :S
END

TO FILL.ARCL :N :SIF :N = 0 [STOP]
MAKE "SAVEX XCOR MAKE "SAVEY YCOR
MAKE "SAVEHEADING HEADING
ARCL :N :S
SETXY LIST :SAVEX :SAVEY
SETH :SAVEHEADING
FILL.ARCL :N - 1 :S
END
```

Learn Another Language

Want to learn another language?

The HAAS procedure has procedure titles written in Dutch. Can you figure out what those titles mean by what they do?

The main procedure shows you some of the Dutch procedure names.

```
TO HAAS
SETUP
LINKERWANG
RIMPEL.LINKS
PU LT 90 FD 40 RT 90 PD
SNOR.LINKS
PU RT 90 FD 40 LT 90 PD
RECHTERWANG
RIMPEL.RECHTS
PU RT 90 FD 40 LT 90 PD
SNOR.RECHTS
PU LT 90 FD 31 RT 90
PU BK 33 PD
```

```
TANDEN
PU FD 39 PD
NEUS
PU BK 4 PD PU FD 12 PD
HOOFD
PU BK 12 PD PU FD 25 LT 90 FD 30 RT 90 PD
OOG
PU RT 90 FD 41 LT 90 PD
OOG
PU LT 90 FD 11 RT 90 PD
PU FD 80 PD
OREN
PU BK 80 PD
END

TO HAAR.L
LT 60
REPEAT 6 [FD 10 LT 10]
PU REPEAT 6 [RT 10 BK 10] PD
RT 60
END

TO RIMPEL.LINKS
RT 180 PU REPEAT 18 [RT 5 FD 2]
PD REPEAT 12 [RT 5 FD 2]
PU REPEAT 30 [BK 2 LT 5]
RT 180 PD
END
```

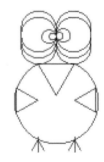

Did you ever see a DODOBIRD? That seemed like a good name for this crazy bird.

Now, what kind of animal can you dream up? Why not do some sketches? Then put them on the computer.

Puff, The Magic Dragon, may give you an idea or two. Puff was sent in as an entry to a Logo animation contest Logy and Morf had some years back. As you will see from the PUFF.LGO procedure, Puff breathes smoke and spits fire.

Up, Up, and Away

Another very popular contest that Logy and Morf held was called the Up, Up, and Away Contest. It celebrated the birthday of the first flight of a hot air balloon.

Young people were told to let their imaginations run wild and create a drawing that featured a hot air balloon. Here's Gretchen's balloon (BALLOON.LGO).

Gretchen was among the winners because her entry was the only one that included animation. The two people in the balloon wave goodbye to you.

Why not try a balloon yourself? Start with a basic balloon shape like this one.

Then see what you can do with it.

How about making the balloon into a turtle that floats over the landscape?

Fly, Fly Away

The Up, Up, and Away Contest was so successful, Logo and Morf held a Fly, Fly Away Contest to see who could create the best drawing of an aircraft. This offered young people another great chance to let their imaginations run wild.

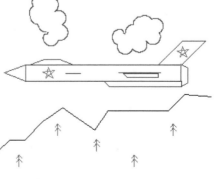

FIREFOX.LGO is a translation of one of the many procedures sent in by young people at the Utah State School for the Deaf. You'll find pictures based on this procedure in the GRAPHICS directory of the CD that came with this book. These may give you some ideas for ways to use this and other procedures mentioned in this chapter.

Here are the three views of X2.LGO, a very creative procedure from an 11-year-old from San Diego.

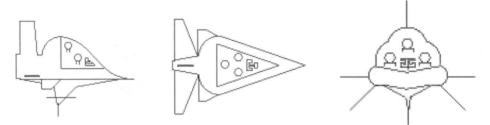

Have you ever been on an airplane? Why not create a picture of it? Or maybe you want to try a helicopter? How about a blimp? Then you can put your favorite advertising message along the side of it.

The Variable Turtle

Here's another use of turtle positions. This draws a turtle any size that you want it to be.

Logy and Morf have used this drawing on software and other things they have published over the years.

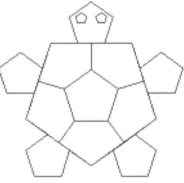

```
TO YPLA :SIZE
TURTLE1
MAKE "P []
REPEAT 6 [TURTLE2]
TURTLE3
END

TO TURTLE1
CS PD HT RT 18
MAKE "TSIZE :SIZE / 3
REPEAT 5 [FD :TSIZE LT 108 REPEAT 3 [FD :TSIZE RT 72] ~
    FD :TSIZE LT 108 FD :TSIZE RT 72]
REPEAT 5 [FD :SIZE RT 72]
END

TO TURTLE2
FD :SIZE / 2 RT 90 FD :TSIZE
MAKE "Q POS
IF :P = [] [MAKE "P POS]
```

210

```
SETXY :P SETXY :Q
MAKE "P :Q BK :TSIZE LT 90
FD :SIZE / 2 RT 72
END

TO TURTLE3
PU FD :TSIZE LT 90 FD :SIZE / 4 LT 18 PD
REPEAT 5 [FD :SIZE / 12 RT 72]
PU RT 18 BK :SIZE / 4 RT 90
PU FD :TSIZE LT 90 FD :SIZE / 4 RT 18 PD
REPEAT 5 [FD :SIZE / 12 LT 72]
END
```

To understand how these procedures work, you have to pick them apart and run them one piece at a time. Try this:

```
TO YPLA :SIZE
TURTLE1
END
```

Before you run this procedure, what do you think it does? What will the turtle draw?

There's one thing you can see right away. Since it uses REPEAT 5, it probably draws some pentagons.

The next thing worth noticing is the use of POS in TURTLE2.

```
TO TURTLE2
FD :SIZE / 2 RT 90 FD :TSIZE MAKE "Q POS
IF :P = [] [MAKE "P POS]
SETXY :P SETXY :Q
MAKE "P :Q BK :TSIZE LT 90 FD :SIZE / 2 RT 72
END
```

This procedure draws the pentagon shapes in the center of the turtles shell. This seems easy enough but you have to remember; this procedure draws any size turtle you want.

TURTLE2 could probably be written using some fancy variables. POS makes it easier. The second line says, "I don't care where you are after doing what it says in the first line. Now, just remember the coordinates where you are and call them Q."

Now let's take a look at :P.

The easiest way to see how :P and the entire YPLA procedure works is to erase all the instructions that include :P. Then run the procedure. What do you see? Everything is there except the pentagon in the center. Now, if you read the procedures carefully, you see how TURTLE2 uses SETXY to draw the center pentagon.

No, this isn't easy. However, don't get discouraged. Exploring like this is what makes it such a *Great Logo Adventure*.

Logo Geography

It started with the idea of Wrapping.

NO, that's a different kind of wrapping!

Some young people in a local elementary school computer club got curious as to what happened when the turtle went off one edge of the screen and then showed up on the opposite edge. Did it travel behind the screen?

This is the same group that explored the soccer ball. They already understood the idea of flattening three-dimensional objects on the two-dimensional screen. So it was easy enough to picture flattening the world into a two-dimensional map, that if they travelled off one edge of the map, they would automatically "wrap" to the same spot on the opposite edge.

But how can you stop the turtle from wrapping?

WINDOW is the command that tells the turtle not to wrap, just keep on going off into the world beyond the screen.

FENCE is the command that stops the turtle at the edge of the screen. It stops the action and tells you that the turtle is "Out of Bounds."

Exploring Texas

Let's get back to geography. You may remember Turtle Town from Chapter 2. Pictures of Turtle Town are in the graphics directory on the CD that came with this book.

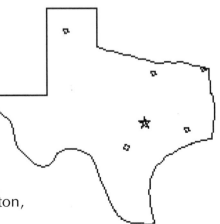

After talking about all sorts of maps, and creating an elaborate Turtle Town game, the students decided to create their own maps on the screen. Here's a map of Texas that they developed. It's part of the TEXAS.LGO procedure

The map of Texas includes the cities of Amarillo, Austin, Dallas, El Paso, Houston,

San Antonio, and Texarkana. And since game design was a very important activity with this group, they made a game out of it.

The GAME procedure, which is only a small part of the complete procedure, describes the game action. Logy and Morf start out at a randomly selected city and have to travel to the target city, also randomly selected.

```
TO GAME
PR [Logy, What direction do we turn?]
PR [How many miles do we have to go?]
WAIT 80
PR [Can you give Logo a hand?]
PR [What direction do they turn?]
MAKE "DIR RW
PR [How far?]
MAKE "TURNS RW
IF :DIR = "LT  [LT :TURNS]
IF :DIR = "RT  [RT :TURNS]
PR [How many miles do they have to travel?]
MAKE "FAR RW  PU
FD :FAR * .187
CHECK
END
```

It took a lot of discussion but the group finally figured out that the actual miles on the screen map were the number of turtle steps times 0.187.

550 miles * 0.187 = 103 turtle steps
(Actually, it's 102.85. But 103 is close enough.)

The game was good practice in guessing directions and drawing mileage to scale. After working with Texas, the group did several other states. Each time, they kept adding new features.

1. Take a look at the Texas procedure and see if you can develop the same type of procedure for your state.

2. Add other landmarks from your state - maybe lakes, rivers, parks, and things.

3. If a player moves from one place to another correctly, have them answer a random question about that place. Think up five or six questions for each location you put on your map.

Can you think of other ways to explore Logo geography?

Recursion

"Well, you sure picked a good subject this time," said Morf, looking a bit puzzled.

"We touched on this before, don't you remember?" replied Logy. "You remember, recursion is when a procedure uses itself as part of the solution."

"Say what?"

Yes, strange as that may seem, a recursive procedure is one that calls itself as part of the total solution. You saw examples of this in earlier chapters.

It is something like the two turtles in the picture. Each turtle is using the other to draw itself.

Is Life Recursive?

Here's a fun procedure to help you make some sense out of recursion, even though it really isn't Logo.

```
TO GET.THROUGH.LIFE
GET.THROUGH.TODAY
GET.THROUGH.LIFE
END
```

Think about it for a moment. This says that to get through life, you have to get through today. Once you are through today, you have to move on, right?

But where?

You can't go backward. You can't stop time. You have to get through life. But to get through life, you have to get through today. Each day is different. So while this may look like a simple loop, it really isn't. Have you ever repeated a day, doing exactly what you did yesterday?

Let's add another twist to this. Let's suppose that when you're standing in front of the Pearly Gates to Heaven, you are asked to take a look at your Book of Life.

Embedded recursion can actually help you with this task. We talk about different types of recursion in the next section. Anyway, to see your Book of Life, all you have to do is add a couple of lines to your life procedure.

```
TO GET.THROUGH.LIFE
IF LIFE = "OVER [STOP]
GET.THROUGH.TODAY
GET.THROUGH.LIFE
PRINT BOOK.OF.LIFE
END
```

It's like every time you GET.THROUGH.TODAY, you write a page in your Book of Life. Only the pages are not printed until LIFE = "OVER. When the procedure stops, all the pages are printed starting with the last page it saved.

This may seem very confusing right now. But it will begin to make sense very shortly.

Tail-end Recursion

Yes, recursion is confusing.

It reminds you of the images you see when you look in two mirrors — without Morf getting in the way, that is. So let's try it with something we know something about.

```
TO MAZE :N
FD :N RT 90
MAZE :N + 5
END
```

This is an example of what you call "tail-end recursion." The recursive call is at the tail-end of the procedure.

To see just how this works, type

```
MAZE 20
```

Now watch what happens.

The turtle goes forward 20 steps and then turns right 90 turns. Then the procedure tells :N (that's 20 to us) to become :N + 5 (that's 25 to us now). Then the procedure says

```
MAZE 25
```

and starts all over again.

MAZE 25 becomes MAZE 30. MAZE 30 becomes MAZE 35, and on and on and on. The screen soon looks something like what you see. And it just keeps on going, gradually filling up the screen.

Of course, we can put a STOP in there if we want.

```
TO MAZE :N
IF :N = 200 [STOP]
FD :N RT 90
MAZE :N + 5
END
```

The first line sets up a conditional test. Each time the procedure runs, it tests :N to see if it equals 200. When :N does equal 200, the procedure stops.

The Turtle's Erector Set

Let's take a look at some other examples

Did you ever play with an Erector Set? Did you ever build bridges? Maybe some buildings?

Well, Logo can help you draw your plans.

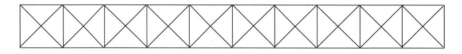

```
TO ERECTORSET :N :X
IF :X = 0 [STOP]
SECTION :N
MOVE :N
ERECTORSET :N :X - 1
END

TO SECTION :N
REPEAT 4 [TRI :N FD :N RT 90]
END

TO MOVE :N
RT 90 FD :N LT 90
END

TO TRI :N
FD :N RT 135
FD :N / SQRT 2 RT 90
FD :N / SQRT 2 RT 135
END
```

Uh, oh!

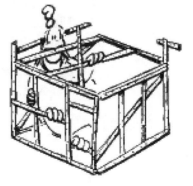

The Italian Turtle

Do you like Italian food? How about spaghetti?

```
TO SPAGHETTI
CIRCLE 5
CIRCLE 4
CIRCLE 3
CIRCLE 2
RT 45
SPAGHETTI
END

TO CIRCLE :N
REPEAT 36 [FD :N RT 10]
END
```

You can make the SPAGHETTI procedure even more variable with a few changes:

```
TO SPAGHETTI :N
CIRCLE :N + 5
CIRCLE :N + 4
CIRCLE :N + 3
CIRCLE :N + 2
RT 45
SPAGHETTI :N
END
```

How about this one?

```
TO SPAGHETTI :N
CIRCLE :N
IF :N = 0 [STOP]
RT 45
SPAGHETTI :N - 1
END
```

This recursive procedure is like some others you have used before. Will it draw spaghetti like the other procedures above? Why? Better yet, why not? What about this one?

```
TO SPAGHETTI :N
IF :N > 200 [STOP]
CIRCLE :N
RT 45
SPAGHETTI :N + 5
END
```

In addition to spaghetti drawings, what else can you do with this circle procedure?

```
TO CIRCLE :N
REPEAT 36 [FD :N RT 10]
END
```

How About a Slinky?

```
TO SLINKY
LT 90
CIRCLES
END

TO CIRCLES
CIRCLE 5
FD 20
CIRCLES
END
```

You might think that recursion is just like a loop, that it just goes around in circles. Well, not quite! Sometimes things aren't what they seem to be.

Embedded Recursion

To check this out, let's look at a procedure that uses "embedded recursion." The recursive call is embedded in the middle of the procedure somewhere, like in the GET.THROUGH.LIFE procedure.

```
TO TEST.RECURSION :N
PRINT [IS THIS RECURSION?]
IF READWORD = "YES [TEST.RECURSION :N + 1]
PRINT :N
END
```

In the TEST.RECURSION procedure, the variable :N is used as a counter. It is used to keep track of your answers to the question, IS THIS RECURSION?

Watch and see. Type

TEST.RECURSION 1

When you start the procedure, the first thing you see on the screen is the question:

IS THIS RECURSION?

READWORD tells Logo to stop and wait for you to type an answer, which it then reads. Type YES. The counter knows that this is your first answer.

Then we come to a test. If the word you typed was YES, then the procedure calls itself. What happens?

You guessed it! There's that question again.

IS THIS RECURSION?

Type YES a few times when you see the question. Then type NO. What happens this time?

When you type NO, the procedure comes to the test. This time the word you typed doesn't match YES and so the computer reads the next line:

PRINT :N

WOW, what happened then?

Why were so many numbers printed? That's what makes recursion different from just a simple loop.

When you first look at this procedure, it seems as if it is going to go around in a loop. Every time it passes the TEST.RECURSION :N + 1 line, the counter is going to add 1. Then, when you type NO instead of YES, you'd think the procedure would simply print the current value of N.

Well, that isn't the way recursion works. Morf has one of his rabbit trails to show you what happens.

Rabbit Trail

22

Recursive Pages

Let's look at this procedure again. You'll need some blank paper, a pencil, and scissors for this one.

Fold the paper in half. Then fold it in half again. And again. Then one last time. Crease the edges nice and sharp and then open up your piece of paper.

Cut the paper along the folds. You should end up with 16 small pieces of paper. Now number these "pages" from 1 to 16 by writing a small number at the bottom of the page.

Get your pencil ready and then type

TEST.RECURSION 1

First, you see the question, IS THIS RECURSION?, on the screen. So write a big 1 on your first piece of paper and put that piece off by itself.

Type YES. What happens?

The question appears on the screen and :N becomes :N + 1 — or 2. Write 2 on your second piece of paper and put that on the pile with your first piece, the one with the 1 on it.

Type YES again.

What does :N become now?

Write 3 on the next piece of paper and put that piece on the number pile. Do this again three more times, writing the new number for :N each time. Put each piece of paper on the top of your growing pile of papers.

Now, when you type NO, what happens on the screen?

You see a list of numbers counting backward, right? From 7 back to 1.

Why?

Look at the screen. There are seven questions shown there. You typed "yes" six times and "no" once. In total, you typed 7 answers.

You should have two stacks of paper now. You have some blank pages left over in one stack, pages 8 to 16. The other stack has the pages you numbered from 1 to 7. Each page has a big number written on it.

Now put the pages back in order from 1 to 16. But how do you do that?

You put page #7 with the big number 7 on it, on top of page 8. You put page #6 on top of page #7, page #5 on top of page #6, and so on until you have all the pages back in a single stack again.

OK! Picture the memory in your computer like that stack of pages. Each time the procedure is run, another page is written to memory. When the procedure is stopped, Logo prints the pages.

Amazing Mazes

Remember the MAZE procedure, the example of tail-end recursion you read about earlier in this chapter?

```
TO MAZE :N
IF :N > 300 [STOP]
FD :N RT 90
MAZE :N +10
END
```

Now look at this procedure.

```
TO AMAZE :N
IF :N > 120 [STOP]
AMAZE :N + 10
FD :N RT 90
END
```

Here's another example of "embedded" recursion.

Will this procedure produce the same picture as the MAZE procedure or will it be different?

Try to picture what it will look like before you run it. Think about how recursion works, about how it reads and acts on procedures. Then start with :N as 50.

This is how Logo reads the procedure the first time.

TO AMAZE 50	
IF 50 > 300 [STOP]	Since 50 is smaller than 300, Logo goes to the next line.
AMAZE 50 + 10	AMAZE 50 becomes AMAZE 60 and AMAZE starts again.
FD 50 RT 90	**This line is held in memory.**
END	

Next, you have:

TO AMAZE 60	
IF 60 > 300 [STOP]	Since 60 is smaller than 300, Logo goes to the next line.
AMAZE 60 + 10	AMAZE 60 becomes AMAZE 70 and AMAZE starts again.
FD 60 RT 90	**This line is held in memory.**
END	

Next, you have:

TO AMAZE 70	
IF 70 > 300 [STOP]	Since 70 is smaller than 300, Logo goes to the next line.
AMAZE 80 + 10	AMAZE 70 becomes AMAZE 80 and AMAZE starts again.
FD 70 RT 90	**This line is held in memory.**
END	

223

and then

```
TO AMAZE 80
IF 80 > 300 [STOP]    Since 80 is smaller than 300, Logo goes to the next line.

AMAZE 80 + 10         AMAZE 80 becomes AMAZE 90 and AMAZE starts again.

FD 80 RT 90           This line is held in memory.
END
```

Each time Logo runs the procedure, it doesn't get to the last line. That's because the procedure calls itself. So it writes each last line on a "page" of the memory stack. It will keep going, writing pages for each line it did not run – AMAZE 90, 100, 110, and finally 300. Then it stops.

As Logo reads the pages, it puts them back in order sending the turtle

```
    FD 300, RT 90
    FD 290, RT 90
    FD 280, RT 90
....back to where she started...
    FD 50, RT 90.
```

So-o-o, are the pictures produced by MAZE and AMAZE the same?

The pictures look the same. The difference is that MAZE starts small and gets larger. AMAZE starts big and gets smaller.

There's another example of embedded recursion on the next page. This procedure produces a crazy drawing.

Why? Can you tell without running it?

```
TO TOWER :SIZE
IF :SIZE < 0 [STOP]
SQUARE :SIZE
TOWER :SIZE - 10
SQUARE :SIZE
FD :SIZE
END

TO SQUARE :SIZE
REPEAT 4 [FD :SIZE RT 90]
END
```

No, this is not like the TOWER procedure from Chapter 6 even though it looks something like it. To see what it looks like, type TOWER and a number for the length of one side of the SQUARE.

How would you change this procedure to make a better looking drawing? As a reminder, here's the TOWER procedure you saw earlier.

```
TO SQUARES :S
IF :S < 0 [STOP]
REPEAT 4 [FD :S RT 90]
FD :S
SQUARES :S - 5
END

TO TOWER :S :T
IF :T = 0 [STOP]
SQUARES :S
TOWER :S :T - 1
END
```

Spirals, Squirals, Polyspis, and Fractals

Do you know what they call the drawings that MAZE and AMAZE produce?

 They're spirals. No, you don't need a telescope to spy on anything.

 Spirals, squrials, polyspis, and fractals draw some of the prettiest drawings you can make using Logo.

MAZE and AMAZE produce square spirals, or squirals.

```
FD 50 RT 90
FD 60 RT 90
FD 70 RT 90
FD 80 RT 90
FD 90 RT 90
```
....and on and on and on.

But what about other types of spirals?

Remember that procedure you wrote to draw any kind of shape?

```
TO POLYGON :SIDE :REPEATS
REPEAT :REPEATS [FD :SIDE RT 360 / :REPEATS]
END
```

OK! Here's a challenge for you. Change this procedure into a recursive procedure that will draw the same kind of picture. How about this?

225

```
TO POLYGON :SIDE :REPEATS
FD :SIDE
RT 360 / :REPEATS
POLYGON :SIDE :REPEATS
END
```

You can make this easier by changing the :REPEATS variable to an :ANGLE variable.

```
TO POLYGON :SIDE :ANGLE
FD :SIDE
RT :ANGLE
POLYGON :SIDE :ANGLE
END
```

OK! If you set :SIDE to 100 and :ANGLE to 120, you will send the turtle on a continuous trip around a triangle.

But that's no fun!   So here's one way to handle it.

```
TO POLYGON :SIDE :ANGLE :AMT
IF :SIDE > 200 [STOP]
FD :SIDE  RT :ANGLE
POLYGON (:SIDE + :AMT) :ANGLE :AMT
END
```

What do you think the AMT variable does?

Well, here's a drawing produced by this procedure.

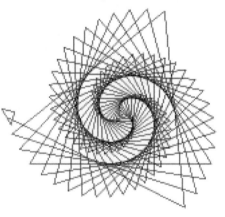

Does it help?

Play around with different numbers for the three variables of the POLYGON procedure. You'll be surprised at the things you can do.

What happens when you change 120 to 123?

POLYGON 1 123 3

POLYGON 1 90 5

POLYGON 5 144 5

POLYGON 1 172 3

There are some more ideas on the next page.

Multiple Spirals

How would you put more than one spiral on the screen at the same time?

Here is a procedure a young student developed. The goal was to create two spirals within the same procedure.

What do you think of it – without running it, that is?

Will this next procedure draw two spirals?

```
TO SPIRAL :N
IF :N > 100 [STOP]
FD :N RT 90
SPIRAL :N + 5
FD 200
IF :N > 100 [STOP]
FD :N RT 90
SPIRAL :N + 5
END
```

It seemed perfectly logical to this student that the turtle would draw the first spiral, move 200, and then draw the second one. What that student overlooked is that the recursive call sends the turtle back to the beginning. The result of this procedure is a mess.

But how would you straighten it out?

One of the things this student overlooked was a very valuable lesson about working with Logo. You need to think in "chunks."

Logo has to process one "chunk" of information at a time. In the procedures below, SPIRAL is one chunk of information. When you want to process more than one chunk of information, you need to add a procedure that will process your chunks in the sequence that you want. This is what SPIRALS does for you.

```
TO SPIRALS :N
SPIRAL :N
PU FD 200 PD
SPIRAL :N
END

TO SPIRAL :N
IF :N > 100 [STOP]
FD :N RT 90
SPIRAL :N + 5
END
```

The SPIRALS procedure draws two spirals. What would you have to do to make it draw four? Six? A variable number?

Polyspis and Inspis

POLYSPI and INSPI are variations on the POLYGON and SPIRAL procedures. You start with the basic POLYGON procedure.

```
TO POLYGON :SIDE :ANGLE
FD :SIDE RT :ANGLE
POLYGON :SIDE :ANGLE
END
```

Let's change this a bit.

```
TO POLYSPI :SIDE :ANGLE
FD :SIDE RT :ANGLE
POLYSPI :SIDE + 3 :ANGLE
END
```

What does POLYSPI do to the POLYGON procedure?

It adds another variable so that you change how much the :SIDE changes.

```
TO POLYSPI :SIDE :ANGLE :INC
FD :SIDE RT :ANGLE
POLYGON :SIDE + :INC :ANGLE :INC
END
```

Try this procedure with various inputs. Then let's change the procedure again. This time, we won't change the :SIDE. We'll change the :ANGLE.

```
TO INSPI :SIDE :ANGLE :INC.
FD :SIDE RT :ANGLE
INSPI :SIDE :ANGLE + :INC :INC
END
```

Now try these. Can you predict what they'll look like?

```
INSPI 10 0 15
INSPI 7 45 17
INSPI 10 4 20
INSPI 10 0 8
INSPI 3 45 30
```

Now try your own ideas. But before we move on, here's one more variation to explore.

Here's the POLY1 procedure.

```
TO POLY1 :SIDE :ANGLE
FD :SIDE RT 90 FD :SIDE RT :ANGLE * 2
POLY1 :SIDE :ANGLE
END
```

How's that different from this one?

```
TO POLY2 :SIDE :ANGLE
FD :SIDE RT 90 FD :SIDE RT :ANGLE
POLY2 :SIDE :ANGLE * 2
END
```

Rabbit Trail

23

String and Wire Art

Have you ever seen string or wire art?

These are beautiful patterns created by wrapping colored string or wire around pins or small nails hammered into a felt-covered board. You can find some very colorful string or wire art kits at a local hobby store.

What's even more fun is to transfer the art patterns to the screen. There you can begin to see the relationships that work together to create the pattern.

First, let's start with a shoe box. Paint the inside of the top using flat black paint. This creates a dull background to show off your string patterns.

The next job is to create an even pattern that you will use to punch tiny holes evenly around the edge of the box top. You can do this very easily on the computer. Here's a recursive procedure that should be pretty easy for you by now.

```
TO PATTRN :DIST :MARKS
IF :MARKS = 0 [STOP]
FD :DIST MARK :DIST
MAKE "MARKS :MARKS - 1
PATTRN :DIST :MARKS
END

TO MARK :DIST
RT 90 FD :DIST / 10
BK :DIST / 5 FD :DIST / 10 LT 90
END
```

This procedure divides the task of drawing a pattern into easily understood chunks. The big chunk is drawing the pattern. The little chunk draws the actual marks.

The variables let you set the number of marks (:MARKS) and the distance (:DIST) between them. For example, if you want to print 20 horizontal marks that are 25 turtle steps apart, type PATTERN 25 20 and press Enter.

Print the patterns and cut them into narrow strips. Then paste or tape them to the edge of your painted box top.

Curves From Straight Lines

Now there are lots of things you can do. For one thing, you can use colored yarn and a needle to make curves from straight lines.

Here's a box top pattern.

1. Start at the lower left hand corner.

2. Push the needle through the corner mark into the box top and then out through the mark at the lower right corner.

3. Move up to the first mark up the right side and push the needle from the outside into the box top.

4. Go to the first mark in from the left corner and push the needle from the inside to the outside of the box top.

Soon you will have a pattern that looks like this, a curve made from straight lines.

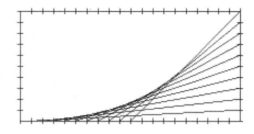

There are lots of other patterns you can make.

Why not try these?

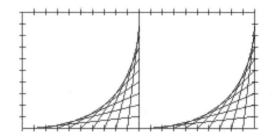

Turn one of those upside down and look what you'll get.

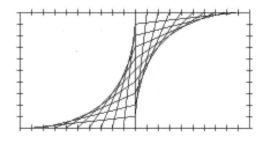

There are all sorts of patterns you can make. If you want to dress them up a bit, try different colors of yarn for different parts of the design.

When you've used up all your old shoe boxes, you can try other designs on the Logo screen.

But, wait a minute! How are you going to do that?

Curves From Straight Lines

Well, let's start with a pencil, a piece of paper, and a straightedge. A ruler makes a good tool for this project.

1. Put the ruler on the paper in a vertical position, so that it's going straight up and down.

2. Draw a line from the bottom of the ruler up to about six inches and back to one-half inch from the bottom.

3. Hold your pencil in place and turn the ruler about 10 degrees.

4. Repeat steps 2 and 3 several times.

Does your drawing look something like this?

Not bad! Here's how you can do that on the computer.

```
TO FANLEFT :DIST :ANGLE
IF :DIST < 0 [STOP]
FD :DIST BK :DIST - 10 LT :ANGLE
FANLEFT :DIST - 5 :ANGLE
END
```

What do you think would happen if you changed the angle and the distance each time a line was drawn?

```
TO LETSFINDOUT :DIST :ANGLE
IF :DIST < 0 [STOP]
FD :DIST BK :DIST - 10 LT :ANGLE
LETSFINDOUT :DIST - 5 :ANGLE + 2
END
```

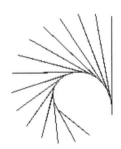

If you can't see the difference here, try changing the number added to the ANGLE.

Here's a challenge for you.

How would you create this drawing?

Here's a hint. Take a look at the angles between the lines.

Here are a few more ideas to play with. How about a FANRIGHT procedure? What would that one do? How would it be different?

What would happen if you combined them?

```
TO SWIRL :DIST :ANGLE
START1
FANLEFT :DIST :ANGLE
START1
FANRIGHT :DIST :ANGLE
START2
FANLEFT :DIST :ANGLE
START2
FANRIGHT :DIST :ANGLE
END
```

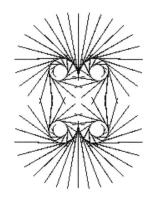

Note that the FANLEFT and FANRIGHT procedures are changed slightly to produce this drawing. Check the recursive statement in each procedure.

```
TO FANLEFT :DIST :ANGLE
IF :DIST < 0 [STOP]
FD :DIST BK :DIST - 5 LT :ANGLE
FANLEFT :DIST - 3 :ANGLE + 1
END
```

```
TO FANRIGHT :DIST :ANGLE
IF :DIST < 0 [STOP]
FD :DIST BK :DIST - 5 RT :ANGLE
FANRIGHT :DIST - 3 :ANGLE + 1
END
```

```
TO START1
PU HOME PD
END
```

```
TO START2
PU HOME RT 180 FD 50 PD
END
```

Another thing you might want to try is to add a START3 and START4 so that you can have figures drawn at 90 degrees and 270 degrees. Here's a few simple ones.

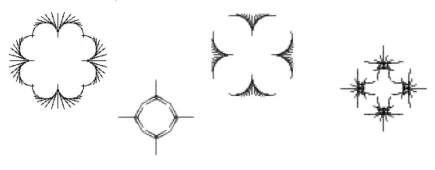

String and Wire Art Procedures

Remember when you did some string and wire art earlier? You never did get around to the Logo procedures, did you? Guess what? You will now!

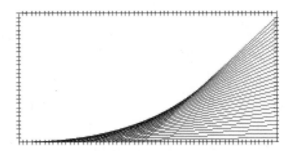

BOXTOP draws the box top. You define the size of the short side and the number of marks to appear on that side. For example:

```
BOXTOP 300 30
TO BOXTOP :DIST :MARK
PU SETX :DIST - :DIST * 2 PD
REPEAT 2 [MARKER :MARK RT 90 REPEAT 2~
    [MARKER :MARK] RT 90]
END
```

The CURVE procedure looks complex. But it is simply the turtle doing the sewing that you did with a needle and colored yarn.

```
CURVE 30 10 -300 0 300 0
```

You draw 30 lines that are 10 steps apart (there's a GAP of 10 steps). You start at :X1 in the lower left where the X-coordinate is 300 and the :Y1 is 0. The turtle moves from :X1 and :Y1 to :X2 and :Y2, then back and forth 30 times.

```
TO CURVE :T :GAP :X1 :Y1 :X2 :Y2
IF :T = 0 [STOP]
PU SETXY LIST :X1 :Y1 PD
SETXY LIST :X2 :Y2
MAKE "X1 :X1 + :GAP
MAKE "Y2 :Y2 + :GAP
CURVE :T - 1 :GAP :X1 :Y1 :X2 :Y2
END
```

```
TO MARKER :MARK
REPEAT :MARK [FD :DIST / :MARK MARKS]
END

TO MARKS
LT 90 FD 5 BK 10 FD 5 RT 90
END
```

Go ahead. Play with a few other combinations. Do the same things on the screen that you did with yarn. What else can you dream up?

What would you have to do to draw the box top patterns shown earlier in this chapter?

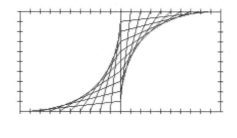

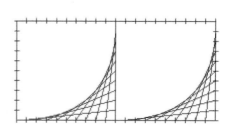

Once you've played with the BOXTOP, the STRING procedures become a bit easier to understand.

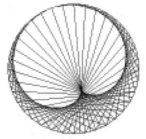
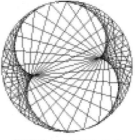

STRING 150 2 2   STRING 150 3 2

```
TO STRING :RADIUS :DIST :HEAD
CS HT MAKE "N 1 PU SETX :RADIUS PD
REPEAT 360 [FD :RADIUS * PI/180 LT 1] PU HOME
REPEAT 36 * :HEAD~
   [
   FD :RADIUS MAKE "P POS HOME HDG
   FD :RADIUS PD SETXY LIST :P PU
   HOME HDG1 MAKE "N :N +1
   ]
END
```

235

```
TO HDG
SETH REMAINDER (:N * 5 * :DIST) 360
END

TO HDG1
SETH REMAINDER (5 * (:N-1)) 360
END
```

Play with these procedures for awhile, trying different variables. Not only do they create some beautiful patterns, they give you a look at how positions and headings can be used.

But before we leave recursion, you can't overlook the fun you can have with fractals.

A Triangle in a Circle

Draw a triangle on the computer – any type of triangle will do.

Now draw a circle around that triangle so that the edge of the circle touches the three points of the triangle.

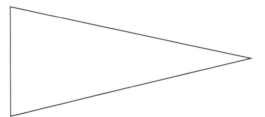

This problem shows a great use of recursion. The CHECK.DIST procedure keeps calling itself until it finds the center of the circle. It then draws the circle touching each corner of the triangle. Without recursion, this would be a difficult mathematical exercise.

Now let's get to it. Just remember, the whole idea behind Logo is to break a problem down into its simplest parts. Start with what you know. Determine what you don't know. Then go find it.

What do you know?

You know that the three points of the triangle are going to be on the edge, or the circumference of the circle. If you can find a point that is the same distance from each of those points, then you have the center of the circle, right?

To make things easier to understand, let's label the points on the circle. Call them A, B, and C.

You have to find point D, a point inside the triangle that is the same distance from A as it is from B and C.

If point D is the same distance from A, B, and C, then point D must be the center of the circle and the three lines, AD, BD, and CD are each a radius of the circle you are supposed to draw.

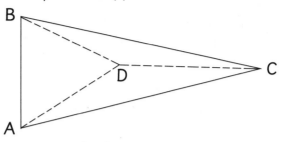

Now, how can you prove that?

Draw the line EF so that it is perpendicular to the middle of line AB.

Perpendicular means that the line EF is at right angles to line AB.

What can you learn from this drawing now?

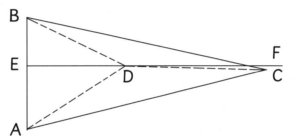

You have two triangles — ADE and BDE — that share one side and have two short sides that are equal. Therefore, the sides AD and BD must be equal.

OK, if you can find the point on line EF that makes these two lines equal to line CD, you have found the middle of the circle you want to draw.

Let's do it.

The Random Triangle

The first step is to create a random triangle, something like you have already drawn.

```
TO RANDOM.TRI
MAKE "POINTA POS
FD 100 RT 120 - RANDOM 30
MAKE "POINTB POS
MAKE "DIST 250 - RANDOM 100 FD :DIST
MAKE "POINTC POS  HOME
END
```

This procedure starts from HOME, POINT A with coordinates 0,0. The turtle goes FD 100 and turns right a random angle, somewhere between 120 and 90. This is POINTB, coordinates 100,0.

The turtle then goes FD between 150 and 250 and sets POINTC. Then the turtle goes HOME. The next step is to draw the perpendicular line.

```
TO RT.ANGLE
SETPOS LIST :POINTA
FD 100 / 2 RT 90
MAKE "POINTE POS
FD 200 PU HOME PD
END
```

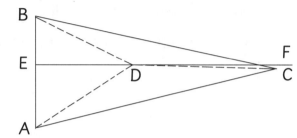

Now you have a drawing something like the one on the last page, but without the dotted lines.

What do you need to know now to complete our circle? You need to find the point D on line EF that is the same distance from B as it is from C. You already know that AD and BD are going to be equal and that each is going to be a radius of our circle.

So if you can make one equal to line DC, the other is automatically equal to DC. The first thing you need for that is a distance procedure.

```
TO DIST :X1 :Y1 :X2 :Y2
OP DIST1 :X1 - :X2 :Y1 - :Y2
END
```

```
TO DIST1 :DX :DY
OP INT SQRT (:DX * :DX) + (:DY * :DY)
END
```

The DIST procedure measures the distance between two sets of coordinates. Logo measures that difference very precisely. So to keep things simple and easy to compare, the output is an integer, a whole number. (It's a lot easier to compare whole numbers than it is to compare long decimals.)

Now let's put the DISTance procedure to work. You'll use it to calculate two distances: the distance between B and D and the distance between C and D. When these are the same, you'll draw our circle.

```
TO CHECK.DIST
MAKE "BD DIST FIRST :POINTB LAST :POINTB ~
    FIRST :POINTD LAST :POINTD
MAKE "CD DIST INT FIRST :POINTC ~
    INT LAST :POINTC FIRST :POINTD LAST :POINTD
TEST :BD = :CD
IFTRUE [HT CIRCLE :POINTD :BD]
IFFALSE [FD 1 MAKE "POINTD POS CHECK.DIST]
END
```

Here are more new commands: FIRST and LAST. Well, actually you've seen them before when you made the POS procedure. This use of FIRST and LAST sort of explains itself.

```
TO POS :LIST
OP LIST FIRST :LIST LAST :LIST
END
```

That's a different way of writing a POS procedure but it gets the job done.

But back to CHECK.DIST. You already know that :POINTB is a list of two coordinates. So FIRST :POINTB must be the first coordinate. And if that's true, then LAST :POINTB must be the last element in the list or the y-coordinate. You'll learn more about characters, numbers, words, lists, FIRST, LAST, and other good stuff later on.

There's one more thing in CHECK.DIST. We used the TEST command:

```
TEST :BD = :CD
IFTRUE [HT CIRCLE :POINTD :BD]
IFFALSE [FD 1 MAKE "POINTD POS CHECK.DIST]
```

You can also write that as

```
IF :BD = :CD  [HT CIRCLE :POINTD :BD] [FD 1 ~
    MAKE "POINTD POS CHECK.DIST]
```

Now let's run through the CHECK.DIST procedure. The first two lines calculate the distances BD and CD. So that you can see how these distances change, the distances are printed in the Listener or Commander window.

Then Logo tests the two numbers. If :BD = :CD is true, if they are equal, Logo draws a circle with :POINTD as the center and a radius of :BD.

If the two distances are not equal, the turtle moves FD 1 and checks the distances again.

```
TO CIRCLE :CENTER :RADIUS
LOCAL "AMT
MAKE "AMT :RADIUS * PI / 180
PU SETXY LIST :CENTER
SETX XCOR - :RADIUS SETH 0 PD
REPEAT 360 [FD :AMT RT 1]
PU SETPOS :CENTER PD
END
```

To put the whole thing together, here's a place to start.

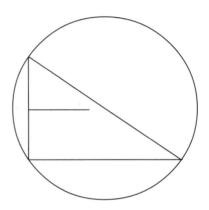

```
TO START
RANDOM.TRI
SETPOS :POINTA
FD 50 RT 90
MAKE "POINTD POS
CHECK.DIST
END
```

Take your time with this procedure. Come back to it when you're ready. This is a good stepping stone to some of the other procedures you'll see in the rest of this book.

Fun With Fractals

Fractals were once thought to be math monsters. No one could figure out what to do with them. But thanks to computers, we now know that these recursive monsters help make beautiful computer graphics.

Take a look at the MTNRANGE.LGO procedure in the Projects directory of the CD that came with this book. That shows you how to draw a random coastline. If you'd like to experiment a bit on your own, take a look at this MEDTRI.LGO procedure.

```
TO MEDIAL.TRIANGLE :X1 :Y1 :X2 :Y2 :X3 :Y3
COOR.TRIANGLE :X1 :Y1 :X2 :Y2 :X3 :Y3
MIDPOINT :X1 :Y1 :X2 :Y2
MIDPOINT :X2 :Y2 :X3 :Y3
MIDPOINT :X3 :Y3 :X1 :Y1
```

```
MIDPOINT :X1 :Y1 :X2 :Y2
END

TO COOR.TRIANGLE :X1 :Y1 :X2 :Y2 :X3 :Y3
SEGMENT :X1 :Y1 :X2 :Y2
SEGMENT :X2 :Y2 :X3 :Y3
SEGMENT :X3 :Y3 :X1 :Y1
END

TO MIDPOINT :X1 :Y1 :X2 :Y2
SETXY (:X1 + :X2) / 2 (:Y1 + :Y2) / 2
END

TO SEGMENT :X1 :Y1 :X2 :Y2
PENUP
SETXY :X1 :Y1
PENDOWN
SETXY :X2 :Y2
END
```

This procedure takes any triangle you define and creates a new triangle drawn from the midpoints of each side.

Here's a challenge for you — something you may want to come back to once you've read more about fractals.

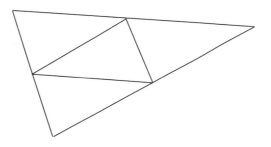

1. Start with a triangle that is about as big as your screen.

2. Can you write a procedure that will draw a triangle at the midpoints of each new triangle you create?

3. Later in this book, you'll get a look at working with three dimensional space where you add a Z axis to X and Y. Think about changing the Z axis of each new triangle you create.

Imagine such a procedure run on a graphics workstation with lots of memory. As the triangles get smaller and smaller, and they begin to tilt in different directions, the picture begins to look like a mountain range. Add some color to make it more realistic. What you get is fractals in action.

C Curves

There are lots of books on fractals that you can read. So rather than try to explain fractals, let's look at how they work. Here's the well-known C curve as a Logo procedure.

```
TO C :SIZE :LEVEL
IF :LEVEL = 0 [FD :SIZE STOP]
C :SIZE :LEVEL - 1 RT 90
C :SIZE :LEVEL - 1 LT 90
END
```

If you look at the procedure, you see that :SIZE is the variable used by FD. :LEVEL is a bit confusing, so let's watch it work first. Type

```
C 5 10
```

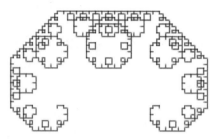

Wow! That's some pattern. Clear the screen and try

```
C 20 3
```

Automatic Startup

OK! Now add the SEE procedure on the next page. When you run SEE, you "see" how the turtle builds such complicated pictures.

```
TO SEE
IF :LEVEL = 11 [STOP]
C :SIZE :LEVEL WAIT 50 CS
SEE :SIZE :LEVEL + 1
END

MAKE "SIZE 10
MAKE "LEVEL 0
```

Hey! Wait a minute.

There's no procedure there at the end for those MAKE statements.

How can that be?

Don't you remember? We talked about how you can have procedures startup and do things when they're loaded into your workspace. In this case, you're telling tell Logo what you want the variables to be without writing a procedure. It saves you the trouble of putting the variables in the procedure title.

Time out for a moment. Here's a question for you. Are those variables local or global? Just checking to keep you on your toes.

242

While you've timed out, here's a couple of other things you can do.

1. To run SEE when it's first loaded, add the variables above and this line:

   MAKE "STARTUP [SEE]

2. Rather than use the SEE procedure, you can edit your procedure in Windows Notepad or in your favorite word processing package. This doesn't work using the MSW Logo Editor.

   ```
   CS C 10 1 WAIT 60
   CS C 10 2 WAIT 60
   CS C 10 3 WAIT 60
   CS C 10 4 WAIT 60
   CS C 10 8 WAIT 60
   CS C 5 10 WAIT 60
   ```

Now when you load the C procedure, it will run six examples to show you how it works.

Figuring Out Fractals

Now, where were we? Run the SEE procedure. You're watching fractals in action.

To help you figure out fractals, here are some tips:

- Write the C and the SEE procedures on pieces of paper as you did in Morf's Rabbit Trail. This will help you follow the action.

- Change WAIT to 100 or 150 — long enough so that you can see the changes from one level to the next.

- Another thing to do is change the LEVEL variable to 5 or 6, large enough so you can watch how the procedure really works. The higher the level, the more complex the picture.

Dragons, Snowflakes, and other Fractals

You'll find some other fractal procedures on the CD - SNOWFLAKE, HILBERT, DRAGON, SRPNSK (that's short for Serpinski) and others.

Take a look at the DRAGON procedure.

```
TO DRAGON :SIZE :LEVEL
LDRAGON :SIZE :LEVEL
END
```

```
TO LDRAGON :SIZE :LEVEL
IF :LEVEL = 0 [FD :SIZE STOP]
LDRAGON :SIZE :LEVEL - 1 LT 90
RDRAGON :SIZE :LEVEL - 1
END

TO RDRAGON :SIZE :LEVEL
IF :LEVEL = 0 [FD :SIZE STOP]
LDRAGON :SIZE :LEVEL - 1 RT 90
RDRAGON :SIZE :LEVEL - 1
END
```

Can you see what the DRAGON procedure does? What a drawing would look like?

Here's a picture for DRAGON 50 1.

What would DRAGON 50 0 look like? Try it and see. For a better look at how DRAGON works, turn on TRACE.

Tracing the Dragon

With TRACE turned on, type DRAGON 50 1 and press Enter.

Then check the Commander window to see the sequence of operations that Logo went through.

```
TO DRAGON 50 1
LDRAGON 50 1
END

TO LDRAGON
IF 1 = 0 [FD 50 STOP]
LDRAGON 50 1 - 1 LT 90
RDRAGON 50 1 - 1
END

TO RDRAGON
IF 1 = 0 [FD 50 STOP]
LDRAGON 50 1 - 1 RT 90
RDRAGON 50 1 - 1
END
```

(NOTE: You can also use the STEP command, which steps you through each command of each procedure. The command is STEP [<procedures to step through>].)

244

Now try DRAGON 20 2

DRAGON 20 3

DRAGON 10 10

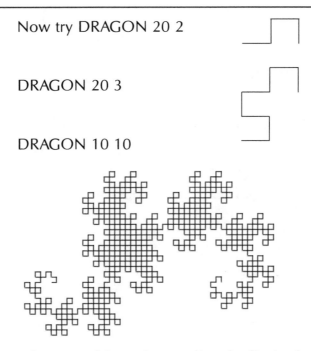

If you have trouble understanding the list in the Trace window, use a pad of paper and make stacks of recursive calls — the same way you did before.

Snowflakes Again

Now take a look at the SNOWFLAKE procedure. Before the snowflakes were made using REPEAT 6 to create a unique six-pointed pattern. These are a bit different.

```
TO SNOWFLAKE :SIZE :LEVEL
REPEAT 3 [RT 120 SIDE :SIZE :LEVEL]
END

TO SIDE :SIZE :LEVEL
IF :LEVEL = 0 [FD :SIZE STOP]
SIDE :SIZE / 3 :LEVEL - 1 LT 60
SIDE :SIZE / 3 :LEVEL - 1 RT 120
SIDE :SIZE / 3 :LEVEL - 1 LT 60
SIDE :SIZE / 3 :LEVEL - 1
END
```

This procedure gets a bit more complex. What would SNOWFLAKE 50 0 look like. No fair trying it on the computer!

Here's one from
SNOWFLAKE 100 4

Here's a picture from
SNOWFLAKE 100 1

Want to see some colorful snowflakes? Try this procedure. It is on the disk that came with this book.

```
TO START
CS PU SETPOS [-100 -100] PD
SETPC [0 0 255]
SNOWFLAKE 300 1 WAIT 30
SETPC [128 128 0]
SNOWFLAKE 300 2 WAIT 30
SETPC [128 0 0]
SNOWFLAKE 300 4
END
```

Hilbert Curve

Now take a look at HILBERT.LGO. It's a bit more complex than SNOWFLAKE or DRAGON – a really good challenge.

```
TO HILBERT  :SIZE :LEVEL
H :SIZE :LEVEL 1
END

TO H  :SIZE :LEV :PAR
IF :LEV = 0 [STOP]
LT :PAR * 90
H  :SIZE  :LEV - 1  0 - :PAR
FD :SIZE
RT :PAR * 90
H :SIZE  :LEV - 1  :PAR
FD :SIZE
H  :SIZE  :LEV - 1  :PAR
RT :PAR * 90
FD :SIZE
H :SIZE :LEV - 1  0 - :PAR
LT :PAR * 90
END
```

The HIL.LGO and LHILBERT.LGO procedures on CD that came with this book offer another look at the Hilbert curve.

Taming the Flicker

For some more complex drawings, take a look at the Sierpinski gasket and carpet procedures that are on the CD (SIERP.LGO). You've got recursive calls embedded all over the place in these procedures.

These include the use of color, which can produce an annoying screen flicker as they are being drawn. An easy way to get rid of the flicker is to shut down the MSWLogo Screen while the fractals are being drawn.

The CARPET procedure gives an example of how you do this. Before the turtle starts drawing, enter the command

ICON [MSWLOGO SCREEN]

When the fractal is complete, display the screen using this command:

UNICON [MSWLOGO SCREEN]

There are a number of examples of fractals in the \projects\chpt9 directory on the accompanying CD, from the simple to the complex. Also, there are many, many books on fractals, from the most basic level to the very complex. Take a look at some of these, especially those that deal with computer art and landscapes.

Logo Trees

RUNNER.LGO, which you'll find on the CD that came with this book, is a great example of recursion. It's also a good example of animating the turtle.

Why not see what you can do with this procedure?

1. Add some color.

2. When the Road Runner reaches the Stop sign, it stops, looks both ways, and then plays two tones. If you have a sound card, why not play a wave file?

3. You'll soon read about changing the shape of the turtle. Why not draw a real Road Runner?

4. Have the Road Runner change directions and travel the other road.

Among other interesting things, RUNNER.LGO uses the classic TREE procedure. It is one of the better known examples of recursion.

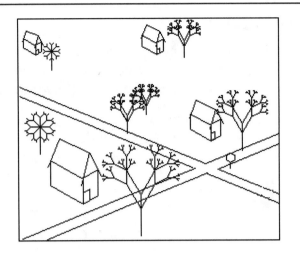

```
TO TREE  :LENGTH
IF :LENGTH < 2 [STOP] LT 45 FD :LENGTH
TREE :LENGTH / 2 BACK :LENGTH RT 90
    FD :LENGTH
TREE :LENGTH / 2 BACK :LENGTH LT 45
END
```

If you can't seem to follow the action here, use Morf's pieces of paper to see how it works. It's really pretty neat! Or maybe you'll find these tree procedures easier to deal with.

```
TO FTREE :SIZE :COUNTER
IF :COUNTER = 0 [STOP]
LT 30 FD :SIZE * 2
FTREE :SIZE :COUNTER - 1
BK :SIZE * 2  RT 60 FD :SIZE
FTREE :SIZE :COUNTER - 1
BK :SIZE LT 30
END
```

```
TO TREE :SIZE :LIMIT
IF :SIZE < :LIMIT  [STOP]
LT 45 FD :SIZE
TREE :SIZE * 0.61803 :LIMIT
BK :SIZE RT 90 FD :SIZE
TREE :SIZE * 0.61803 :LIMIT
BK :SIZE LT 45
END
```

These are in the TREES.LGO procedure on the CD that came with this book. You'll also find some good examples of recursion in the next chapter.

The Great Math Adventure

"When I'm doing my arithmetic homework, it seems more like a pain in the neck than a Great Math Adventure."

True enough! But think about this for a moment! What part of your life does not involve mathematics, some form of calculation, counting, or measurement?

What about time, the counting and measurement of seconds and hours? Or distance, the measurement of space in inches and feet, or centimeters and meters? What about music, measured in frequencies?

Think about Logo and the computer for a moment. Everything you do on the computer is translated into electrical signals that become a mathematical code of zeros and ones.

Everything you have been doing so far in our *Great Logo Adventure* has been part of turtle geometry, right? I hate to tell you this, but that's mathematics.

Just what is mathematics? Is it just some number tables that you have to memorize? Is it just a bunch of formulas and equations?

Or is it a way to express ideas and relationships using common symbols such as +, -, *, /, and others? That sounds like a language, doesn't it?

Isn't it sort of like Logo? A way to explore and express ideas on and off the computer? What you read on the screen is expressed by numbers, by a mathematical code that is translated into electrical signals.

If you had to communicate with people who don't speak English, how would you do it? What if they were aliens who didn't speak at all?

One way to start is through the use of numbers, music, and mathematics.

Counting is something everyone does in one way or another. Musical tones all have numerical frequencies as you may remember. Sounds set up vibrations. So even if you can't hear the sounds, you can feel them. Believe it or not, that's how some deaf people enjoy music.

To carry this idea a bit further, humpback whales sing. The use of mathematics is helping scientists analyze their songs.

So look beyond your homework into all the realms where numbers and math are used. Who knows? Maybe by the time you finish this book, you may just agree that math is a universal language.

Come on! Let's start with arithmetic.

Logo Arithmetic

Remember back in the first Rabbit Trail where you took a Turtle Walk. You used the multiplication symbol then.

FD 10 * 5

What would happen if that line said

FD 10 + 5 or

FD 10 - 5 or

FD 10 / 5

Try these commands using variables.

MAKE "A 50
MAKE "B 100
MAKE "C :A + :B
FD :A + :B or FD 100 + 50

FD :C / :A * 10

That's FD 50 + 100 divided by 50, or 3. 3 * 10 = 30 or FD 30.

How about FD :C / (:A * 3)

Does this instruction do the same thing? Why? Or why not?

When Logo looks at a command that uses arithmetic, it does the arithmetic in the standard mathematical order: multiplication and division followed by addition and subtraction.

So, when Logo reads that line, the first thing it sees is FD :C or FD 150. This is divided by 50 * 3 or 150. So you have FD 150 / 150 or FD 1. Looks like the parentheses change things.

Parentheses are among the Logo delimiters that can be used to change the order of operations.

"Delimiters. That's a funny word!"

It may seem a bit strange. But when you think about it, that's just what they do. Delimiters define the limits of an operation. Take a look.

The commands listed below use arithmetic signs to tell the turtle to go FD 200.

FD 100 + 1000 / 10
FD 10 * (5 + 15)
FD (20 - 10) * (18 + 2)

Write down some other commands that will take the turtle FD 200. Make sure you use parentheses in your examples. Then test them out.

Positive and Negative Numbers

When you add or multiply two positive numbers together, what do you get? You get another positive number. That makes sense, doesn't it?

Add a positive and a negative number together. What do you get? Why not try it and see.

    SHOW 10 + (-2)
    8

    SHOW 10 + (-12)
    -2

What about multiplication?

    SHOW 10 * -2
    -20

    SHOW -10 * -2
    20

Adding and Multiplying Negative Numbers

How can that be? Multiply two negative numbers and the answer is positive?

This is something worth talking about. How can two negatives make a positive?

One way to look at the subject of positive and negative numbers is to see how the turtle handles such things. Check out the coordinate system again, especially the GRID.LGO procedure you saw in Chapter 8.

    FD 50   That's easy. The turtle moves (+) 50.
    BK 50   The turtle moves back (-) 50.

What happens when you ask the turtle to go BK -50

Rabbit Trail
25

Positive and Negative Numbers

Here's another way to make some sense out of positive and negative numbers.

Make a game out of them or just make up a demonstration. You'll need:

- some scissors.

- sheets of paper in at least two colors.

- markers to write on sheets of paper.

You're going to play a game of high finance.

Cut out a bunch of paper strips – at least five of each color for each player – about the size of a dollar bill. Next you need to mark the strips for what they are worth. There are four colors in the example shown below. Two colors will work also.

Color	Description	Value
White	Asset	+1
Red	Debt	- 1
Yellow	Asset	+5
Green	Debt	- 5

Assets are things that people own. They have a positive value. Debts have a negative value; like when you borrow money from the bank to buy a home or a car.

Now you're ready to start your game or demonstration. You can call it "Wall Street Trader," where you will buy and sell companies. Maybe you can play "Banker" where players trade for things in their own small town. Make up your own rules; as simple or as complicated as you want. The whole idea is to see what happens when you use positive and negative numbers.

Here's how it works:

3 * 5	I give you three of my yellow assets.
3 * -1	I give you three of my red debts.
-2 * 5	I take two of your yellow assets.
-3 * -5	I take three of your green debts.

After you have made several trades, how are you doing? Subtract your debts from your assets. Do you have more than when you started or less?

More important, does this help make sense out of positive and negative numbers?

Engineering Notation

"You're getting complicated again. What's with this notation stuff?"

Engineering notation – some people call it exponential notation – is simply a way of writing very big numbers.

Decimal numbers include a part of a whole number, such as 1.25, 3.24, 89.23. Logo lets you use decimals such as

    FD 100.125 BK 21.75

Logo writes very big and very small numbers using engineering notation such as 1.0E-21.

COOKIE.LGO is a simple game that adds some fun to mathematics. It's a great test to see who can make the most money selling cookies. The full procedure is on the CD that came with this book. Only a few of the subprocedures are listed here. You'll need to look at the whole thing to understand what's going on.

Right now, let's just focus on that strange stuff in the Cost procedures:

```
TO COSTA
OUTPUT 1.E-2*(19 + RANDOM 7)
END

TO COSTB
OUTPUT 1.E-2*(12 + RANDOM 8)
END

TO COSTC
OUTPUT 1.E-2*(9 + RANDOM 7)
END
```

Engineering notation looks strange all scrunched together like that. But it's not all that complicated. It's really pretty easy.

Time to experiment.

Try playing around with some engineering numbers.

```
SHOW 1.E+2*9
900

SHOW 1.E+5*9
900000
```

SHOW 1.E+14*128
1.28E+16

What kind of answer is 1.28E+16?

If you play around with engineering notation, you'll discover how it works. Try adding lots of numbers to 1.E. Subtract a bunch also. What happens?

1.28E+16 is 128 with 14 zeros, sixteen places to the right of the decimal point.

What's SHOW 1.E-14 * 128?

Mathematics doesn't have to be dull, meaningless stuff. It can be fun. It can even get exciting! It can even get weird!

Mathematical Operations

There are lots of other ways you can use arithmetic with Logo. Here are the math commands used in MSW Logo.

SUM	DIFFERENCE	MINUS
PRODUCT	QUOTIENT	REMAINDER
INT	ROUND	SQRT
POWER	EXP	LOG10
LN	SIN	RADSIN
COS	RADCOS	ARCTAN
RADARCTAN		

Let's take a look at some examples:

FD SUM 50 50

What do you think that means? You're right - FD 100. Forward the sum of 50 and 50 or 50 + 50. How about

FD DIFFERENCE 300 200

Forward the difference between 300 and 200 or 300 - 200.

FD PRODUCT 10 10

Forward the product of 10 times 10 or 10 * 10.

FD QUOTIENT 1000 10

Forward the quotient of 1000 divided by 10 or 1000 / 10.

FD REMAINDER 1000 300

Forward the remainder of 1000 divided by 300. How much is that?

MSW Logo uses INT for integer. But what's an integer? That's a whole number, one without decimals or fractions.

> FD INT (121.8 - 21.1)

Forward the integer of 121.8 - 21.1. 121.8 - 21.1 equals 100.7. But, since the command is FD INTeger, or whole number, the decimal is dropped and you're left with FD 100.

> FD ROUND 121.8 - 21.5

Forward 121.8 - 21.5 rounded off. That equals 100.3, which rounds to 100.

Change that to

> FD ROUND 121.8 - 22.1

That equals 99.7, which is rounded to 100.

All these examples would be much simpler if they just said FD 100. After all the arithmetic is done, they each tell Ernestine, the turtle, to go FD 100.

So what?

Well, what if you want to add or multiply a bunch of variables?

> FD SUM (PRODUCT :A :X)(QUOTIENT :B :Y)
> REPEAT (PRODUCT :A :B) [FD SUM :C :D RT 90]

You'll see some examples of this type of thing later on.

Factorials

Factorials give you the chance to explore recursion again as well as multiplication. A factorial is the product of all the whole numbers from 1 to whatever.

For example, factorial 5 is just another way of saying 5 * 4 * 3 * 2 * 1 which equals 120.

To write that as a procedure:

```
TO FACTORIAL :N
IF :N = 1 [OUPUT :N]
OUPUT :N * (FACTORIAL :N - 1 )
END
```

The easiest way to make sense of this is to use the recursive pages approach like you did with AMAZE in the last chapter.

When you type FACTORIAL 5, this is what Logo sees.

```
TO FACTORIAL 5
IF 5 = 1 [OUPUT 5]
OUPUT 5 * (FACTORIAL 5 - 1 )
END
```

This is saved on the first page as the procedure is called again in the third line: OUPUT 5 * (FACTORIAL 5 - 1). This time, it reads

```
TO FACTORIAL 4
IF 4 = 1 [OUPUT 4]
OUPUT 4 * (FACTORIAL 4 - 1 )
END
```

This continues until the second line of the procedure reads

```
IF 1 = 1 [OUTPUT 1]
```

Then Logo reads back through the pages:

```
5 * 4 = 20 * 3 = 60 * 2 = 120 * 1 = 120
```

The Tangram Procedures

Now let's take a closer look at something else you've seen before. Do you remember the Tangram puzzles? Well, let's take a look at the procedures to draw the Tangram pieces you saw earlier. They're on the CD that came with this book in the \procs\chpt10 subdirectory.

```
TO TRIANGLE.RT  :SIDE
TO TRIANGLE.LT  :SIDE
TO SQUARE.LT  :SIDE
TO SQUARE.RT  :SIDE
TO MED.TRI.RT  :SIDE
TO MED.TRI.LT  :SIDE
TO SMALL.TRI.RT  :SIDE
TO SMALL.TRI.LT  :SIDE
TO PARGRAM.LT  :SIDE
TO PARGRAM.RT  :SIDE
```

To give you an idea of what you can do with tangram shapes, try this procedure.

```
TO TANGRAM  :SIDE
SETH 90 TRIANGLE.LT :SIDE
FD :SIDE SETH 0
TRIANGLE.LT :SIDE
```

```
FD :SIDE SETH 270
SMALL.TRI.LT :SIDE
FD :SIDE / 2 SETH 225
MED.TRI.RT :SIDE
SQUARE.LT :SIDE FD :SIDE1
PARGRAM.LT :SIDE
END
```

This procedure uses the different shape procedures to make one big shape. Which one?

You'll have to run the procedure to see.

Fun With Tangrams

Enough of this stuff. Let's have some more fun with tangrams! Put two small triangles together. What shape do you get? Can you make a square from the two small triangles? How about a larger triangle? A parallelogram?

Put the parallelogram and two small triangles together. What shape is that? Can you make a square? What about a trapezoid?

"A what?"

"A Trap-e-zoid! That's another shape, Morf. It's like a parallelogram but it only has one set of parallel sides instead of two."

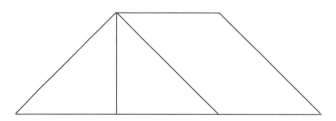

"That's no trap-e-whatever. That's a picture of the pup tent we use out in the back yard!"

"Get serious, Morf! Can you make a triangle using five pieces of the puzzle?

Check out the CD that came with this book for more ideas on what to do with tangrams.

Making Crazy Shapes

Why not have the computer think up some shapes for you?

These might come out a bit crazy. But who cares? That's the fun of having the turtle do things for you. That's why CRAZY.SHAPES was included in the TANGRAM.LGO procedure.

```
TO CRAZY.SHAPES :SIDE
SHAPES :SIDE
MOVE :SIDE
CRAZY.SHAPES :SIDE
END

TO SHAPES :SIDE
MAKE "SHAPE RANDOM 10
IF :SHAPE = 0 [TRIANGLE.RT :SIDE]
IF :SHAPE = 1 [TRIANGLE.LT :SIDE]
IF :SHAPE = 2 [MED.TRI.RT :SIDE]
IF :SHAPE = 3 [MED.TRI.LT :SIDE]
IF :SHAPE = 4 [SMALL.TRI.RT :SIDE]
IF :SHAPE = 5 [SMALL.TRI.LT :SIDE]
IF :SHAPE = 6 [SQUARE.RT :SIDE]
IF :SHAPE = 7 [SQUARE.LT :SIDE]
IF :SHAPE = 8 [PARGRAM.RT :SIDE]
IF :SHAPE = 9 [PARGRAM.LT :SIDE]
END

TO MOVE :SIDE
MAKE "MOVE RANDOM 5
IF :MOVE = 0 [SETH HEADING + 45]
IF :MOVE = 1 [SETH HEADING + 90]
IF :MOVE = 2 [FD :SIDE]
IF :MOVE = 3 [FD :SIDE / 2]
IF :MOVE = 4 [FD (:SIDE / SQRT 2 ) / 2]
END
```

SHAPE :SIDE and MOVE :SIDE offer a very simple method for selecting something at random. Other methods are coming up.

RANDOM, Picking, and Shuffling

There's that RANDOM command again. It takes one input. Also, do you remember that in MSW Logo, RANDOM selects a number between zero and the number you input.

There are times that you want to randomly rearrange a list, like a sequence of numbers, letters, cities, or whatever — like shuffling a deck. To do that, you have to give RANDOM a little help.

Here's a procedure to do just that. It has some new commands that you'll get into a bit later. But since we're talking about RANDOM, go ahead and try it out now. You'll find lots of uses for it.

```
TO SHUFFLE :DECK
MAKE "X []
REPEAT COUNT :DECK [CHECK MAKE "DECK BUTFIRST :DECK]
REPEAT (RANDOM 4) [MAKE "X LPUT FIRST :X BUTFIRST :X]
OP :X
END

TO CHECK
IFELSE (RANDOM 3) = 1 [MAKE "X FPUT FIRST :DECK :X] ~
    [MAKE "X LPUT FIRST :DECK :X]
END
```

Why not see what happens when you deal a shuffled list of shapes?

```
TO DEAL
CS
MAKE "LIST SHUFFLE [SQ TRI HEX]
RUN :LIST
END

TO HEX
REPEAT 6 [FD 50 RT 60] WAIT 60
END

TO SQ
REPEAT 4 [FD 50 RT 90] WAIT 60
END

TO TRI
REPEAT 3 [FD 50 RT 120] WAIT 60
END
```

Now that we've confused you with this procedure, let's confuse you even more. There's another way to shuffle things around. You saw that in the SHAPES :SIDE procedure.

```
TO SHAPES :SIDE
MAKE "SHAPE RANDOM 10
IF :SHAPE = 0 [TRIANGLE.RT :SIDE]
    on through...
```

```
IF :SHAPE = 9 [PARGRAM.LT :SIDE]
END
```

In effect, this procedure shuffles the Tangram procedures. It makes the variable :SHAPE a random number. It then matches the random number with the conditional statement to find a procedure to run.

Using SHUFFLE, the whole thing would be a bit easier.

One last point of confusion. There's also a PICK command that randomly selects an element from a word or list. For example:

```
MAKE "CHOICES [A B C D E]
SHOW PICK :CHOICES
D
```

Go ahead and explore how you could use all these choices. They all do things a bit differently. So you've got lots of choices for whatever you want to do.

Squares and Square Roots

Look back at the TRIANGLE.RT procedure. Got any idea what the SQRT 2 means?

That number is used to figure out how long the two short sides of the triangle are. The left side is the longest side, right? And you know that you have two equal sides connected by an angle of 90 degrees.

A long time ago, some mathematician figured out that when you know the long side of a triangle that has two equal sides and a right angle, then the short sides equal

<Long side> / SQRT 2

There are lots of rules like this for triangles and other shapes. You've already figured out a bunch of them.

"But what does SQRT 2 mean?"

Actually, it stands for the square root of 2. That sounds a lot worse than it really is. It doesn't have anything to do with the square shape. It's part of an arithmetic problem that asks what number, multiplied by itself, gives you the answer of 2.

What's SQRT 100? SQRT 9? SQRT 16?

Think about it for a minute. What number multiplied by itself equals 100?

$$10 * 10 = 100$$

What number multiplied by itself equals 9?

$$3 * 3 = 9$$

What number multiplied by itself equals 16?

$$4 * 4 = 16.$$

Now let's turn the square around. Square roots are like saying, "Here's the answer. Tell me what the question is. Here's 16, tell me what number multiplied by itself gives me that answer?"

So let's take a look at another question: 4 multiplied by itself equals what? MSW Logo has a POWER command.

FD POWER 4 2

That's like saying forward 4 to the power of 2, or 4 squared, or 4 times 4.

FD POWER 10 3

This is like saying Forward 10-cubed or 10 * 10 * 10 or 10 to the power of 3. The 2 in POWER 4 2 and the 3 in POWER 10 3 are called "exponents." This might make you think that POWER and EXP (or EXP) are the same. EXP is a trigonometric function that calculates the natural base e (2.7183. . .) raised to the power specified by its input.

"I didn't understand a word of that."

Walking Distance

Let's first do some coordinate calculations to follow up on a Chapter 8 project.

Do you remember in Chapter 2 when you explored Turtle Town? You were asked to draw a map to your friend's house.

Now let's figure out the distances between two houses. Let's use Logy's and Morf's homes.

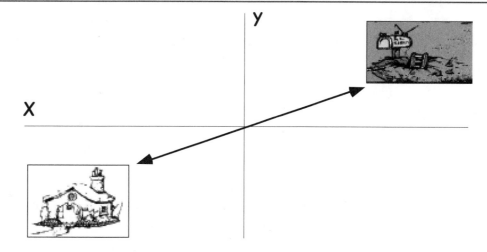

If you know the coordinates of each home, it's easy to use Logo and trigonometry to calculate the distance between the two homes. (You'll get into trigonometry in the next section.) Here's a variation of the DISTance procedure.

```
TO DIST  :X1 :Y1 :X2 :Y2
OP DIST1 :X1 - :X2 :Y1 - :Y2
END

TO DIST1  :DX :DY
OP SQRT (:DX * :DX ) + (:DY * :DY )
END
```

Logy's home is at [-100 -80] and Morf's Den is at [150 60]. What's the distance between the two homes?

```
SHOW DIST -100 -80 150 60
286.530975637888
```

This answer is fine if you're flying between homes. But since you're walking, you've still got some figuring to do.

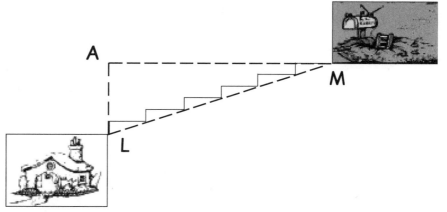

Walking between the two homes means that you have to go up one block, turn right, go another block, turn left, and so forth. That's not the same as the straight line distance from L to M.

So how can you calculate the walking distance?

1. Start with what you know.

2. Define what you need to know.

3. Go find it.

You know the coordinates of each home, and you calculated the distance between the two homes.

*   Logy's Home is at [-100 -80].

*   Morf's Home is at [150 60].

*   The direct distance between the two homes is 286.53.

You also know that turn from one block to the next, that the total distance you must walk going North (top of the screen) is the distance from L to A. The total distance you will walk going East (right side of the screen) is the distance from A to M.

Think about this. You also know the coordinates of point A. Take the Y coordinate of Morf's home and the X coordinate of Logy's home, and where are you?

Point A is at [-100 60].

The easy way to calculate the walking distance would be to use the DIST procedure. Rather than do that, let's write a procedure to calculate the total walking distance.

```
TO WALK.DIST
(LOCAL "MX "MY "LX "LY "WALK)
MAKE "MX 150
MAKE "MY 60
MAKE "LX -100
MAKE "LY -80
MAKE "WALK ABS (:LX - :MX) + (:LY - :MY)
(PR [THE WALKING DISTANCE IS] :WALK)
END
```

The walking distance is 390 steps.

You can use the DIST procedure to prove this. First calculate the distance from Logy's Home to A.

DIST -100 -80 -100 60 = 140

Now from Point A to Morf's Home.

DIST -100 60 150 60 = 250

One last test: does 286.53 squared equal 140 squared plus 250 squared.

SHOW SQRT 140 * 140 + 250 * 250
286.530975637888

Works for me!

A Quick Look at Trigonometry

"You know, you can't really get away from trigonometry if you're going to explore angles. In simplest terms, trigonometry is the study of triangles. And what's a triangle other than three connected angles?"

Trigonometry – *trig* for short – also includes the study and use of what they call trigonometric functions. These functions include strange names such as sine, cosine, tangent, arctangent, and cotangant. They describe the functions of an angle that is described in terms of the ratios of pairs of sides or angles in a right triangle. You remember the right triangle, don't you?

A right triangle includes one right angle – right angles are 90 degrees – and two acute angles. Acute angles are less than 90 degrees. Obtuse angles are more than 90 degrees.but less than 180 degrees.

So here's a right triangle:

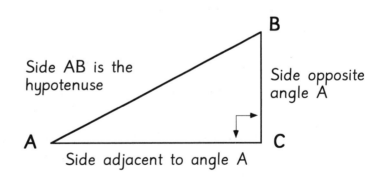

A gentleman of Ancient Greece named Pythagoras came up with the rule that lets you determine the length of any side of a right triangle if you know the length of any two sides. The relationship that Pythagoras came up with says that side AC squared plus side BC squared equals the hypotenuse, side AC, squared.

$$A2 + B2 = C2$$

Remember the DIST procedures?

```
TO DIST  :X1 :Y1 :X2 :Y2
OP DIST1 :X1 - :X2 :Y1 - :Y2
END

TO DIST1  :DX :DY
OP SQRT (:DX * :DX ) + (:DY * :DY )
END
```

Gee, when you look at those procedures, it seems as if trigonometry does have something to do with the coordinate system – which, of course, it does. Does that DIST1 procedure look familiar?

```
SQRT (:DX * :DX ) + (:DY * :DY)
```

is the same as

```
SQRT :DX2 + :DY2
```

which looks just like the Pythagorean theorem above. If you take the

```
SQRT A2 + B2
```

What will you get? Morf got the square root of C.

Defining Trig Functions

Once you know how the different sides of a right triangle relate to each other, you can define the trigonometric functions in terms of their right triangle relationships. Using the angles A, B, and C in the right angle shown previously, here's the definitions of functions with MSW Logo commands:

Sine (sin):	Sine of angle A = the ratio between the side opposite angle A and the hypotenuse. BC / AB.
Cosine (cos):	Cosine angle A = the ratio between the adjacent side and the hypotenuse. AC / AB
Tangent (tan):	Tangent angle A = the ratio between the opposite side and the adjacent side. BC / AC
Arctangent: (Arctan)	Arctangent angle A = The inverse of the tangent or the ratio between the adjacent side and opposite side. AC / BC

Using this information, you can define just about any trig function you may need. It also may help you understand some of the more complex procedures and commands in MSW Logo.

There are many books on trigonometry, if you really want to dig into it. There are also books on advanced Logo that talk about it much more than space allows in this book. For now, let's take a quick look at trigonometry in action.

Morf's TV Antenna

Here's a problem that uses the sine function.

Morf has a TV antenna that is twelve feet tall. The instructions say that to keep it steady, he has to use four wires, each at a 65 degree angle from the ground.

How much wire does he need to buy?

Here's what the antenna looks like. Just remember that there are four wires and not just two as shown here.

The sine of angle A equals the opposite side (the height of the antenna) divided by the hypotenuse (the length of the wire).

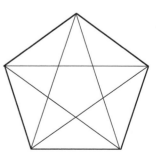

SINE A = 12 / WIRE LENGTH

or

TOTAL WIRE = (12 / SINE A) * 4

In Logo, that's written as

SHOW (12 / SIN 65) * 4
52.9621401101996

Looks like Morf needs about 13-1/4 feet of wire for each of the four wires.

Side of the Star

Do you remember the problem with the stars back in Chapter 7? You started with a pentagon like this:

REPEAT 5 [FD 100 RT 72]

How did Ernestine know that the side of the star was 160? Maybe you can figure it out now.

What do you know about that pentagon and the star?

The sides of the pentagon are 100.

267

The three angles at each corner equal 36 degrees.

Now, how can you prove that the long side of the shaded triangle is 160?

From HOME in the lower left, type

LT 18 FD 100 RT 108 / 2 FD 80

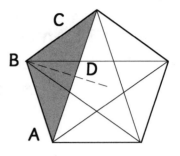

You already know that the big angle in the shaded triangle is 108. In Chapter 7, you proved that it's 180 - 72. So you cut that angle in half and go FD 80 – any distance, just so long as you cross the long side of the triangle.

You're left with two right angles, ABD and CBD.

Now you can calculate half of the long side of the shaded triangle using this trigonometric function.

COSINE 36 = ADJACENT / 100 (hypotenuse)

To put this in Logo terms:

SHOW 100 * COS 36 or
80.9016994374947

Now let's do some checking.

Using the Pythagorean theorem of A2 + B2 = C2, you can calculate the length of the short side of the right triangle BD.

1002 = 80.92 + What?

SHOW SQRT (POWER 100 2) - (POWER 80.9 2)
58.7808642331839

To check this out, try this:

REPEAT 5 [FD 162 RT 144]
LT 36
REPEAT 5 [FD 100 RT 72]

FD 100 RT 72 + 54 (Half the inside angle of 108)
FD 58.78
RT 90
FD 80.9

Where are you?

The length of the long side of the shaded triangle is 80.9 * 2 or 161.8, which is just about 162. Ernestine likes to work with rounded numbers. So now you know where she got it.

This is a bare taste of trigonometry. But maybe as you look at some of the procedures in the \projects\chpt10 and the Logolib subdirectory, they won't seem quite so strange now.

You never know. You might just be able to figure them out and do some really neat things with them.

Here's a challenge for you. Do you remember the "From the Center" exercises. You found the center point of different polygons. Now that you've had some experience with trigonometry, can you find out the distance from the edge to the center of any of the shapes?

But first, let's check out a few other Logo commands.

Counting Numbers and Stuff

COUNT is another very useful Logo command. It outputs the number of elements in its input. That input can be a word or a list.

SHOW COUNT "LOGO
4   (There's four letters in LOGO.)

SHOW COUNT [LOGY AND MORF]
3   (There's three words in the list.)

Here's an example from a procedure we talk more about in Chapter 12. Since you're only interested in the first command, the one using COUNT, we left that second part off. Let's see if we can use the REPEAT command to help make some sense out of COUNT.

REPEAT (COUNT :NUMS2) - 1 [...

You have a variable named :NUMS2. So for our explorations, let's make :NUMS2 equal to a list of numbers.

MAKE "NUMS2 (LIST 22 11 30 567 982)

SHOW :NUMS2
Result: [22 11 30 567 982]

SHOW COUNT :NUMS2
Result:5

REPEAT (COUNT :NUMS2) - 1 [FD 100 RT 90]

What would this command draw? You should know that. You learned about this shape back in Chapter 3.

Items, Members, and Things

There are some other neat things you can do with words and lists. In the example above, you used the COUNT of the variable :NUMS2 to create a square. You can also select an item from a word or list and use that, too.

Here's an example. I bet you can guess what this is going to look like. It also tells you what ITEM does in a Logo procedure.

```
REPEAT ITEM 3 :NUMS2 [SQUARE RT 12]

TO SQUARE
REPEAT ( ( COUNT :NUMS2 ) - 1 ) [FD 100 RT 90]
END
```

What do you think ITEM 3 :NUMS2 is?

You know that :NUMS2 is a list — [22 11 30 567 982]. So what is ITEM 3 :NUMS2?

Another double-dip ice cream cone if you said 30.

ITEM outputs the third element of the variable :NUMS2. It doesn't matter whether the variable is a word or a list.

```
SHOW ITEM 2 "CAT
     A

SHOW ITEM 2 7861236
     8
```

Get the idea?

In the :NUMS2 example, you knew what NUMBER you were looking for — the third element, or 30. But what if you didn't know?

Logo lets you ask. Take a look.

```
TO CHECK :X
IFELSE MEMBERP :X :NUMS2~
    [REPEAT ITEM 3 :NUMS2~[SQUARE RT 12]] [SQUARE]
END

TO SQUARE
REPEAT ( ( COUNT :NUMS2 ) - 1 ) [FD 100 RT 90]
END

MAKE "NUMS2 [22 11 30 567 982]
```

In the CHECK procedure, Logo asks if :X is a member of the variable :NUMS2. If it is, it runs the REPEAT command

[REPEAT ITEM 3 :NUMS2 [SQUARE RT 12]]

If not, it just runs the SQUARE procedure.

Logo picks up these instructions from the IFELSE command. It's like saying if a condition is true, then do this, or else do this.

Ask Logo

You just saw MEMBERP. It asks if THING1 is a member of THING2. THING is the same as the dots in a variable, remember?

SHOW MEMBERP 1 [1 2 3 4]
TRUE

SHOW MEMBERP "CAT [DOG CAT RABBIT]
TRUE

SHOW MEMBERP "A "CAT
TRUE

There's also a MEMBER command. If "thing2" is a word or list, it shows the portion of THING2 from the first instance of THING2 to the end. If THING1 is not part of THING2, MEMBER outputs an empty word or list, whatever THING 1 is.

Does this have you nice and confused? Try it out! You're getting good at this by now.

Well, there are a number of other questions you can ask Logo. Your version of Logo may use a ? rather than a P at the end of the commands; MEMBER?, for example.

EQUALP
    Are two words or lists equal or identical? For example:
    IF EQUALP :X (ITEM 3 :NUMS2) [REPEAT ....

EMPTYP
    Is a word or list empty (") or ([ ])? For example:
    IFELSE EMPTYP :NUMS2 [STOP] [REPEAT .....

If :NUMS2 is an empty list STOP, else run the REPEAT command.

NUMBERP
    Is the object a number? For example:
    IF NUMBERP (ITEM 3 :NUMS2) [REPEAT ....

If ITEM 3 :NUMS2 is a number, then continue with the REPEAT command. Otherwise skip it and go on to the next line.

WORDP

Is something a word?

LISTP

Is something a list?

Logical Operations

There are three other primitives you need to look at before you leave Logo arithmetic: AND, OR, NOT.

AND

AND tests to see if all the conditions following the command are true.

```
MAKE "X 210
MAKE "Y 724
MAKE "Z 910
IF AND :X > 200 :Y < 800 [FD 100]
```

The conditions are true so the turtle moves forward 100.

Where you have more than two conditions, the commands and the command AND must be enclosed in parentheses.

```
MAKE "Z 555
IF (AND :X > 200 :Y < 800 :Z >500) [FD 100]
```

The conditions are true so the turtle moves forward 100.

OR

Where AND tests if all conditions are true, OR tests to see if any of the conditions is true. If you have more than two conditions to test, use parentheses as shown below.

```
IF OR :X > 200 :Z >1000 [FD 100]
IF (OR :X > 200 :Y < 800 :Z >1000) [FD 100]
```

Because at least one of the conditions is true, the turtle moves forward 100.

You could rewrite the Serpinski curve procedure from the last chapter using OR by changing

```
IF :LEVEL = 0 [FD :SIZE STOP]
IF :SIZE < 2 [FD :SIZE STOP]
```
  to
```
IF OR (:LEVEL = 0)(:SIZE < 2) [FD :SIZE STOP]
```

NOT

If the condition is false, NOT outputs True. In other words:

IF NOT :Z > 1000 [FD 100]

Since Z is not greater than 1000, the turtle moves forward 100.

Math Challenges

Math Challenges may sound a bit like homework, but these problems are fun!

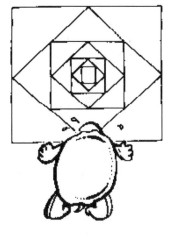

Here's a fairly easy challenge for you. Draw a series of squares within squares like the ones that are causing Logy to shake her head. It's tricky, sure. But it's really not that tough.

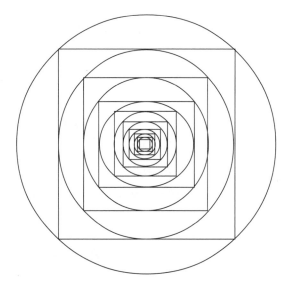

Here's another bit of a challenge to see what you've learned so far.

This drawing is a Mandala. People in India believe this is a symbol of the endless universe. Take some time to figure out how this procedure works. It's an interesting exercise in turtle geometry. (MANDALA.LGO in the \procs\chpt10 subdirectory.)

OK! After you get the Mandala procedure all figured out, try doing the same thing using triangles instead of squares. If you get bored with that, there are more math challenges in the \projects\chpt10 directory on the CD.

Rotating Planes in Space

"No, Morf. This is not about rotating or rolling your favorite Biplane. This is about moving shapes through space."

Do you remember the picture below? You saw it in Chapter 3 and also in Chapter 9, only it didn't have the dotted-line square in the picture then.

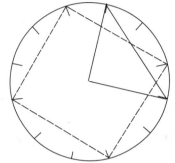

The original idea was to use string and make a triangle; first from 12:00 o'clock to 3:00 o'clock, the center, and back to 12:00 'oclock. Next you moved to 1:00 o'clock and made the triangle shown in the picture. Then you moved to 2:00 o'clock and so one, all the way around the clock.

The triangles moved around an axis that was at the center of the string clock. When you did the same thing with squares, they moved around on an axis at the center of the square.

Can you write Logo procedures that show the shapes rotating around an axis?

Sure you can! Take a look at ROTATE.LGO in the \procs\chpt10 subdirectory of the CD. Type START to begin the show.

This procedure shows squares and cubes rotating around an axis. It also gives you another example of trigonometry at work.

How about a challenge or two?

1. These procedures show the "side view" of the shapes rotating around a vertical axis. Write procedures to show a top view of the shapes rotating around the axis — as if you were looking down on the shapes.

2. Write procedures for other shapes, such as a rotating triangle. Use different types of triangles.

3. What about moving a pyramid through space?

Well, maybe you had better leave that job to the next project.

How About Turtle CAD

When some junior high students saw the work that the third grade students had done creating and folding soccer ball patterns, they wondered if it would be possible to work in three dimensions on the

Logo screen. They were thoroughly familiar with the two dimensions of the x - y coordinate system.

Could this be expanded to serve three dimensions: X, Y, and Z?

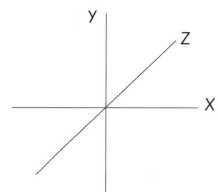

Yes, it can. In addition, the resulting procedure offers a good look at property lists, an often confusing feature of Logo.

In the procedure listed on the following pages, (ECONOBOX.LGO on the CD) the basic unit is the coordinate point as defined by the POINT procedure. Points have letter names and x, y, and z coordinates to position them in three-dimensional space.

Take a look at the DIAMOND and CAR procedures. To display a 3-D object, you must define each point in space and each line. Once you have defined all the required points by name and position, you can construct shapes like this one.

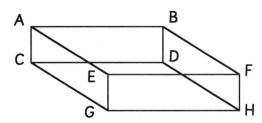

The FIGURE procedure takes the shape name and a list of two-point lists; for example, [[A B][A C][A E][B F][B D] [C D][C G]…]. The two-point lists represent the line segments of the shape with each letter representing an endpoint.

Here's a simple procedure to develop a pyramid. Each point is defined along with the lines linking those points.

```
TO PYRAMID
POINT "A [0 0 0]
POINT "B [0 0 50]
POINT "C [50 0 50]
POINT "D [50 0 0]
POINT "E [25 50 25]
FIGURE "PYRAMID [[A B][B C][C D][D A][A E]
    [B E][C E][D E]]
END
```

The procedure allows you to create as many shapes as you want. Each can be as complex as you want. But only one can be manipulated at a time.

Once you have defined your shape, you can expand it or contract it, rotate it, magnify it, shrink it, and then restore it to its original shape.

To expand a shape, use EXPAND. Tell the procedure which shape to expand, which axis the expansion will operate on, and how much to expand it.

MAGNIFY is very similar to EXPAND. However, you don't specify an axis since the figure is magnified in all directions.

ROTATE operates on a plane: xy, xz, or yz. Specify the shape, the plane, and the degrees of rotation you want to see. As you move your shape through space, the turtle remembers the position of your shape and moves it from its last position. When you want to start over with a new shape, or start from your shape's original position, use

RESTORE "*<figure name>*.

To get you started, there are three examples provided in the procedure below: a diamond, a pyramid, and an econobox-like car.

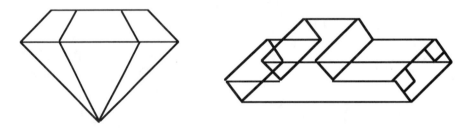

Type DIAMOND or CAR to see a front view of the figures. Then rotate the figures using commands such as:

ROTATE "<figure name> "XY 45
ROTATE "<figure name> "YZ 30

Now you're ready to start off on your own.

Understanding Property Lists

For the longest time, Property Lists were a major source of confusion — until Logy and Morf discovered a way to read them.

Put the PROPerty of :PROPERTY, which has the value of :VALUE, with the name :NAME. It helped when they saw PPROP written as a procedure.

```
TO PPROP :NAME :PROPERTY :VALUE
MAKE (WORD :NAME CHAR 32 :PROPERTY) :VALUE
END
```

Another way to look at the PPROP procedure is to use some more familiar terms.

```
PPROP "TEXAS "CAPITAL "AUSTIN
PPROP "TEXAS "ABBREVIATION "TX
PPROP "TEXAS "CITIES [HOUSTON DALLAS
    AMARILLO EL PASO]
PPROP "TEXAS "REGION "HILL.COUNTRY
```

Put the property of CAPITAL with the value of AUSTIN with the name, TEXAS. Put the ABBREVIATION TX with TEXAS. Put the cities of Houston, Dallas, Amarillo, and El Paso with Texas.

In the POINT procedure used on the previous pages, you have

```
PPROP :POINTNAME "POINT "TRUE
PPROP :POINTNAME "ORIG :COORDS
```

Put the property of POINT with the value of TRUE with the name :POINTNAME.

Put the property of ORIG with the value of COORDS with the name :POINTNAME. Take a look at the RESTORE procedure to see how this is used.

It's not nearly as scary as you think!

Now that you have the properties defined, what can you do with them? For one thing, you can recall them using the GPROP procedure. That's exactly what's done in the RESTORE procedure.

```
TO GPROP :NAME :PROPERTY
OUTPUT THING (WORD :NAME CHAR 32
    :PROPERTY)
END
```

This outputs the THING (the value) defined in the PPROP procedure. For example:

GPROP "TEXAS "CAPITAL results in AUSTIN.

GPROP (FIRST :N9) "ORIG results in the original coordinates for :NAME.

The THREED procedures are one good examples of property lists. Play around with them on your own. You're bound to find other uses.

Animating Multiple Turtles

"Wow, working with one turtle was bad enough. But working with hundreds?

"That's worse than working with rabbits!"

Simulating Multiple Turtles

Yes, there are lots of turtles in MSW Logo, 1024 of them. You can animate them, change their shapes, add sound effects, and all sorts of things.

But before you start getting busy with animating all those turtles, let's take a look at how you can use just one turtle to simulate multiple turtles that do lots of different things. It's a great review of things you've been doing up until now. And it will give you some ideas for working with UCB Logo, which only has one turtle.

The KALEIDOSCOPE procedure (KALEID.LGO) shows a good use of coordinate, color, and other commands. The resulting picture looks as if it were drawn by multiple turtles.

```
TO KALEID :ANG :CNT
IF :CNT < 1 [STOP]
SETPC (LIST (RANDOM 128)+128 (RANDOM 128) ~
    +128 (RANDOM 128)+128)
;Try SETPC RANDOM 16 with other Logos
MOVE
KALEID :ANG + 5 :CNT - 1
END
```

The pen colors for red, green, and blue are set from 128 to 255 (0 to 127 plus 128). You may recall that the higher the number, the lighter the color. The lighter pen colors go with the darker screen colors set in the START procedure below. In that procedure, the colors are set randomly from 0 to 100 to produce a darker screen color.

```
TO START
CS HT
SETSC (LIST RANDOM 100 RANDOM 100 ~
    RANDOM 100)
;Try SETBG RANDOM 16 with other Logos
KALEID 0 50
WHATNOW
END
```

In the MOVE procedure, the turtle remembers it's coordinates and then moves. The four simulated turtles each move in the four quadrants (the four quarters) of the screen based on the (+) positive and (-) negative values assigned to the X and Y variables.

```
TO MOVE
(LOCAL "X1 "Y1 "Y2 "Y2)
MAKE "X1 XCOR
MAKE "Y1 YCOR
FD RANDOM 100 RT :ANG + 15
MAKE "X2 XCOR
MAKE "Y2 YCOR
PU SETPOS (LIST (- :X1) :Y1) PD
SETPOS (LIST (- :X2) :Y2)
PU SETPOS (LIST (- :X1) (- :Y1)) PD
SETPOS (LIST (- :X2) (- :Y2))
PU SETPOS (LIST :X1 (- :Y1)) PD
SETPOS (LIST :X2 (- :Y2))
PU SETPOS (LIST :X2 :Y2) PD
END
```

Below is the MSW Logo procedure for running the procedure again. It creates a typical Windows dialog box where you can click on your response to run the kaleidoscope again or quit.

```
TO WHATNOW
CT MAKE "ANS YESNOBOX [AGAIN?] ~
    [RUN THE KALEIDOSCOPE AGAIN?]
IFELSE :ANS = "TRUE [START][CT STOP]
END
```

Try this procedure with non-windows versions of the language.

```
TO WHATNOW
CT
PR [ANY KEY TO RUN IT AGAIN, ESC TO TERMINATE]
IF RC = CHAR 27 [CT STOP] [START]
END
```

If you press the Esc key – CHAR 27 – the text is cleared and the procedure stops. Any other key and the START procedure is called.

The drawing shown below was made with the KALEID2.LGO procedure. This procedure includes a couple of different ways of simulating multiple turtles. Imagine what this would look like if added different colors to it.

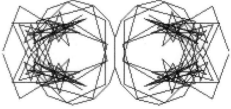

In fact, why not give that a try!

Independent Turtles

The MULTI.LGO procedure in the \procs\chpt11 subdirectory is another good example of using coordinate commands in a procedure. In the KALEIDOSOPE procedure, the simulated turtles all acted according to plan. In MULTI.LGO, you tell each one what to do.

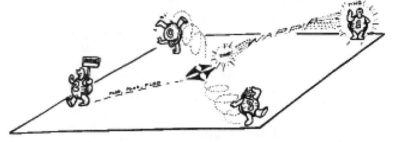

Four turtles are defined in this new procedure even though only one is actually used. The SETUP procedure defines each turtle by defining its position and heading. XCOR, YCOR, and HEADING are each spelled out for each turtle so you can see how this procedure works.

Type START to begin. Then ASK a turtle – 0, 1, 2, or 3 – to do something.

You'll notice that ASK requires a turtle number (:TNUM) and a :COMMAND.LIST. So be sure to enclose your instructions to the turtle in brackets.

ASK 2 [REPEAT 4 [FD 100 RT 90]]

If nothing else, this little exercise is a great little demonstration of what you can do with turtle positions and headings.

A New Target Game

There's a new target game in \procs\chpt11 called ZAP.LGO. This is a more practical application of simulated turtles. Ernestine gets the chance to shoot herself down.

This simple procedure is also just the beginning of what you can do with this game. There are lots of things you can do to dress it up. But first let's see how it works.

The ZAP procedure get's you started. It tell's you what you have to do.

To start the actual game, press Z.　

The Z procedure sets up the game. Turtle 0 is put in a random position on the screen. It's pen is put down so that it will draw a short line to show you the direction in which it's moving.

Your job is to guess the direction and speed of your turtle to intercept the first turtle. The target turtle is going to keep moving across the screen in the direction it's heading, once you guess how to catch it.

You have to set the heading to intercept Turtle 0. And you have to set the speed. You'll get used to the speed by trial and error. The higher the speed, the greater the chance for error. Try keeping it in the 5 to 20 range.

Once you enter the direction and speed, the computer takes over. If you come within 10 turtle steps of Turtle 0, you'll get the CHEERS procedure. Otherwise, you'll have to try again.

Read the procedures carefully. Then try this game a few times.

- What can you do to make it easier?

- How would you make it harder?

- What would you do to make the CHEERS procedure a bit flashier. Printing Congratulations is a bit dull.

There are lots of things you can do to make this game better. Go do it!

Simulations

Before we go too far, there is another realm to explore, the realm of simulations. Among other things, simulations are ways to get the computer to act out your "What if?" wishes. Actually, you have already been simulating multiple turtles. Maybe now you can get the simulated turtles to simulate others kinds of behavior.

You've heard about aircraft simulators. These are computer-controlled airplane cockpits that allow airline pilots to train in all sorts of emergency situations without ever leaving the ground.

You may have gone to arcades where they have driving or flying simulators. And, of course, there are the flight simulator software programs you can buy for your own computer.

Logo Science

An interesting use of simulators is in analyzing behavior. For example, how would a mouse find its way out of a maze.

One way that researchers discovered was that every time this one mouse came to a wall, it turned right. It eventually found its way out.

You'll find a behavior simulation on the CD that came with this book, BEHAVIOR.LGO. This offers three animal simulations: Find By Smell, Find by Sight, Chase and Evade.

The "Find" simulations are rather straight forward. The Chase and Evade simulation is fun. Will Find.By.Sight catch Avoid.By.Smell before Avoid can get out of the playing area?

Here's a challenge! BEHAVIOR.LGO uses one turtle to simulate the actions of two. Change the procedures to actually use two turtles.

Cellular Behavior

Another interesting simulation can be found in CELLS.LGO. This is an example of Logo used in medical education. The START procedure lists a message that was posted on CompuServe's Logo Forum.

CELLS.LGO is the response.

Three groups of cells are drawn randomly on the screen. The turtle always seeks out the red cells on which additional cells are grown.

Your Challenge

Create an AVOID procedure. Currently, the turtle will move right over the green and blue cells to find the red ones. Your job is to create a procedure that makes the turtle move around the green and blue cells while still seeking the red cells.

Yes, it can be done. Give it a try.

Working With Multiple Turtles

OK! You've got the idea. Now the question is: how do you go about doing that – work with multiple turtles, that is?

In MSW Logo, there are 1024 turtles numbered from 0 to 1023. To talk to a specific turtle, use the SETTURTLE command. Or why not write a simple TELL procedure? In that way, you keep talking the same language as you did when simulating multiple turtles.

```
TO TELL :TNUM
SETTURTLE :TNUM
END
```

You can set the heading, position, size, and pen control for each turtle, but not the pencolor. All the turtles use the same pen color.

We started this book with a race between the tortoise and the hare. So how about a race just for turtles? Ernestine and her cousins love to race.

```
TO RACE
TELL RANDOM 4 FD RANDOM 10
TELL 0 IF YCOR > 200 [PR [TURTLE 0 IS THE WINNER!] STOP]
TELL 1 IF YCOR > 200 [PR [TURTLE 1 IS THE WINNER!] STOP]
TELL 2 IF YCOR > 200 [PR [TURTLE 2 IS THE WINNER!] STOP]
TELL 3 IF YCOR > 200 [PR [TURTLE 3 IS THE WINNER!] STOP]
RACE
END
```

```
TO START
TELL 0 PU SETPOS [-100 -150] ST
TELL 1 PU SETPOS [-50 -150] ST
TELL 2 PU SETPOS [0 -150] ST
TELL 3 PU SETPOS [50 -150] ST
RACE
END
```

This race procedure is very simple. All it does is place four turtles in a race from the bottom to the top of the screen.

1. Why not draw a race track on which the turtles can run?

2. Why not add some pizzazz to the announcement of a winner? Some flashing lights? Maybe some music?

3. Change the shapes of the turtles into race cars.

Changing the Shape of the Turtle

What about changing the shape of the turtle? This is where animation and multimedia starts to creep into Logo.

CAR.LGO and BIPLANE.LGO are procedures you can use to change the shape of the turtle. You can edit the procedures to make them bigger or smaller depending on how you are going to use them.

Morf's just an old fashioned guy who likes the old stunt planes. So he made one of his own. He also made bitmap files of the race car and the biplane that you'll find in the graphics directory, in case you want to use it as a turtle shape.

Let's stick with the racing theme.

1. Run the CAR procedure.

    The car image is displayed.

2. Pick up the pen and move to the lower left corner of the car image.

    PU SETXY -2 -6

3. Type BITCUT 25 45

    The car image disappears. It is cut to the clipboard.

    More about loading and cutting graphic images in the next section. For now, let's focus on the turtle.

4. Type BITMAPTURTLE

    The car image is taken from the clipboard and "mapped" or changed into a turtle.

    Now you can drive your race car around the screen.

    PD FD 100 HOME

Remember, you raised the pen before you cut the image to the clipboard. You have to put it back down again before you can start drawing.

Saving Your Drawings

Before you go too far, there's something important you need to know.

- You've written a procedure to create a great drawing.

- You already know about saving the procedure.

- What about saving the drawing?

You were introduced to this idea in Chapter 2. Let's explore this some more using Morf's biplane, OK? BIPLANE.LGO is in the \procs\chpt11 subdirectory. Erase everything else in your workspace using the ERALL command. Then load the biplane. After it is loaded into Logo, type BIPLANE and press Enter.

   Morf's biplane is displayed.

You can save this drawing as a bitmap using the Bitmap menu or the BITSAVE command. However, you'll be saving one humongous file, typically over 2 megabytes. Most of that will be wasted white space. To check this out:

1. Click on the Bitmap menu.

   The Bitmap menu is displayed.

2. Select SaveAs...

   The SaveAs dialog box is displayed.

3. Type the name of the image. Name it whatever you want, for example TEST.BMP. Then click on OK.

   The image is saved as a BMP file.

Now that the picture is saved, go take a look at its size, using the Windows File Manager, Explorer, or MS-DOS. Pretty big, isn't it?

So let's cut it down. You do this by reducing the active area to something just larger than the picture. As we said earlier, unless you redefine the active area as something smaller, MSW Logo sets it as 1000 pixels (turtle steps) wide by 1000 high.

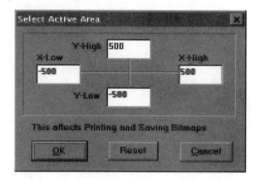

How big does it have to be to accommodate Morf's biplane? You'll have to do some exploring to determine that. The first place to look is at the procedures. What do they tell you about the dimensions of the drawing?

Or you can just guess?

1. With the biplane displayed on the screen, type ST to show the turtle.

   The turtle is displayed near the tail of the biplane.

2. Lift the pen using PU. Then estimate how far it is to just beyond the propeller. For example, type SETX 100.

   The turtle moves to the left just beyond the propeller.

3. Good guess! Now you want to move down to just below the wheels. How far do you think that is?

   Type SETY - <your guess>. How'd you do?

4. Now you are at the lower left corner of the picture.

   You've got two of the four numbers required for the active area.

5. How high above 0 does the biplane extend? One way to experiment is to try using BITCUT.

   BITCUT 100 50

   That doesn't quite do it, does it?

6. Try something just a bit bigger. How about 102 and 56?

   The entire biplane is cut. Works for me!

7. Type CS and run the biplane procedure again.

   The biplane graphic is displayed.

8. Open the Bitmap menu and select Active Area... You can also use the SETACTIVE AREA command.

   SETACTIVEAREA [<Xlow Ylow Xhigh Yhigh>]

   SETACTIVEAREA [-100 -25 2 31]

9. Now open the Bitmap menu and select SaveAs...

   The current directory is displayed.

10. Save the new active area as TEST.BMP, writing over the existing file.

    This new BMP file is much smaller, isn't it?

Now you have a BMP image that you can use as a turtle. However, you've still got a problem!

When you start moving a bitmap image around the screen as a turtle, you'll notice that the turtle trail comes from the lower left corner of the bitmap. That's where the center of the turtle would be if it were visible.

However, you're going to run into trouble when you want to turn. The picture doesn't turn the way that Ernestine does. Try it.

   FD 1OO RT 90 FD 100

Looks like the car went into a 100 step skid sideways. If you're using the biplane, it all of the sudden became a helicopter.

To show the car or biplane facing other directions, you have to add additional bitmaps. The easiest way to add these is to load your bitmap into a program such as Paintbrush (it comes with Windows) or Paint Shop Pro, a popular shareware product that's included on the CD that comes with this book. Rotate the bitmap and save each view as a separate bitmap.

But then, how do you load each bitmap into Logo? Let's take a look at that next.

Animating the Turtle

Graphics are much more fun when they seem to come to life. Animating the turtle gives you the chance to play movie producer, director, script writer, and even actor all at the same time.

Making movies isn't really all that complicated. Even with all the exotic computer-generated special effects, movies are simply a series of still pictures or photographs that are run in front of a lens at speeds generally from 32 to 64 frames (or pictures) per second.

Take a look at ANIMATE.LGO in the \procs\chpt11 subdirectory. Type START to watch a simple stick figure appear to wave its arms.

When you look at the procedure, you see that the arms are drawn and then erased. The turtle turns 10 degrees and then repeats the process. If the motion seems too slow on your computer, take out the WAIT 2 commands.

For some other example of turtle animation, see Puff, the magic dragon, and Gretchen's Balloon. You saw them in Chapter 8.

Animating Other Shapes

An easy place to start animating other shapes is with a bouncing ball. There are five colored balls in the graphics directory on the CD that came with this book. Copy those <color>.BMP files into your MSW Logo directory. Then we can get down to business.

Let's start with one bouncing ball and a procedure named BOUNCE.LGO.

```
TO START
BITLOAD "REDW.BMP
BITCUT 32 32
BITMAPTURTLE
MAKE "HGHT 200
PU SETY :HGHT
BOUNCE :HGHT
END
```

```
TO BOUNCE :HGHT
IF :HGHT < 20 [HOME STOP]
DOWN
UP :HGHT
BOUNCE :HGHT - 20
END

TO DOWN
IF YCOR = 0 [STOP]
BK 5 WAIT 1
DOWN
END

TO UP :HGHT
IF YCOR = :HGHT [STOP]
FD 5 WAIT 1
UP :HGHT
END
```

Most of this is old stuff. The new commands are right there at the beginning of the START procedure. This time you're going to load another image into Logo and then change it into a turtle.

```
BITLOAD "REDW.BMP
BITCUT 32 32
BITMAPTURTLE
```

These commands are key to changing the shape of the turtle.

1. BITLOAD *<Bitmap File>* Loads a graphics file such as REDW.BMP

   You can load just about any graphic image into MSW Logo. It doesn't have to be something you created in Logo. It can be clip art from another program. It can be a photograph or artwork that you scanned into the computer. There's only one catch.

   Graphics files must be in the BMP format.

   You can use the Paintbrush program that comes with Windows, SNAGIT, or *Paint Shop Pro*, shareware programs included on the CD, to convert graphics from other formats to the BMP format.

   BITLOAD is like LOADPIC, LOADPICT, LOADSNAP and similar commands used in other versions of Logo.

2. BITCUT *<width>* *<height>* cuts the rectangular shape that you define to the clipboard.

You can cut rectangular shapes of most any size and then change them into turtles. This is particularly useful when you want to precisely position a larger graphic as a background on which you draw other designs or as the background over which you move other turtles.

Graphics programs as well as clip art and scanning utilities usually show or allow you to ask the size of a graphic image. If you don't know the size of the image, MSW Logo offers the advantage of the BITLOADSIZE command. This tells you the width and the height of the bitmap you loaded into Logo.

BITCUT is like the SNAP command used in some other versions of Logo.

3. BITMAPTURTLE maps, or changes, the bitmap image to Turtle 0 or to the turtle number set by the SETTURTLE command. More on multiple turtles is coming up.

Before we go too far, take a look at what you've got here. The red ball appeared and began to bounce, gradually coming to a stop. Now you've got a red ball sitting on a white background. This is your turtle. Ernestine is taking a rest.

Give the turtle a few commands to see how it works with this new shape. You'll see that the turtle's pen is in the lower left corner of the shape. To get a better idea of what you're dealing with, change the screen color.

What happens?

Now it's easier to see that the turtle doesn't actually turn the way that Ernestine does. It just moves off in the direction in which you send it.

After you play around with the red ball turtle, see what else the other Bounce procedures offer. They're in the \projects\chpt11 subdirectory of the CD that came with this book.

From One to Two Turtles

Here's another procedure that can get you started on a billiards game.

Here you have a red ball and a white ball that bounce around the table and off of each other when they collide. It's the BILRDS.LGO procedure in the \procs\chpt11 subdirectory on the CD. This procedure goes a step beyond the bouncing ball procedure.

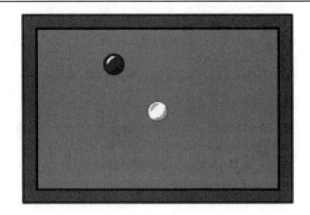

```
TO SETUP
...
SETBITINDEX 0
BITLOAD "REDG.BMP
BITCUT 32 32
SETTURTLE 0
BITMAPTURTLE
...
SETBITINDEX 1
BITLOAD "WHITEG.BMP
BITCUT 32 32
SETTURTLE 1
BITMAPTURTLE
...
END
```

When you start working with multiple turtles you have to add some additional commands. Other versions of Logo have their own way of doing this. MSW Logo may seem to be a bit more complicated. But actually, it tells you more about what's actually going on inside Windows.

- SETBITINDEX <index> indexes or reserves a space on the clipboard for the next image to be cut (up to 1024 images).

- BITLOAD loads the bitmap image from your hard drive.

- BITCUT cuts the image to the clipboard as the indexed image.

- SETTURTLE <number> identifies the turtle by number.

- BITMAPTURTLE maps the most recently indexed image to turtle number identified by SETTURTLE.

In the BILRDS.LGO procedure, two balls images are set up as turtles 0 and 1.

- What would it take to make a realistic billiard game?

- How would you make a pocket billiards game?

Racing Cars

Early in this chapter when you first read about working with multiple turtles, you played with a RACE procedure. Let's fix up that procedure so you're racing multiple cars rather than multiple turtles.

Take a look.

```
TO START
CS
REPEAT 4 ~
    [
    SETBITINDEX REPCOUNT - 1
    BITLOAD "RACECAR.BMP
    BITCUT 30 58
    SETTURTLE REPCOUNT - 1
    BITMAPTURTLE
    ]
SETTURTLE 0 PU SETPOS [-100 -150] ST
SETTURTLE 1 PU SETPOS [-50 -150] ST
SETTURTLE 2 PU SETPOS [0 -150] ST
SETTURTLE 3 PU SETPOS [50 -150] ST
RACE_CAR
END

TO RACE_CAR
SETTURTLE RANDOM 4
WAIT 20
FD RANDOM 20
IF YCOR > 200 [FLAG STOP]
RACE_CAR
END

TO FLAG
(PR "TURTLE TURTLE [IS THE WINNER!])
MAKE "ANS YESNOBOX [RACE] ~
    [WANT TO RACE AGAIN?]
IFELSE :ANS = "TRUE [START] ~
    [CS CT PR [SEE 'YA AT THE RACES.]]
STOP
END
```

This is quite a bit different from the first RACE procedure.

First of all, the RACE_CAR procedure is much simpler. There's really no reason to test all four turtles after each step. You only need to test the last one that moved.

Did that turtle — or car — go past the Y coordinate of 200 or not? If so, the FLAG procedure is called.

The TURTLE command tells you which turtle is active. In this case, the active turtle is the one that crossed the finish line first.

> (PR "TURTLE TURTLE [IS THE WINNER!])

Why [FLAG STOP]?

When the winning car crosses the 200 Y-coordinate, the FLAG procedure takes control from the RACE procedure. When you stop the FLAG procedure, control passes back to where Logo left the RACE_CAR procedure. The next line says RACE_CAR, which isn't exactly what you wanted.

In the FLAG procedure, when you left-click on NO in the RACE_CAR box, the first thing that happens is that the screen and text are cleared. When you clear the screen or type NOBITMAPTURTLE, the turtle reverts back to her original form.

What About REPCOUNT

When you want to use one or more other shapes as the turtle, you have to have a way to know which bitmap works with which turtle. Let's review for a minute.

To talk to each turtle, you use the SETTURTLE command —SETTURTLE 0, SETTURTLE 1, all the way up to SETTURTLE 1023, if you want.

To help match bitmaps to turtles, you use the SETBITINDEX command.

```
REPEAT 4 ~
    [
    SETBITINDEX REPCOUNT - 1
    BITLOAD "RACECAR.BMP
    BITCUT 30 58
    SETTURTLE REPCOUNT - 1
    BITMAPTURTLE
    ]
```

SETBITINDEX takes one input, an index number. In the START procedure, there's a new way of assigning that number. It's the REPCOUNT command.

REPCOUNT outputs the number of repeats including the current one. It starts at number 1. Since the goal of the procedure is to match the index numbers with the turtle numbers (that start at 0), the START procedure uses REPCOUNT - 1.

The next step is to load the race car bitmap and cut it to the clipboard.

```
BITLOAD "RACECAR.BMP
BITCUT 30 58
```

Next, you match the bitmap index to a turtle. Again, you use the REPCOUNT command to count the four race cars.

```
SETTURTLE REPCOUNT - 1
BITMAPTURTLE
```

Finally, you assign the bitmap that is currently on the clipboard to the selected turtle using BITMAPTURTLE. This process is repeated four times to assign a race car bitmap to each of four turtles.

Awfully simple? Or simply awful?

You find a number of examples of REPCOUNT in the \projects\chpt11 subdirectory.

Keyboard Control

In a game or an animated show, you may want the user to provide a direction, a distance, or some other form of response while the procedure is running. Most versions of Logo use READCHAR or RC, READWORD or RW, READLIST or RL. Each of these commands stop the action and awaits your input. Nothing happens until you type a character, a word, or a list.

MSW Logo provides another form of keyboard control. This one is an example of Windows modeless programming that you'll read more about in the next chapter.

To get you started, here's a simple procedure for doodling on the screen.

```
TO DOODLE
CS
MAKE "STEP 0
KEYBOARDON [COMMAND ]
SETFOCUS [MSWLOGO SCREEN]
ST
END
```

```
TO COMMAND
MAKE "KEY CHAR KEYBOARDVALUE
IF :KEY = "R [RIGHT 30]
IF :KEY = "L [LEFT 30]
IF :KEY = "U [PENUP]
IF :KEY = "D [PENDOWN]
IF :KEY = "C [DOODLE]
IF :KEY = "Q [CS KEYBOARDOFF]
FD :STEP
IF NUMBERP :KEY [MAKE "STEP :KEY]
END
```

To run the procedure, type DOODLE and then press a number key to set the speed of the turtle. Make sure the Caps Lock key is On. Then press and hold any key to move the turtle forward. You can then change directions or lift the pen up whenever you want.

This procedure introduces some new commands: KEYBOARDON, SETFOCUS, and KEYBOARDVALUE. KEYBOARDON allows you to trap events, such as pressing a key, that take place in the window that has "focus." That's the window that's selected at the time; the one with the highlighted title bar. Other windows have a grey title bar.

Want to see which window has focus? Use the GETFOCUS command.

1. Open MSW Logo.

2. Click in the Commander window.

3. Type GETFOCUS. What happens?

4. Type EDALL in the Input Box.

5. Type SETFOCUS "EDITOR in the Input Box. Which title bar is highlighted?

Typically, the Commander window has focus when you're running Logo procedures. Logo interprets the commands and executes them one after the other. KEYBOARDON traps events that take place in the MSW Logo screen, which is why you must SETFOCUS to that screen.

KEYBOARDVALUE outputs the ASCII value of the key that is pushed. You'll read about the ASCII code, CHAR, and ASCII commands in the next chapter. Here's a variation of DOODLE that shows you how those values are used.

DOODLER doesn't care if the Caps Lock key is on. The numbers in the list (in the brackets) are the upper and lower case ASCII values of the first letter of each command.

```
TO COMMAND :KEY
IF MEMBERP :KEY [70 102] [ FD 30 STOP ]
IF MEMBERP :KEY [66 98] [ BK 30 STOP ]
IF MEMBERP :KEY [82 114] [ RT 30 STOP ]
IF MEMBERP :KEY [76 108][ LT 30 STOP ]
IF MEMBERP :KEY [67 99] [ CS STOP ]
IF MEMBERP :KEY [81 113] [ QUIT STOP ]
END

TO DOODLER
ICON "COMMANDER
SETFOCUS [ MSWLOGO SCREEN ]
KEYBOARDON [ COMMAND KEYBOARDVALUE ]
END

TO QUIT
KEYBOARDOFF
UNICON "COMMANDER
END
```

To get your keyboard back to normal, use KEYBOARDOFF. This disables the trapping of events by KEYBOARDON.

For another look at how these keyboard control commands can be used, take a look at the MIDI.LGO procedure in the Examples directory. This was set up when you installed MSW Logo.

Controlling the Turtle's Speed

There are times when the turtle seems to go too fast. For example, if you have a fast Pentium computer, the DOODLE procedure moves along pretty fast even when the STEP variable is 1.

There are various ways to handle that using WAIT commands and other timing procedures.

```
TO TIMER :TIME
IF :TIME = 0 [STOP]
TIMER :TIME - 1
END
```

If your version of Logo doesn't have speed control, put a TIMER procedure in between moves the turtle might make. It's one simple way to slow things down.

For better control, here's a procedure from George Mills, the person responsible for MSW Logo.

```
TO DOKEY
MAKE "KEY CHAR KEYBOARDVALUE
IF :KEY = "+ [MAKE "DELAY :DELAY - 50]
IF :KEY = "- [MAKE "DELAY :DELAY + 50]
IF :DELAY < 50 [MAKE "DELAY 50]
SETUP.TIMER
END

TO DOSTEP
FD 10
END

TO MAIN
MAKE "DELAY 1000
SETUP.TIMER
KEYBOARDON [DOKEY]
SETFOCUS [MswLogo Screen]
END

TO SETUP.TIMER
SETTIMER 1 :DELAY [DOSTEP]
END
```

Now go see what you can do.

More Logo Animation

Another way to create animation is to use different turtles, each showing part of an action. Here are three very simple drawings of a soldier walking.

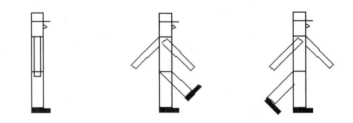

Look at the SOLDIER.LGO procedure. If you have a fast computer, run START and watch the soldier as he seems to walk across the screen.

Whoever saw a marching turtle?

SOLDIER.LGO is a very simple start that you can build upon. It uses STAND.BMP, LWALK.BMP, and RWALK.BMP to march across the screen.

```
TO START
SETUP
SETTURTLE 0
SETX -200 ST WAIT 30
CT PR [FORWARD, MARCH!]
WAIT 10
REPEAT 15 [MARCH]
CT PR "HALT
SETTURTLE 0 ST
END

TO MARCH
LOCAL "X
MAKE "X POS HT
SETTURTLE 0
ST SETPOS :X
WAIT 10 FD 25
MAKE "X POS HT
SETTURTLE 1
ST SETPOS :X
WAIT 10 FD 25
MAKE "X POS HT
SETTURTLE 2
ST SETPOS :X
WAIT 10 FD 25
MAKE "X POS HT
END

TO SETUP
CS CT
SETBITINDEX 0
BITLOAD "STAND.BMP
BITCUT 30 110
SETTURTLE 0
BITMAPTURTLE
PU SETH 90 HT
SETBITINDEX 1
BITLOAD "RWALK.BMP
BITCUT 80 110
SETTURTLE 1
BITMAPTURTLE
PU SETH 90 HT
SETBITINDEX 2
BITLOAD "LWALK.BMP
```

```
BITCUT 80 110
SETTURTLE 2
BITMAPTURTLE
PU SETH 90 HT
END
```

The SETUP procedure loads the three bitmaps, cuts each to the clipboard, and assigns each to a turtle. The MARCH procedure tells each turtle to take a step forward and then tells the next turtle where it is so that it can take a step from that position.

You can add additional views to make the action smoother. You can also create pictures using MS PAINT or another graphics program and then animate those pictures.

Flying the Firefox

Do you remember the FIREFOX procedure? You might want to run it from the CD that came with this book if you don't remember. In the graphics directory, you'll find twelve separate files for each view of the Firefox.

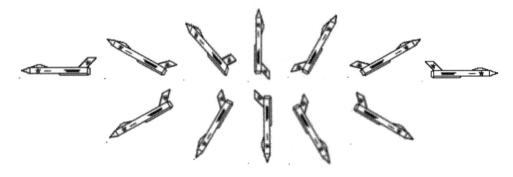

Each bitmap file (*.BMP) is named for the direction it is headed: N.BMP for North, ENE.BMP for East North East, and so on.

There's also another one called HIT.BMP. You can use this one for when you Zap the Firefox.

Ready to start flying? Take a look at the FLY.LGO procedure in the \procs\chpt11 subdirectory on the CD. Read the START procedure to learn how to fly the jet.

Here are three of the procedures that control the flight of the Firefox. They show another use of the Keyboard commands.

```
TO FLY
CS READY
MAKE "STEP 0
KEYBOARDON [CONTROL]
SETFOCUS [MswLogo Screen]
TELL 3 PU RT 90 SETX -400 ST
ICON "COMMANDER
END

TO CONTROL
MAKE "XY POS
MAKE "KEY CHAR KEYBOARDVALUE
IF :KEY = "R [RT 30 MAKE "H HEADING HT ~
    TURN PU SETPOS :XY SETH :H ST STOP]
IF :KEY = "r [RT 30 MAKE "H HEADING HT ~
    TURN PU SETPOS :XY SETH :H ST STOP]
IF :KEY = "L [LT 30 MAKE "H HEADING HT ~
    TURN PU SETPOS :XY SETH :H ST STOP]
IF :KEY = "l [LT 30 MAKE "H HEADING HT ~
    TURN PU SETPOS :XY SETH :H ST STOP]
IF :KEY = "Q [QUIT STOP]
IF :KEY = "q [QUIT STOP]
FD :STEP
IF NUMBERP :KEY [MAKE "STEP :KEY]
END

TO QUIT
KEYBOARDOFF
UNICON "COMMANDER
CS
END
```

Logo Flight Simulator

With all this talk about airplanes, why not develop a flight simulator?

It's not really that hard to do. You can use the Firefox graphics or you can develop new ones.

Of course, you'll need to create an airport graphic with maybe a hanger, airstrip, and trees. It's easier if you create this as a picture file and then just load the picture rather than have this drawn each time you decide to go flying.

Now let's go flying. The simplest thing to do is make a group of key controls for the aircraft: Up, Down, Level flight, Slow Down, Speed up, Stop.

301

You want the aircraft to start rolling down the runway, picking up speed as it goes. When you think you're going fast enough, you want to take off. If you're not going fast enough and you try to take off, you crash. Make sure you create a picture of a crash scene.

How fast is fast enough? That's something you can set with a conditional statement.

When you're flying around the screen, you want to be able to go through some maneuvers. To add some realism to your simulator, you can add speed changes if the plane climbs or dives.

In real flying, if a plane starts to climb and doesn't maintain its speed, it stalls. The opposite is just as bad. If you go into a dive and start going to fast, you may not be able to pull in time. Last but not least, you want to be able to bring the plane down on the runway and have it roll to a stop.

There's nothing that hard here. It's just going to take some planning and experimenting to make it work as much like a real airplane as you want.

Masking

You've got one more problem, however. And it can get a bit tricky to solve it.

The problem is masking.

When you cut an image to the clipboard, you cut a rectangle. The Firefox images all have a picture of the jet on a white background. That's not so bad if you're flying in a white sky. But when you start flying over a multi-colored landscape, that can become a problem.

There's a short introduction to masking on the CD in the \projects\chpt11 subdirectory. SPRITE.LGO introduces you to the Bitmodes in which MSW Logo operates, and to the BITMODE commands.

Check it out and see what these features can do for you.

You're getting pretty good at this stuff now; changing shapes and all. So why not try a few other things using your own multiple turtle procedures?

Talk To Your Computer

Just when you thought you were getting good at this, here comes a whole new Logo world to explore, the world of list processing. It's one of the more interesting things about the Logo language. In fact, while most people think about Logo as a graphic language, it is actually based on Lisp, a list processing language. Turtle graphics were added later.

Logo is called a high level language. The first real computer language was machine language, which meant programming the computer using 0's and 1's. Then came assembly languages followed by other early computer languages that became known as "number crunchers." Everything they do deals with numbers: money, inventories, counting, calculating, and things like that.

Logo is different. It uses "symbolic computation" that allows you to process ideas.

Just what does symbolic computation mean? Actually, it gets sort of complicated. For our purpose – which is to keep things simple – let's just say it means that in addition to numbers, you can process words and lists of words, numbers, and things.

You can add two lists together or add words to a list. And you can teach the computer to remember them. This is very important to the study of Artificial Intelligence, or AI. You'll get introduced to that later in the this chapter.

In the meantime…

Did you ever talk to your computer?

Here's a short and simple procedure to get you started. Type it, or load it (TALK.LGO), and then run it. What happens?

It's like a short conversation, isn't it? But, no, you're not really talking to the computer.

```
TO TALK
CT PRINT [HI! WHAT'S YOUR NAME?]
MAKE "NAME READWORD
MAKE "REPLY SE :NAME~
    [MY NAME IS ERNESTINE.]
PRINT SE [I DON'T THINK WE'VE MET,] :REPLY
PRINT [HAVE YOU EVER TALKED TO A ~
    COMPUTER?]
TEST READWORD = "NO
IFFALSE [PRINT ~
    [WOW! DO YOU TALK TO TURTLES, TOO?]]
IFTRUE [PRINT [OH BOY!  A BEGINNER.]]
END
```

Logo Sentences

Take a look at the TALK procedure. There's really only one thing new there.

Do you see how SENTENCE works? SENTENCE, or SE for short, takes two inputs and prints them together. These can be two words, two lists of words, or a combination of words, lists, characters, or numbers. The output is a list.

PRINT SE [I DON'T THINK WE'VE MET,] :NAME

I DON'T THINK WE'VE MET, is a list that is the first input. The variable :NAME is the second. This is the word you typed when the procedure asked you for your name.

When you want to add more than two inputs to SENTENCE, or when you add additional inputs to PRINT, TYPE, SHOW, WORD, or LIST, use parentheses.

For example:

PR (SE :NAME ", [HOW ARE YOU?])

Let's say that :NAME is the variable with the value of Ernestine. This line is displayed as

ERNESTINE, HOW ARE YOU?

While it may seem strange, Logo treats the comma as a separate word. Anything that follows a single quotation mark is considered to be a word. That word ends with a space.

Logo Numbers, Characters, Words, and Lists

OK! You've explored a bit with Logo numbers, characters, words, and lists. You've played a bit with a few list processing commands too. But there is much, much more to list processing.

So let's review where we've been. It may seem strange, but when you're exploring so many different things, there are times when you have to look back to know where you're going. This is one of those times.

"First, what do you really mean by list processing?"

"One of the really neat things about Logo is that it allows you to process information, or data, in many different forms. It can be numbers, words, lists of other words and lists, property lists, or arrays."

Numbers

Let's start with Logo numbers.

Numbers consist of one or more integers, decimals, or exponents such as engineering notation. Remember integers? Integers are "whole" numbers such as 3, 25, 423, or 1,324,598. Fractions and decimals are not whole numbers. They are parts of whole numbers, even if you have something like 1.5. 1.5 is part of 2, isn't it?

All the commands shown below use whole numbers.

FORWARD 5	SETH 45
REPEAT 4	SETH 0
RIGHT 20	SETH -90

Characters

Logo can also display alphabetic and numeric characters using the CHAR or ASCII (American Standard Code for Information Interchange) primitives. You've may have heard about ASCII code before. It is a standard code that is used by computer manufacturers to display a set of 128 characters numbered from 0 to 127. These codes describe all the punctuation marks, upper and lower case letters. There's also a high-level set of codes that go from 128 to 255.

Take a look.

SHOW CHAR 65 displays the letter A.

SHOW CHAR 67 displays the letter C.

SHOW CHAR 49 displays the number 1.

SHOW CHAR 32 displays a space.

Yes, there's even a code for a blank space.

CHAR followed by a code number displays the letter, number, or punctuation mark for the specific ASCII code. But, no, you don't have to memorize ASCII code.

If you ever want to find out the ASCII code for a something, type

SHOW ASCII <character>

SHOW ASCII "A displays 65.

SHOW ASCII "a displays 97.

Upper and lower case letters each have different codes. That's because they're different shapes.

Try a few ASCII and CHAR commands so that you get a good feel for what they do.

ASCII Art

You may have seen cute little characters added to e-mail and other messages – things like a happy face (:>) or the sad face (:>(Some people do it like this: :-) or :-(

There are all sorts of these little additions. It's a way to add some expression to what can sometimes be dull on-line text.

And, yes! You can add these touches to your procedures. For example, you can display your signature every time you create a picture.

```
TO SIGNATURE
CT TYPE [GRAPHICS BY JIM]
TYPE CHAR 32
TYPE CHAR 40
TYPE CHAR 58
TYPE CHAR 62
PR CHAR 41
END
```

Run this procedure and

GRAPHICS BY JIM (:>)

is printed in the Commander window.

You can also write it like this:

```
TO ARTIST
(TYPE [GRAPHICS BY JIM] CHAR 32 CHAR 40~
    CHAR 58 CHAR  62) PR CHAR 41
END
```

Spacing

Before you leave this procedure, there's something else to look at.

```
(TYPE [GRAPHICS BY JIM] CHAR 32 CHAR 40~
    CHAR 58 CHAR 62) PR CHAR 41
```

Why not include everything with the TYPE command? Why change to the PRINT command at the end? Or, why not just use PRINT in parentheses?

307

```
(PR [GRAPHICS BY JIM] CHAR 32 CHAR 40
    CHAR 58 CHAR 62 CHAR 41)
```

TYPE and PRINT do essentially the same thing, except that TYPE does not add a space between the characters or a carriage return at the end of the line.

- TYPE prints the string of characters all on one line. You must include a PRINT or SHOW command at the end of the command line to move to the next line.

- PRint and SHOW add a space between each character and a carriage return after printing the string of text, which sends the cursor to the next line.

Try these commands:

```
TYPE "TRY TYPE "THIS
```

What happened? Nothing – because there wasn't a PRINT or SHOW command at the end. So try this:

```
TYPE "TRY TYPE "THIS SHOW "
TRYTHIS
```

There is no space between the two words. What about

```
SHOW "TRY SHOW "THIS
TRY
THIS
```

One more time, this time with a single space after the backslash. What happens?

```
(TYPE "TRY "\ "THIS) SHOW "
```

What happens when you insert two spaces after the backslash? What's that tell you about the backslash?

Play around with the spacing when using different commands. This comes in handy at times, especially if you want to start displaying some fancy ASCII artwork.

```
|\   /|
| \/ |
| /\ |
|/   \|
|o   o|
|\../ |
\/ -- \/
 \__/
```

When you want to run text procedures such as ARTIST, ASCII, and SIGNATURE, open the Commander window. That's where they are displayed. Either drag the edge up, or left-click on the middle of the three boxes on the right of the Title bar.

Take a look at ASCII.LGO file \procs\chpt12 subdirectory for an interesting twist on ASCII art.

This one's a famous movie title of some years back.

Adding More Pizzazz

After TurtleBusters, why not add some Pizzazz to your signature? Try this:

```
TO SIGNATURE
CT  REPEAT 10 [TC 32]
TC 71 TC 114 TC 97 TC 112 TC 104 TC 105 TC 99
TC 115 TC 32 TC 66 TC 121 TC 32 TC 74 TC 105
TC 109
FLASHER 1 1
END

TO TC :C
TYPE CHAR :C
END

TO FLASHER :X :Y
CT  REPEAT :X [PR "]
REPEAT :Y [TC 32]
TC 71 TC 114 TC 97 TC 112 TC 104 TC 105 TC 99
TC 115 TC 32 TC 66 TC 121 TC 32 TC 74 TC 105
TC 109 PR "
MAKE "X :X + 1
MAKE "Y :Y + 5
IF :X > 24 [MAKE "X 1 MAKE "Y 1]
WAIT 3 FLASHER :X :Y
END
```

Put your own name in this procedure (FLASHER.LGO) and then run it. If you can't find a list of the ASCII codes, why not write a procedure that prints them out for you?

That's not as hard as you might think. So why not give it a try. You can do it.

This new SIGNATURE procedure is a step in the right direction, but it really isn't that flashy. What else can you add to this?

Adding Some Real Pizzazz

But what about the graphics screen? Why not see what you can do to add a flashy signature to your drawings on the graphics screen?

LABEL is one of those commands that means different things in different versions of Logo. In MSW Logo, LABEL's input, which may be a word or a list, is printed on the graphics screen.

To define the font in which the word or list is to be displayed, you have two choices:

1. Open the Select menu and left-click on Font.

   The Font selection window is displayed.

Here you can select the Font. This defines what the text is going to look like. Left-click on a font to see what it looks like in the Sample window.

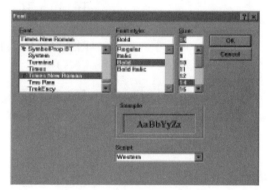

You can change the style of the font to display:

- regular type.

- type in italics

- bold type

- bold italics.

The third window is where you select the size you want to display. Type is measured in points, 72 points to the inch. This book is printed in 14 point Times New Roman to give you some idea of size. The Sample window also helps you select the size you want.

The other method for selecting a font is to use the SETTEXTFONT command.

SETTEXTFONT [[font] *<attribute list>*]

The input to the MSW Logo command, SETTEXTFONT, describes a font and the attributes it is to display: the size of the type and whether it is to be in bold, italics, underlined, etc.

MSW Logo gives you a wide range of attributes that define exactly how the text is to appear. These include:

```
SETTEXTFONT
[
[Font]
Height
Width
Orientation
Weight
Italic
Underline
StrikeOut
CharSet
OutPrecision
ClipPrecision
Quality
PitchAnd-Family
]
```

The on-line help file describes each of these attributes. However, you don't have to use any of them if you don't want to. You can accept the default values. Just type

SETTEXTFONT [<*font name*>]

You may want to specify the size of the type. So type the name of the font followed by a height and width.

SETTEXTFONT [[HELV] 24 16]
LABEL [Graphics by Morf!]

MSW Logo prints in upper and lower case. It also prints in the direction the turtle is facing.

Why not experiment with the font attributes? See what type of crazy pizzazz you can come up with. Then you can get back to list processing.

Logo Words

Logo words are easy. They're anything between a quotation mark to the left and a space on the right. However, there can not be any spaces in a word.

Just remember that when you identify a Logo word, you must use a quotation mark in front of it. You don't have to do that with numbers. Logo treats 3 as a number just as it treats 325491587 as a number.

As you have seen, Logo treats a single letter or a punctuation mark as a word. It treats

PRINT "T the same as

PRINT "Tyranosaurus

Of course, it isn't really strange at all once you think about it. "A" is a word, isn't it? It's one of the three articles in the English language. The other two are "an" and "the."

What about the word "I?"

A Logo word is any combination of letters, numbers, and punctuation marks with no spaces.

SHOW "ABC_456
    displays ABC_456.

SHOW "A93HK8
    displays A93HK8.

SENTENCE and WORD

As you saw in the TALK procedure, SENTENCE produces a list. However, WORD, produces another word.

To see the difference, try something like this:

PRINT WORD "A "B
PRINT SENTENCE "A "B

or this:

PRINT WORD 1 2
PRINT SE 1 2

Hmmmm, what would happen if we did this:

MAKE "A WORD 1 2
MAKE "B WORD 3 4
PRINT :A + :B

Try this:

MAKE "C WORD :A :B
PRINT :C

What happened? Bet you got 1234, right? So let's do some testing to see what we've got here.

        PRINT NUMBERP :C

or

        IF NUMBERP :A [PRINT "TRUE]

Remember NUMBERP? If you want to review, go back to the *Great Math Adventure* chapter.

The statements above tell Logo that if :A is a number, print TRUE. Another way to say this is:

        IF NOT NUMBERP :C [PRINT "FALSE]

Even though you created a word from :A and :B, it's still a number, right?

Before we leave this confusion, let's mess it up some more. What would this line print?

        PRINT (WORD 1 CHAR 32 2 CHAR 32 3)

The result would look something like a sentence but would actually be a word.

        1 2 3

This actually reads as 1 space 2 space 3, because the spaces are deliberately inserted as characters. In Logo, that's a word.

Just to check the difference, try it this way:

        PRINT (WORD 1 2 3)

Where'd the spaces go?

Just to be absolutely sure, try this one:

        MAKE "CHECK (WORD 1 CHAR 32 2 CHAR 32 3)
        SHOW WORDP :CHECK

The result True is displayed. So I guess that the output is a word, not a list.

Lists

Lists are elements within square brackets — [ ]. A List can include words, numbers, or other lists. Of course, if a List contains a list, both have to be enclosed in brackets.

PRINT [This is a list.]
> displays
>> This is a list.

PRINT [1 2 3 this is also a list_A B C?]
> displays
>> 1 2 3 this is also a list_A B C?

What about this?

PRINT [1 2 3 [this is also a list_A B C]]

Here's a list within a list that displays as

1 2 3 [this is also a list_A B C]

Do you remember the difference between how PRINT displays lists and how SHOW displays them? Check it out.

Creating Lists

You can, of course, create lists. You started this in Chapter 8 when you used SETPOS LIST :X :Y. Now lets try something different:

MAKE "SAMPLE (LIST 1 2 3 45 98 "PR "JIM)
SHOW :SAMPLE

[1 2 3 45 98 PR JIM] is displayed.

In the previous section on words, you asked if :CHECK was a word?

MAKE "CHECK (WORD 1 CHAR 32 2 CHAR 32 3)
SHOW WORDP :CHECK

Now change that second line to

SHOW LISTP :CHECK

What's the response going to be, TRUE or FALSE?

LIST or ( )

When do you use the LIST command? When do you use brackets? Why does SETPOS LIST :X :Y work when SETPOS [:X :Y] doesn't?

There is a very simple but very important rule that explains this. Brackets do not execute what's inside them. They merely list the contents. LIST makes things happen.

Remember this when writing procedures.

314

Logo Postcards

Has your family ever been on a vacation and sent lots of postcards to friends back home? Those cards seem to be all the same, don't they.

Dear _____,
Here we are in wonderful _____. We're having a great time _____ and _____. The weather is very _____. We'll be home _____. See you then.
Love,

_____

Wouldn't it be nice to have a procedure to print your cards for you.

```
TO SETUP
PRINT [WHO IS THIS CARD FOR?]
MAKE "FRIEND READWORD
PRINT [WHERE ARE YOU WRITING FROM?]
MAKE "VAC READWORD
MAKE "VAC WORD :VAC ".
PRINT [WHAT ARE YOU DOING?]
MAKE "ACT1 READWORD
PRINT [WHAT ELSE?]
MAKE "ACT2 READWORD
MAKE "ACT2 (WORD :ACT2 ".)
PRINT [HOW'S THE WEATHER?]
MAKE "WEA READWORD
MAKE "WEA WORD :WEA ".
PRINT [WHEN WILL YOU BE HOME?]
MAKE "ARR READWORD
MAKE "ARR WORD :ARR ".
PRINT [HOW WILL YOU SIGN THE CARD?]
MAKE "SIG READWORD
END
```

Now we'll print this information on the postcards.

```
TO POSTCARD
SETUP CT TS
PRINT SE [DEAR] :FRIEND
PRINT "
TYPE SE [HERE WE ARE IN WONDERFUL] :VAC
    PRINT [WE'RE HAVING]
TYPE SE [A GREAT TIME] :ACT1 TYPE SE "AND
    :ACT2) PRINT "THE
TYPE SE [WEATHER IS] :WEA PRINT SE [WE'LL BE
```

```
            HOME] :ARR
     PRINT [SEE YOU THEN.]
     PRINT "
     PRINT [LOVE,]
     PRINT "
     PRINT :SIG
     END
```

Do you remember the difference between PRINT and TYPE?

TYPE prints its input without adding a carriage return at the end the way that PRINT does. TYPE lets you print text more like you do with word processing software. PRINT only allows you to print one string of text on a line. Of course, you can also write the line as

PR (SE [A GREAT TIME] :ACT1 "AND :ACT2 "."THE)

See! There's usually an easier way if you'll look for it. But there's still a problem with the postcard procedure.

Making Headlines

Look at any book on Logo and usually you'll find a procedure that picks parts of speech and combines these into sentences – something like this:

```
     TO HEADLINES
     MAKELISTS
     PRINTHEADLINES
     END

     TO MAKELISTS
     MAKE "ADJ [HAPPY GLAD ANXIOUS GOOD SINCERE]
     MAKE "NOUN [SANTA PEOPLE FRIENDSPARENTS]
     MAKE "VERB [GAVE RECEIVED SPREADSHARED  WISHED]
     MAKE "OBJ [GIFTS LOVE CHEER GLADNESS JOYHAPPINESS]
     END

     TO PRINTHEADLINES
     PR (SE PICK :ADJ PICK :NOUN PICK :VERB PICK :OBJ)
     WAIT 10
     PRINTHEADLINES
     END
```

When you type HEADLINES, the first thing that Logo does is run the MAKELISTS procedure to make up lists of words: ADJ, NOUN, VERB, and OBJ. Then the next procedure is called.

PRINTHEADLINES tells the computer to PRint a SEntence - but what sentence? PICK is a command that randomly selects an item from a list. So it randomly picks elements from the four lists and prints them as a sentence.

Some versions of Logo don't have a PICK command. You can write one like this:

```
TO PICK :WORDS
OUTPUT ITEM (1 + RANDOM (COUNT :WORDS)) :WORDS
END
```

That's fine. But what's with all the parentheses?

To understand any Logo statement, you start at the left and move to the right, one command at a time. OUTPUT takes one input. That input is ITEM.

ITEM takes two inputs: a number and something else, like the 4th list, the 2nd word. The next thing you see after ITEM is in parenthesis. That means that

(1 + RANDOM (COUNT :WORDS))

is all one element. RANDOM typically selects a number between 0 and, in this case COUNT :WORDS. But again, what about all those parentheses?

The easiest way to read those is to start with the parentheses on the inside:

(COUNT :WORDS)

The first task for PICK in the PRINTHEADLINES procedure is to select an adjective – PICK :ADJ. So, in the first case, (COUNT :WORDS) temporarily becomes

(COUNT :ADJ)

How many adjectives (:ADJ) are inside the brackets in the MAKELISTS procedure? There are five adjectives, right? So, if you COUNT the ADJectives, you get 5. Substitute 5 in the original procedure and here's what you get:

(1 + RANDOM (5)) which is the same as 1 + RANDOM 5 after you take the unneeded parentheses away.

1 + RANDOM 5 gives you the five numbers 1, 2, 3, 4 and 5. So now we have:

OUTPUT ITEM RANDOM 5 :WORDS

or

OUTPUT a randomly selected item from the five words in the ADJ list.

Now the following line begins to make a bit more sense:

PR (SE PICK :ADJ PICK :NOUN PICK :VERB PICK :OBJ)

Logo is going to print a random ADJ, a random NOUN, a random VERB, and a random :OBJ. You'll get sentences like

HAPPY SANTA GAVE CHEER
GLAD PEOPLE RECEIVED GIFTS
ANXIOUS PARENTS WISHED JOY
HAPPY PARENTS SPREAD LOVE
HAPPY PEOPLE GAVE GIFTS
SINCERE FRIENDS SHARED LOVE
ANXIOUS PEOPLE RECEIVED CHEER

Explore these headlines some more, why don't you? Make a longer headline using five or more words. Combine words and lists. You can even throw in a sentence or two.

The main thing is to explore, to learn, and to have some fun doing both.

Word Games

Logo postcards and headlines may seem a bit silly. But what about a word game – like the game of Nim. This also gives you the chance to see more Windows commands in action.

Nim is a game the computer always wins. Can you figure out why? Take a look at the NIM.LGO procedure in the \procs\chpt12 subdirectory to find the answer.

Before you start digging into the windows programming tools used in Nim, here's a couple of challenges for you.

1. Change the game so that the computer does not always win.

2. Word games aren't very pretty. Why not change this into a graphic game where you pick real stones, or trees, or shapes?

3. Set up different rows of objects so the player has to select which row to select from?

What other things can you dream up?

Windows Programming

"Logy, I'm having enough trouble learning Logo for Windows. Now you want me to learn Windows programming?"

"Well, not exactly. However, to use some of the features of MSW Logo, you have to learn a few of the things about what makes windows programming different from other Logo programming. What follows are a few examples to explore. For a better description, read the Windows Functions section of On-line Help."

Up until now, you've seen how Logo reads one line at a time and then interprets that line from left to right. That's the Modal mode where the application is in control. Windows programming supports two modes or methods of programming, Modal and Modeless.

Modal Mode

Those of you who have done some DOS programming before are familiar with the Modal mode. This is where the program or procedure controls the action. It is the type of programming used in the NIM procedure.

DIALOGCREATE is used to stop the action of a procedure while it asks you for some information. In the case of NIM, it asks you to pick a number.

DIALOGCREATE creates a dialog box in which you can add radiobuttons, scrollbars, listboxes, checkboxes, and the other types of input devices you see in windows applications. DIALOGCREATE is similar to the WINDOWCREATE command described overleaf, except it will not return to the calling procedure until the dialog is closed.

Dialog boxes aren't the only devices that stop the action. NIM shows you examples of some others: the YESNOBOX and the MESSAGEBOX. There's also the QUESTIONBOX. Change the OVER procedure to something like this and see what happens.

```
TO OVER
PR [There is one stone left. I win again.]
MAKE "ANS QUESTIONBOX [Nim] [Want to play again?]
IFELSE (FIRST FIRST :ANS) = "Y [NIM][CT PR [Bye for now!]]
END
```

319

Modeless Mode

The Modeless mode is just the opposite of Modal mode. In the Modeless mode, the Window (user) is in control. This takes some getting used to but is a very important idea.

In the Modeless Mode, you use the WINDOWCREATE command as in the MODELESS procedure listed below.

```
TO START
CS CT
PR [Let's draw a shape.]
PR [How many sides should it have?]
MODELESS
END

TO MODELESS
WINDOWCREATE "ROOT "SELECTOR ~
    "SELECTBOX 250 0 100 180 []
GROUPBOXCREATE "SELECTOR "NIM 10 10 80 140
RADIOBUTTONCREATE "SELECTOR "NIM "ONE ~
    [ONE] 20 15 60 15
RADIOBUTTONCREATE "SELECTOR "NIM "TWO~
    [TWO] 20 30 60 15
RADIOBUTTONCREATE "SELECTOR "NIM
    "THREE [THREE] 20 45 60 15
RADIOBUTTONCREATE "SELECTOR "NIM ~
    "FOUR [FOUR] 20 60 60 15
RADIOBUTTONCREATE "SELECTOR "NIM ~
    "FIVE [FIVE] 20 75 60 15
RADIOBUTTONCREATE "SELECTOR "NIM ~
    "SIX [SIX] 20 90 60 15
RADIOBUTTONCREATE "SELECTOR "NIM
    "SEVEN [SEVEN] 20 105 60 15
RADIOBUTTONCREATE "SELECTOR "NIM ~
    "EIGHT [EIGHT] 20 120 60 15
RADIOBUTTONCREATE "SELECTOR "NIM ~
    "NINE [NINE] 20 135 60 15
RADIOBUTTONSET "ONE "TRUE
RADIOBUTTONSET "TWO "FALSE
RADIOBUTTONSET "THREE "FALSE
RADIOBUTTONSET "FOUR "FALSE
RADIOBUTTONSET "FIVE "FALSE
RADIOBUTTONSET "SIX "FALSE
RADIOBUTTONSET "SEVEN "FALSE
RADIOBUTTONSET "EIGHT "FALSE
```

```
RADIOBUTTONSET "NINE "FALSE
BUTTONCREATE "SELECTOR "GAME "OK ~
    35 150 25 20 [EXECUTE]
END

TO EXECUTE
IF RADIOBUTTONGET "ONE [HT GREET STOP]
IF RADIOBUTTONGET "TWO [ST GREET STOP]
IF RADIOBUTTONGET "THREE [CS REPEAT 3 ~
    [FD 50 LT 120] GREET STOP]
IF RADIOBUTTONGET "FOUR [CS REPEAT 4 ~
    [FD 50 LT 90] GREET STOP]
IF RADIOBUTTONGET "FIVE [CS REPEAT 5 ~
    [FD 50 LT 72] GREET STOP]
IF RADIOBUTTONGET "SIX [CS REPEAT 6 ~
    [FD 50 LT 60] GREET STOP]
IF RADIOBUTTONGET "SEVEN [CS REPEAT 7 ~
    [FD 50 LT 360/7] GREET STOP]
IF RADIOBUTTONGET "EIGHT [CS REPEAT 8 ~
    [FD 50 LT 45] GREET STOP]
IF RADIOBUTTONGET "NINE [CS REPEAT 9 ~
    [FD 50 LT 40] GREET STOP]
END

TO GREET
PR [How about that!]
END

TO DEL
WINDOWDELETE "SELECTOR
END
```

In MODELESS, the dialog box created by WINDOWCREATE doesn't need to be deleted. You can continue to press buttons to draw all the shapes you want.

Type DEL to delete the dialog box.

This is barely a taste of what you can do with windows and dialog boxes. To learn more, explore the on-line help files for each of these new commands. Most importantly, explore the examples given for each command. For example, here's a slight variation of the DODRAW procedure listed for the LISTBOXADDSTRING command.

```
TO DEL
WINDOWDELETE "MYWINDOW
END
```

```
TO DODRAW
;SELECT FIGURE FROM LISTBOX AND THEN ~
   CLICK ON DRAW BUTTON
CS
IF EQUALP [TRIANGLE] LISTBOXGETSELECT ~
   "MYLIST [REPEAT 3 [FD 100 RT 120]]
IF EQUALP [SQUARE] LISTBOXGETSELECT ~
   "MYLIST [REPEAT 4 [FD 100 RT 90]]
END

TO START
WINDOWCREATE "MAIN "MYWINDOW ~
   "MYTITLE 0 0 100 100 []
LISTBOXCREATE "MYWINDOW "MYLIST ~
   25 0 50 50
LISTBOXADDSTRING "MYLIST [TRIANGLE]
LISTBOXADDSTRING "MYLIST [SQUARE]
BUTTONCREATE "MYWINDOW "MYDRAW ~
   "DRAW 25 50 50 25 [DODRAW]
END
```

For a better example, take a look at the MODELESS procedure in the Examples\Windows directory that was setup when you installed MSW Logo.

More Fun With Text

Among the first things you did in this book was to make different shapes. Well, how about making word shapes? That means making shapes out of the text you print on the screen. In addition to being a fun project, it gives you some practice with some new list processing commands.

Here's an easy one to start with. It's on your Sourcebook diskette as WORDTRI.LGO. What's the new command?

```
TO WORDTRIANGLE :WORDS
IF :WORDS = " [STOP]
PR :WORDS
WORDTRIANGLE BUTFIRST :WORDS
END
```

This procedure simply prints :WORDS and then calls itself BUTFIRST :WORDS. BUTFIRST, BF for short, means it prints everything BUT the FIRST element of the variable :WORDS. You'll see how this works as we go along.

WORDTRIANGLE "LOGOADVENTURES

The result:

LOGOADVENTURES
OGOADVENTURES
GOADVENTURES
OADVENTURES
ADVENTURES
DVENTURES
VENTURES
ENTURES
NTURES
TURES
URES
RES
ES
S

And this raises some questions:

- What would happen if :WORDS was a list? What would you have to change to drop the first letter of each word?

- What would you have to do to have the procedure drop the last letter?

Maybe if you turn that triangle around, you'll get some ideas.

Turning It Around

Have the procedure print the first letter, then the first and second, then the first three, and so on. Along the way, you'll see how some other list processing commands work. (This is WORDTRI2.LGO on the Sourcebook diskette.)

You've already seen the command FIRST. It selects the first element of a word or list. In the START procedure, after clearing all the text, Logo prints the FIRST element of the variable :WORDS. If you use the same variable again, an L is displayed.

```
TO START :WORDS
CT PR FIRST :WORDS
MAKE "LINE WORD (FIRST :WORDS) (FIRST BUTFIRST~
    :WORDS)
PR :LINE
REST BF BF :WORDS
END
```

After the L is displayed, Logo makes a new word, :LINE, by combining FIRST :WORDS with FIRST BUTFIRST :WORDS. What would that be?

In the WORDTRIANGLE procedure, you found out that BUTFIRST :WORDS printed everything but the first element of :WORDS. Using the traditional Logo parsing technique, start at the right with FIRST. That takes one input, which is BUTFIRST :WORDS. BUTFIRST :WORDS removes the first element but leaves the rest of the variable there. So what does FIRST BUTFIRST do?

You got it. It prints the first element in BUTFIRST :WORDS, or 0. So here's what you have when the START procedure runs:

```
L
LO
```

This sets up the new triangle. Since you don't want to repeat these steps, you move on to the REST procedure for the rest of the triangle.

```
TO REST :WORDS
IF :WORDS = " [STOP]
MAKE "LINE WORD :LINE (FIRST :WORDS)
PR :LINE
REST BF :WORDS
END
```

If you'll follow the printout below, you'll see how it works. REST picks up the variable :LINE from START. After START has run, :LINE has a value of . :WORDS has a value of

```
                                              L
GOADVENTURES                                  LO
MAKE "LINE WORD :LINE (FIRST :WORDS)          LOG
                                              LOGO
Make "LINE a word by combining LO and FIRST   LOGOA
:WORDS or G. This keeps repeating: LOG, then  LOGOAD
LOGO, etc. Get the idea? Here's what it looks  LOGOADV
like:                                         LOGOADVE
                                              LOGOADVEN
We've got one more triangle to check out. How  LOGOADVENT
would you make this one?                      LOGOADVENTU
                                              LOGOADVENTUR
                                              LOGOADVENTURE
                                              LOGOADVENTURES
```

A Logo Tree

Pick your way through this one. You've been through the other two so this one should be easy.

```
TO START :WORDS
CT  TC ((COUNT :WORDS) / 2) PR FIRST :WORDS
```

```
MAKE "LINE (WORD (FIRST :WORDS) ~
    (FIRST BF:WORDS) (FIRST BF BF :WORDS))
TC ((COUNT :WORDS) / 2) - 1 PR :LINE
REST BF BF BF :WORDS
END
TO TC :N
IF :N < 1 [STOP]
REPEAT ROUND :N [TYPE CHAR 32]
END

TO REST :WORDS
IF :WORDS = " [STOP]
IF COUNT :WORDS = "1 ~
    [MAKE "WORDS WORD :WORDS CHAR 32]
MAKE "LINE (WORD :LINE (FIRST :WORDS) (FIRST BF~
    :WORDS))
TC ((COUNT :WORDS) / 2) - 1 PR :LINE
REST BF BF :WORDS
END
```

You've already explored COUNT. This tells you that to make an even tree shape, you have to type blank spaces (CHAR 32) to take you to the middle of :WORDS – COUNT :WORDS / 2. The rest shouldn't be too difficult to follow.

```
        L
      LOG
     LOGOA
    LOGOADV
   LOGOADVEN
  LOGOADVENTU
 LOGOADVENTURE
LOGOADVENTURES!
```

Once you get that one figured out, you're on your own. What other word shape procedures can you make?

How about changing all the FIRST commands to LAST, and all the BUTFIRST commands to BUTLAST. What happens? Can you rewrite these three procedures using LAST and BUTLAST?

How about making a square in the middle of the screen? Have the procedure repeat printing a phrase until it completes a square. Can you make a circle?

The Amazing Oracle

Here's a fun game to play on a group of friends or on a class. The Oracle thinks up a story. The object of the game is to figure out the story by asking the Oracle direct questions that can be answered by Yes or No.

Well, the Oracle is sneaky. Take a look at the procedures and see if you can figure out how it works. Then take another look. Because the Oracle gives you some ideas on how to use LAST and BUTLAST to handle lists.

```
TO ORACLE
CLEARTEXT TEXTSCREEN
PR [I'M THINKING OF A STORY. ASK ME DIRECT  QUESTIONS,]
PR [THOSE I CAN ANSWER WITH YES OR NO.]
PR [THEN I'LL TELL YOU WHAT IT IS.]
QUIZ
END

TO QUIZ
PR "
PR [WHAT'S YOUR QUESTION?]
MAKE "QUESTION READLIST
IF NOT (LAST LAST :QUESTION) = "? [PRINT ~
    [QUESTIONS MUST END WITH A QUESTION ~
    MARK.] QUIZ]
IF MEMBERP ~
    (LAST BUTLAST LAST :QUESTION)~
    [A E I O U]    [PR "YES QUIZ STOP]
IF (LAST BUTLAST LAST :QUESTION) = "Y ~
    [PR "MAYBE QUIZ STOP]
PR "NO
QUIZ
END
```

Oracle begins by asking you for a question.

    MAKE "QUESTION READLIST

When you type a question, you are actually typing a list. This list becomes the variable :QUESTION. Logo then checks to see if you added a question mark.

    IF NOT (LAST LAST :QUESTION) = "? [PRINT
        [Questions must end with a question mark.] QUIZ]

What this says is that if the LAST character of the LAST word in the list is not a question mark, print the statement and return to the top of the QUIZ procedure.

Now take a look at this one.

    IF MEMBERP (LAST BUTLAST LAST :QUESTION)
        [A E I O U] [PR "YES QUIZ]

That really does makes sense because what this statement says is if the next to the last — last but last — character of the last word of the sentence is a member of the list [a e i o u], print Yes and then call the QUIZ procedure again.

If the next to last character is not a member of the list, Logo reads at the next line.

    IF (LAST BUTLAST LAST :QUESTION) = "Y [PR
        "MAYBE QUIZ]

This time, Logo asks if the next to last character is 'y. If so, Logo prints Maybe and calls the QUIZ procedure again.

By the way, what's LAST :QUESTION? This question gives you a clue. If the next to last character is neither a vowel or 'y, Logo prints 'No and calls QUIZ again.

Now do you know how the Oracle works? It simply answers your questions based on the last letter in the last word. You're actually the one who makes up the story. And some of them can get pretty crazy.

Now that you've had a healthy taste of list processing, take a look at the Data Structure Commands in the MSW Logo On-line Help file. This will give you an overview of the other list processing commands. You'll be using more of them in the next exercise.

Time-out for a few experiments first. They're really a review, but you know how Morf hates tests.

Try this one:

    SHOW LAST "TEST
    (You can use SHOW or PRINT)

What do you think is going to be shown (or printed)?

    SHOW FIRST "TEST

What's this going to show?

How about these?

    SHOW BUTFIRST "TEST
    SHOW BF [THIS IS A TEST.]
    SHOW LAST BF [THIS IS A TEST.]
    SHOW LAST FIRST BF [THIS IS A TEST.]

One HUGE Gold Star if you said S for that last one.

Try a few of your own. Using the commands of FIRST, LAST, BUTFIRST, and BUTLAST, you can pick any letter of any word in a list.

Word Sums

"What's two plus two?"

"How easy can you get? It's four, of course!"

"How'd you get the answer?"

"I added two plus two and got four. What do you think?"

"Did you add 2 + 2? Or two plus two? If you're talking about Logo, there is a difference you know."

"Well, I never really thought about that."

"OK, let's give it a whirl."

Adding words together is a great exercise in list processing. Here's a brief description of how it works.

WORDSUM "THREE "SIX

WORDSUM counts through a list to see where the words THREE and SIX are located. They are in the third and the sixth position. So, Logo then adds

3 + 6 = 9

Finally, Logo counts to the ninth position in the list and prints that word as the answer: NINE.

Logo does one more thing with this procedure; that's to determine if there if the number is a 'teen. In the problem above, it isn't, so Logo simply printed the answer. But let's take a look at another example:

WORDSUM "EIGHT "SIX

We know the answer is 14. To print it, Logo went to the TEENS procedure and output

The answer is fourteen.

Take a look at the full procedure;WORDSUM.LGO in \procs\chpt12. Look it over and then let's take it apart.

The first question, as you start to look at WORDSUM, is what do :NUMS1 and :NUMS2 equal.

Turn on TRACE and then run the procedure again. This allows you to follow the recursive calls of SET1 and SET2. Then you go to ADDNUMS.

Another way is to just explore the procedure on paper. Start with what you know.

```
WORDSUM "EIGHT "SIX
:NUM1 = EIGHT
:NUM2 = SIX
:NUMS = [ZERO ONE TWO THREE FOUR
    FIVE SIX SEVEN EIGHT NINE]
```

From the WORDSUM procedure:

```
MAKE "NUMS1 SET1 :NUM1 :NUMS
MAKE "NUMS2 SET2 :NUM2 :NUMS
```

If you have trouble stepping through these first two lines, just add the following before ADDNUMS in WORDSUM.

```
MAKE "NUMS1 SET1 :NUM1 :NUMS
MAKE "NUMS2 SET2 :NUM2 :NUMS
PR :NUMS1
PR :NUMS2
IGNORE RC
```

This will print the variables :NUMS1 and :NUMS2 and stop until you press a key to continue. This gives you a chance to check on what's going on.

```
:NUMS1 equals EIGHT NINE
:NUMS2 equals ZERO ONE TWO THREE  FOUR FIVE SIX
```

Make sure you understand how those variables were selected before proceeding.

```
TO ADDNUMS
MAKE "NUMS1 SE :NUMS1 :NUMS
MAKE "NUMS3 (FIRST :NUMS)
REPEAT (COUNT :NUMS2) - 1 [MAKE "NUMS1 BF
    :NUMS1 IF (FIRST :NUMS1) = (FIRST :NUMS)
    [MAKE "NUMS3 FIRST BF :NUMS]] IF :NUMS3 =
    "ZERO [TYPE [THE ANSWER IS] PR (FIRST
    :NUMS1)] [TEENS]
PR [PRESS ANY KEY TO CONTINUE.]
END
```

Knowing :NUMS1 and :NUMS2, you can write down what the first two lines of ADDNUMS will equal. Again, if you can't figure it out, add the print lines again:

```
MAKE "NUMS1 SE :NUMS1 :NUMS
MAKE "NUMS3 (FIRST :NUMS)
PR :NUMS1
PR :NUMS3
IGNORE RC
```

The third line is where things get a little complicated. But you know all those commands. So just start from the right and move through the line, one command at a time.

```
REPEAT (COUNT :NUMS2) - 1
```

Let's say you typed WORDSUM "EIGHT "SIX. What would :NUMS2 be?

```
[ZERO ONE TWO THREE FOUR FIVE SIX]
```

So, COUNTS :NUMS2 - 1 is what? I get six, what do you get? So the line starts with REPEAT 6. Now what?

The next command is

```
MAKE "NUMS1 BF :NUMS1
```

First of all, what's :NUMS1?

```
EIGHT NINE ZERO ONE TWO THREE FOUR FIVE
    SIX SEVEN EIGHT NINE
```

What is BF :NUMS1? Remember, BF is BUTFIRST. So BF :NUMS1 is the list above without the first element, or

```
NINE ZERO ONE TWO THREE FOUR FIVE
    SIX SEVEN EIGHT NINE
```

Next, you come to:

```
IF (FIRST :NUMS1) — that's now NINE, right?
IF (FIRST :NUMS1) = (FIRST :NUMS)
    [MAKE "NUMS3 FIRST BF :NUMS]
```

:NUMS is defined in the SETUP procedure. What's FIRST :NUMS? Does it equal FIRST :NUMS1? No. So the procedure repeats again.

On the sixth repeat, what is FIRST :NUMS1?

Four, right?

What has :NUMS3 become? It became ONE on the third repeat cycle. Since :NUMS3 does not equal ZERO, the TEENS procedure is called.

Since FIRST :NUMS if four, the answer is FOURTEEN.

Awfully simple? Or simply awful?

"Wow! What can't you do in Logo?"

"Well, Morf, the most important lesson is "Never say never." You and I aren't experts, but have you ever found anything you can't do if you put your mind to it?

There is a WDTEEN.LGO procedure on the diskette that comes with this book that gives you another look at how this same type of addition can be done. You may like it better than the one used here.

But, after all, that's what this book is all about. You can almost always find another way to do something, and it just may be a lot easier.

Another thing you've got to realize is that we have just scratched the surface of what you can do with Logo. There is so much, much more you can do."

"OK, we're wasting time! What's next?"

Logo and Artificial Intelligence

The whole idea of artificial intelligence gets very confusing. It makes you wonder, just what is intelligence? And how can it be artificial?

This is not the place to discuss whether computers can or ever will be able to really learn. Leave that to the computer scientists and philosophers.

For our purposes, computers of today don't really learn. It is the software that computers run that make them appear to learn. So, if you look at it, the learning is really kind of artificial. Maybe we can agree that this is a type of artificial intelligence.

There are some examples of procedures that "learn" on the CD that came with this book. There's the well-known Animal guessing game in \procs\chpt12 – ANIMAL.LGO. This is a procedure where you teach Logo to recognize animals by the descriptions you type.

Have you ever played the game States and Capitals? Someone names a state. You have to name the capital of that state. This edition of the game shows how the computer can appear to be learning (STATES.LGO in \procs\chpt12).

By now you should have little if any trouble figuring out how this procedure works. Sure, it might take some time. But you can do it.

The main feature of this game is "lists within lists within lists." First, there is the list of States and Capitals – SLIST. If you ever want to erase this list and start over, type INIT.

Secondly, there is a list that matches each state with its capital – GROUP.

Thirdly, there is a list of each state generated from the variable :QUEST and one for each capital that comes from :ANSWER.

Together, these look like this:

MAKE "SLIST [[[Oklahoma] [Oklahoma City]]
    [[New York] [Albany]]
    [[Texas][Austin]]
    [[Massachusetts][Boston]]
    [[California][Sacramento]]]

Logo "learns" new states and capitals from the TEACH procedure.

The first thing that TEACH does is ask you to create the variables, :QUEST and :ANSWER. It then creates a new empty list named GROUP.

    MAKE "GROUP []

Next, it adds the state (:QUEST) to the :GROUP list.

    MAKE "GROUP LPUT :QUEST :GROUP

LPUT and FPUT are interesting commands. They are used to add words or other lists to a list. For example:

    LPUT "Logo [MSW]
        results in the list [MSW Logo].

    FPUT "MSW [Logo]
        also results in the list [MSW Logo].

In the case of States and Capitals, LPUT tells Logo to add :QUEST at the end of the list :GROUP. Once you have the state listed, you need to add the capital.

    MAKE "GROUP LPUT :ANSWER :GROUP

This line adds :ANSWER as the second list within the list :GROUP.

MAKE "SLIST LPUT :GROUP :SLIST

And finally, this line adds the list of two lists to the master list :SLIST.

Time to experiment.

Change the TEACH procedure to add a third element to the GROUP list, maybe the county of the capital or the population of the state?

How would you change the other procedures to ask about that third element?

Go ahead – try it. It's really not that hard.

Rather than look for the LAST element of the GROUP list, you might want to look for the LAST BUTLAST element, or the FIRST BUTFIRST element, or select an ITEM from a list that matches something else.

What's Next

"Seems we just got started and here we are. And there are so many other things to do." .

Well, there has to be something left for you to explore on your own. You can start with the projects on the CD that came with this book. This is what Logy and Morf like best, exploring new ways to do things, finding new and better ways to make things work.

By now you can do just about anything you want with MSW Logo. What you don't know, you can find – in the on-line help files or in the Example procedures that came with MSW Logo.

Want to explore some more? You'll find a number of interesting Logo sites on the Internet. There's Logy and Morf's Home Page at http://www.cyberramp.net/~jmul

Other addresses include:

http://www.softronix.com

for information on MSW Logo and other products from George Mills.

For more information about UCB Logo, use the Logo news group or discussion group as described below. Brian Harvey is a regular participant in these forums.

There is a Logo news group at comp.lang.logo. There's also an on-line Logo mailing list, actually a discussion group. To subscribe, send

subscribe logo-l   as the subject to majordomo@gsn.org

There should be no other text in your message - no signature either.

One of your best sources of information about Logo and Logo products is the non-profit organization:

The Logo Foundation
250 West 85th Street
New York, New York 10024
(212)579-8028

E-mail: michaelt@media.mit.edu
http://el.www.media.mit.edu/groups/logo-foundation

Most important! What ever you do, enjoy your very own

GREAT LOGO ADVENTURE!

Digging Into Logo

Believe it or not, you've just started to dig into Logo.

As you continue digging on your own, there's one important thought to keep in mind. The procedures offered in this book and on the CD that comes with it are how other people solved a problem. That doesn't mean that these solutions are the best way to do things. They may not be the easiest or the most efficient way. These are just places for you to start on your own adventures.

What's On Your CD

This book is just the beginning. There are more than 300 procedures, graphic files, posters, and projects to explore - all in six directories on the CD that came with this book. There's more on

Animation
Perspective drawing
Number Systems
Logo Physics
The Historical Turtle
Exploring Pi

You'll find a variety of games for all ages including

Logo baseball
Logo football
Logo basketball
Hide 'N Seek

All of these files are listed in seven directories. Copy them to your hard drive or use them from the CD.

\	This appendix.
\Acrobat	Acrobat Reader 3.0 is installed
\graphics	Graphics files in BMP format.
\logo	Free Logo software
\procs	MSW Logo procedures from the book.
\projects	Other procedures, articles, posters, and projects.
\util	Acrobat Reader, graphics, and other utilities ready to install on your hard drive.

\Graphics

This directory includes all the BMP files listed in the book plus many of the individual graphics used in posters and PDF files.

\Logo

MSW Logo for all Windows systems. Type the name of the file for your computer and then follow the instructions displayed on the screen.

msw32b52.exe	This is the 32bit kit for Windows 95 and Windows NT.
msw32s52.exe	This is for those running Win32s in Windows 3.1x. Win32s is not included.

msw16b52.exe	The 16bit kit for those running Windows 3.1x or Windows 95 in 16-bit mode.
msw16s52.exe	This is for those running Windows 3.1 on IBM XT and other 286 computers.
mswtut52.exe	An on-line video tutorial for beginners 3.5 MB compressed.

UCB Logo is more like "classic Logo" in that it does not include multiple turtles, music, or multimedia features. Two UCB Logo packages are included on the CD, one for the Macintosh and the other for PCs.

ucblogo_seax.hqx	Compressed files for the Macintosh.
blogo.exe	Compressed files for the PC.

Blogo.exe includes three Logo programs:

ucblogo.exe	runs in MS-DOS on 286-and-up PCs. It uses extended memory if you have it, so you can run large Logo programs.
bl.exe	runs on any MS-DOS PC, but is limited to 640K.
ucbwlogo.exe	runs on Windows 95 and Windows NT only.

Copy the UCB Logo file for your computer into an empty directory on your hard drive and then inflate it. To install UCB Logo, type install. Read the Readme and UCBLogo.txt files for more information on how to setup and run UCB Logo.

\procs

The procedures from the book are listed in this directory by chapter. The graphic procedures were developed on a Pentium PC running Windows 95 at a screen resolution of 1024 x 768. If you cannot display that resolution, use the MSW Logo ZOOM command or menu to zoom out so that the graphics appear correctly on your screen.

\projects

This directory includes approximately 150 Logo procedures, posters, and project files listed by chapter. The PDF files can be viewed and printed using the Acrobat Reader. Click on the PDF file to open it and the Acrobat Reader.

\util

This directory contains some useful free and shareware utilities for working with book, Logo, and graphics files.

AR32E30.EXE	Acrobat Reader for the PC.
AR	Acrobat Reader for the Macintosh.
GA15T.EXE	GIF Animator for Windows 95
GIFCON.EXE	GIF Animator for Windows 3.1.
GIFCON32.EXE	GIF Animation for Windows 95
PSP311.EXE	Paint Shop Pro, Graphics utility for the PC.
PW118.ZIP	Allows you to run 32-bit applications under Windows 3.1.
SNAGIT40.ZIP	A graphics capture and conversion utility for Windows 95.

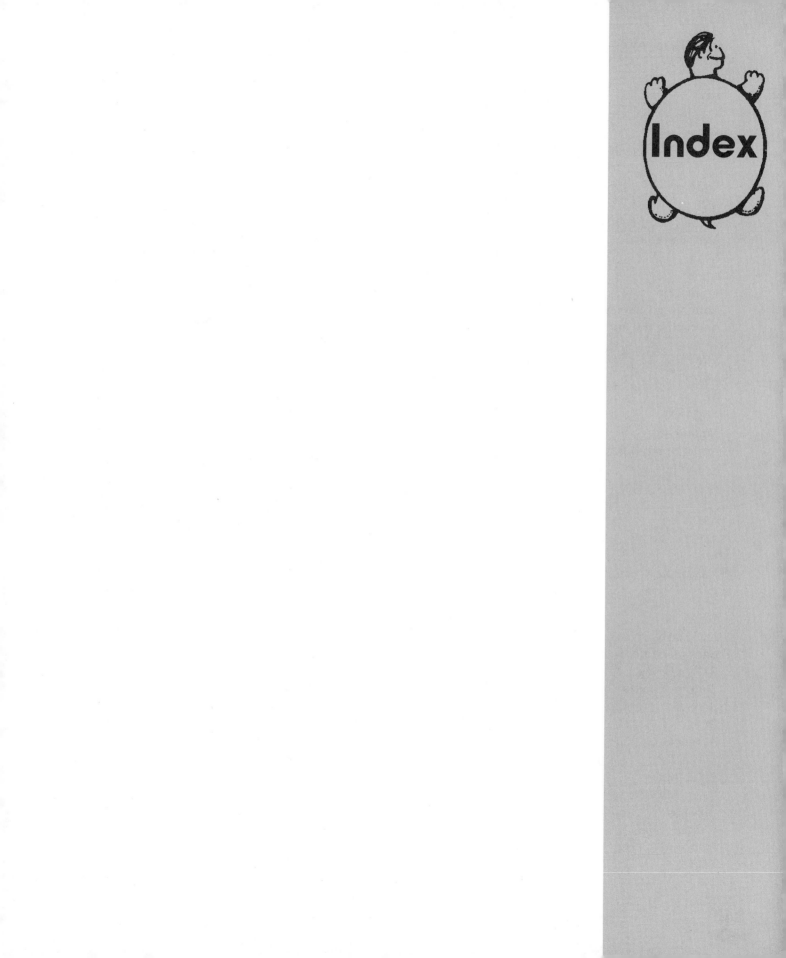

Index

ORDER FORM

Please send .... copy(s*) of The Great Logo Adventure ($24.⁹⁵each) at a total cost of $................ plus $3 S&H

If I am not completely satisfied I can return the book for a full refund within 15 days of delivery.

Name ....
Company ....
Address ....
City ....
State ....
Zip ....
Daytime phone no. ....

☐ check or money order enclosed

☐ visa   ☐ mastercard

Acc. no. ....
Expiration date..
Signature ....

*Discounts are available for orders of 3 or more: contact the publisher

Fill and return to:
Doone Publications
7950 Hwy 72W, #G106, Madison, AL 35758 USA
Tel: 1-800-311-3753, Fax: 205-837-0580
e-mail: asmith@doone.com
web: www.doone.com